C000134728

IN THE SERVICE
OF THE KING

William Thornton Keep, 1789-1883.
A miniature showing him in later life.

IN THE SERVICE OF THE KING

The Letters of William Thornton Keep,
at Home, Walcheren, and in the Peninsula, 1808-1814

Edited by Ian Fletcher

SPELLMOUNT
Staplehurst

To Roy and Joy Newton

British Library Cataloguing in Publication Data:
A catalogue record for this book is available from the British Library

Copyright © Ian Fletcher 1997

ISBN 1-873376-79-0

First published in the UK in 1997 by
Spellmount Ltd
The Old Rectory
Staplehurst
Kent
TN12 0AZ

The right of Ian Fletcher to be identified as the author of this work
has been asserted by him in accordance with the
Copyright, Designs and Patents Act 1988

All rights reserved. No part of this publication may be reproduced, stored in a retrieval
system or transmitted in any form or by any means, electronic, mechanical, photocopying,
recording or otherwise, without prior permission in writing from
Spellmount Ltd, Publishers.

Printed in Great Britain by
TJ International Ltd
Padstow, Cornwall

CONTENTS

ILLUSTRATIONS

1. An officer of the 28th (North Gloucestershire) Regiment, c.1811.

2. Arthur Wellesley, 1st Duke of Wellington, 1769-1852. After a painting by Heaphy.

3. Sir Thomas Picton, 1758-1815. Picton was Keep's brigade commander during the Walcheren Expedition in 1809 when he was serving in the 77th Regiment.

4. The interior of the fort at Berry Head showing the old barrack mounds with a capped well at bottom left. Keep was stationed here with the 28th, before leaving for the Peninsula in 1812.

5. British infantry at drill. Private soldiers, wearing their white fatigue jackets, are shown the rudiments of drill by sergeants under the watchful eyes of officers right.

6. The battle of Vittoria, June 21st 1813. The battle was Keep's first action in the Peninsula. This superb painting by Beadle shows Robinson's brigade attacking the village of Gamara Mayor.

7. British cavalry smash into the French rearguard during the closing stages of the battle of Vittoria.

8. The battlefield of Maya, as seen from the main ridge along which the 92nd Highlanders fought. The French attacked from left to right along the track visible on the left. The rocky height on the right was where Moyle Sherer and his piquet were overrun and taken.

9. Maya. The rocky spur, described by Keep, where he fought and saved one of the 28th's colours on July 25th 1813. The French swarmed up this spur before driving the 28th down the other side into the valley of the Baztan.

10. The battle of the Nivelle, November 10th 1813. Simkin's painting shows the 85th Light Infantry, attacking French redoubts.

11. Wellington and his staff on the Rhune mountain during the battle of the Nivelle, after a painting by Thomas Heaphy. The artist travelled to the Peninsula to paint a number of Wellington's officers, many of whom appear in this most detailed painting. Wellington's pose is virtually identical to that in plate number 2 in this book, which was also painted by Heaphy.

12. The western sector of the battlefield of St Pierre, as seen from the main road to the north of the Chateau Larralde. Keep was severely wounded whilst fighting in the trees to the right of this picture. Captain Hartman, of the 28th, led the light company out into the field in the distance to skirmish with the French.

13. Number 13, Rochester Row, Camden Town, London, Keep's house from 1841 until his death in 1884. Keep used to re-enact his old battles in the back garden of the house with his friend, Henry Alexander, an old comrade in the 28th.

MAPS

ACKNOWLEDGEMENTS

I would like to express my thanks to Colonel R.E. Whatmore (Retd), curator of the Regiments of Gloucestershire Museum, for his help. The museum is in possession not only of the copies which William Thornton Keep made of his own letters, but also the miniature of him which appears in this book. As well as other fine exhibits, the museum also has a beautiful watercolour of Charles Cadell, who served in the Peninsula with William Keep. I would also like to thank Mr David Grant, for reading through the manuscript and for the liberal use which he made of his red pen. My publisher, Mr Jamie Wilson, was, as usual, most supportive throughout.

Above all, however, I would like to express my most sincere thanks to Professor Roy Newton and his wife, Joy, for without them there is little doubt that the letters of William Thornton Keep would never have seen the light of day. Joy took up the threads of Keep's story many years ago before entrusting me with seeing it through to publication. Both Roy and Joy were a constant source of encouragement and assistance and it was with great pleasure that I took them both to the Peninsula in the late summer of 1996 to escort them round the battlefields and haunts that William Keep would have known so well. Indeed, we enjoyed a marvellous day at Maya where, on a beautiful, warm Sunday afternoon, we stood on the very spot where Keep saved one of the colours of the 28th Regiment. Roy was also responsible for tracing Keep's final resting place, now sadly overgrown, in Highgate Cemetery. I thank both Roy and Joy immensely and hope this book lives up to their expectations. Thanks.

Introduction

William Thornton Keep was born on October 16th 1791, two years before the start of the conflict which, until 1914, was known as 'The Great War'. To the people of Britain the war was actually a series of conflicts with France which, apart from a short period of peace following the Peace of Amiens in 1802, lasted right up until the final overthrow of Napoleon Bonaparte, Emperor of the French, in 1815. During the period from 1793 to 1815 Britain proved Napoleon's most dogged opponent on land and sea. She also kept the fires of Britain's allies — Austria, Prussia and Russia — continuously burning by stoking them regularly with supplies of specie. It was during this momentous era that William Keep chose the martial path which was eventually to present to us this most informative, graphic and entertaining set of letters, written without the benefit of hindsight and allowing us a glimpse of past events through the eyes of one of those who helped forge them.

William Thornton Keep was the eldest of some twenty children born to William Alexander and Honora Margaretta Keep, although sadly, just six of them lived to adulthood. He was baptised at St Martin-in-the-Fields. His father worked in the War Office and doubtless kept a close eye on his son's progress and on the events which were to shape his life. One gets the feeling that he did not come from a particularly wealthy family despite his father's occupation, and despite the fact that his brother, Samuel Nicholas, was a lawyer. There are frequent references in the letters to his mother of her 'troubles and difficulties', which were obviously financial. Army pay was frequently in arrears, particularly in the Peninsula and this appears to have been a constant problem for Keep, even when in England, as his letters clearly indicate. Nevertheless, with a little help from his friends and family he was able to survive the long periods of inactivity at home and the rigours of campaign life in Holland and the Peninsula where an officer in the British army needed almost as much in his purse as he needed courage in the field.

Britain's military contribution to the downfall of Napoleon was patchy, certainly in the years prior to 1808 when the British army embarked upon its most successful and certainly its most telling contribution to the allied war effort, the Peninsular War, which was fought between 1808 and 1814. This six-year conflict saw the British army fight what was arguably the most successful campaign in its long and illustrious history. It also saw the rise to fame of one of its greatest — if not the greatest — commanders, Arthur Wellesley, later 1st Duke of Wellington. The success of the campaign is reflected in some of the great battle honours which date from Wellington's era, such as Vimeiro, Busaco, Salamanca and Vittoria, names which adorn the Colours of scores of great British regiments.

It was this astonishing success which sparked off a hitherto unparalleled flow of journals and diaries written by eye-witnesses of these great events as Wellington's veterans, eager to relate their part in the overthrow of Napoleonic France, put pen to paper or dictated their reminiscences to more literate friends.

These memoirs today form the core of most of the research into the Peninsular War. The letters of William Thornton Keep, previously unpublished, add to our understanding not only of the battles and campaigns in which he took part, but also of the day to day life of a soldier in the early 19th century. Indeed, many of the aspects to which he refers, such as barrack life and training, often go overlooked as each correspondent sought to concentrate on campaign life only.

Keep's letters are in no way unique but they differ perhaps from many Georgian memoirs inasmuch as they provide us with a vivid and extensive portrait of life at home in England as well as on campaign. The officers and men of those British army regiments which remained in Britain whilst Wellington's army marched in triumph across Spain and Portugal must have craved their share of glory and the news which they received from the Peninsula must have served only to increase their anxiety. Keep was no different and in fact his frustration must have been even more acute as his regiment, the 28th, saw more than its fair share of action in the Peninsula. Therefore, one can feel the excitement building within as orders arrive for his regiment's departure to the theatre of war in Spain.

But here we are jumping ahead of ourselves, for Keep's first regiment, into which he was commissioned at the age of seventeen on April 21st 1808, was the 77th Regiment and his first overseas service took him not to the dusty plains of the Iberian Peninsula but to the damp, malaria-ridden marshes of Walcheren where, in the summer of 1809, he was to be struck down with the same wasting fever that laid low and saw off hundreds of other British soldiers. The so-called 'Walcheren Fever', in fact, was still taking its toll some four years later when British reinforcements, seemingly recovered from their toils in the marshes, arrived in the Peninsula in the spring of 1813 only to fall prey to a recurrence of the fever which had apparently lain dormant and which awoke with a vengeance once in Spain.[1]

William Keep wrote six letters from Walcheren, or Flushing to be precise, which capture some of the disenchantment of what was a dismal failure of a campaign. Indeed, the fortunes of the British army at the time were not overly inspiring even in the Peninsula, where Wellesley, having now become Lord Wellington following his victory at Talavera, was beginning a period of fourteen months without battle during which he fought not only the French but the many doubters at home and in his own camp who questioned the wisdom of remaining any longer in the Peninsula on what appeared to be a hopeless cause. As we know all too well, the campaign was eventually a great triumph but this was not clear until after the battle of Vittoria on June 21st 1813. It was here that Keep saw his first action with the 28th, as part of Rowland Hill's 2nd Division. Keep had joined the regiment on August 29th 1811 after having been forced to resign from the 77th following a bout of Walcheren Fever, contracted during the ill-fated campaign

---

[1] The 1st and 3rd Battalions of the 1st Foot Guards, for example, were hit by an outbreak of low fever shortly after joining Wellington's army in the main theatre of war in the Peninsula in December 1812. During the first seven months of 1813 the brigade lost no fewer than 800 men dead. Although the fever was diagnosed as being low fever there is little doubt that many of the men were still suffering from the effects of the fever contracted at Walcheren, some 2500 of the 1st Foot Guards having served there. (See Fletcher, *Gentlemen's Sons*, pp.150-151.)

there in the late summer of 1809. Keep later fought at the battle of Maya, on July 25th 1813, one of the three battles of the Pyrenees, at the battle of the Nivelle and at the battle of St Pierre on December 13th 1813, the final day of the battle of the Nive. Here he was badly wounded by a French musket ball which struck him in the mouth and lodged at the back of his neck. His description of being wounded is one of the most graphic I have ever read and, given the severe nature of the wound, it is remarkable that his powers of description remained intact and that he was able to describe the incident in such a lucid manner.

His is one of the few descriptions of the fight at the pass at Maya where, as we will see, he saved one of the regiment's Colours by flinging himself down one side of the ridge. The description of this battle is particularly satisfying, not least because of its graphic detail, but because it clears up one or two mysteries which surround the battle, such as the exact ground over which it was fought, and the length of time which, as he himself says, the battles take to develop. It was at Maya that Moyle Sherer, author of *Recollections of the Peninsula*, was taken prisoner whilst fighting with a piquet of his regiment, the 34th. Sherer was an acquaintance of Keep's, serving together as they did in Hill's 2nd Division, and he is mentioned in some of the letters, a happy coincidence. It is not often that we find famous diarists mentioned in the letters of other such soldiers.[2]

But what sort of army was William Thornton Keep joining in 1808? When he was commissioned on April 21st 1808 events in Spain were only just coming to the boil and it would be another three months or so before British troops began to land in Portugal. Optimism was high but perhaps not too well founded. The victory in Egypt in 1801 seemed a distant memory whilst even Sir John Stuart's significant victory at Maida in July 1806 had been somewhat overshadowed by the ill-fated attack on Buenos Aires the following year. Egypt too had seen an inglorious reverse at El Hamet in 1807. So, apart from the victories in Egypt and at Maida, and in far-off India under the command of Sir Arthur Wellesley, there was little cause for great optimism at the beginning of the Peninsular War. Nonetheless, the small army, once again under Wellesley, set about its task with relish.

There is little doubt that the success of the British army in the Peninsula rests firmly with the prowess of its infantry. Each infantry battalion in 1808 consisted of ten companies, eight of which were battalion or centre companies and the other two consisting of one grenadier company and one light infantry company. On paper each of these companies consisted of 100 men, giving a total of 1,000 men in each battalion. However, apart from the three regiments of Foot Guards, this was rarely the case. In fact, the average strength of a British infantry battalion in the Peninsula has been put at 550.[3] The composition of an infantry battalion makes interesting reading, not only as regards strength but also the height and ages of the men themselves. The grenadier company of the battalion traditionally consisted of the tallest men in the battalion. However, in the 57th Regiment, for example, in

---

[2] *Recollections of the Peninsula*, by Captain Moyle Sherer, was first published in London in 1832. He was also the author of *Sketches in India*.
[3] Philip Haythornthwaite, *Wellington's Military Machine*, p.28

May 1809, out of 852 men there were just two men measuring six feet tall.[4] Some 443 men, over half the battalion, were just 5 feet 5 inches tall. By today's standards this represents little height at all but it is quite evident that what the British soldier lacked in height he made up for with guts, and lots of it, for there was nothing so fearful in the Peninsula than a bayonet-wielding British soldier. Indeed, the image of the charging, yelling redcoat is one of the more enduring images, not only of the Napoleonic period but of British military history in general. And yet in reality there was very little bayonet work done in the Peninsula. Indeed, it was more often the mere sight of long red ranks of British soldiers with lowered bayonets that won the day for Wellington. Having delivered their customary volley from a two-deep line, the British infantry would give a mighty cheer before charging home against the French columns with their bayonets, leaving the enemy with little choice but to break and run, something which happened with almost tiresome regularity on the battlefields of Portugal and Spain.

Wellington's tactic of the two-deep line over the French column was much more than simply a victory based purely on a mathematical equation. Granted, his line would always be able to bring more firepower to bear on the French than the enemy's dense columns, but it was also his subtle use of the ground, his employment of a heavy skirmishing line, and his use of artillery to disorder the columns which were as much a winning tactic as the actual contest of musketry. In fact, it is now generally accepted that, far from being unaware of the mathematical disadvantage under which the French troops laboured in their attacks on Wellington's positions, they did, in fact, use the columnar formation merely as a means of movement and that they did try to deploy into line once the British line had been discovered. However, as Wellington's troops were invariably tucked away safely on the reverse slopes of his positions, the French never really knew when to deploy and on those occasions when they did attempt it, they were simply too late and the British volleys hustled them back neatly and quickly into their columnar formations.

Another favoured tactic employed not only by Wellington's men but by all the combatant armies in the Napoleonic period was the infantry square, often four ranks deep, against which it was virtually useless to throw cavalry, the horses being most reluctant to try and break in past the four ranks of bristling bayonets. There were, of course, some instances of cavalry breaking squares but these are so extremely rare that their names spring to mind quickly and easily — Garcia Hernandez, for one, being perhaps the most famous of the age. William Keep never needed to employ this tactic and certainly, once the fighting in the Peninsula moved into the Pyrenees, there was little or no scope at all for the employment of cavalry on either side.

When Keep joined the 77th Regiment the officers of the British army were still wearing the cocked hat and long-tailed coat. In the case of the 77th the scarlet coat had yellow facings and the officers silver lace. Other ranks had a single lace

---

[4] Captain Woolwright, *History of the 57th Regiment*, p.400. Co-incidentally, the 57th (West Middlesex) Regiment later amalgamated with the 77th (East Middlesex) Regiment, Keep's first regiment.

loop with a black stripe. Officers wore white breeches with black gaiters or with a variety of boots. A crimson sash denoted the officer's status as did a brass gorget which hung around his neck on his chest. A black silk stock was worn also. The cocked hat came complete with a large white over red plume and black cockade. Battalion company officers carried the 1796-pattern infantry officers' sword, with a straight 32-inch blade. Flank company officers took to wearing the curved 1803-pattern infantry officers' sabre. By the time William Keep joined the 28th Regiment in August 1811 new designs were already being submitted for a new uniform which, although introduced in 1812, saw little use in the Peninsula, save with those units which came out very late in the war, or with officers who had specifically sent home requesting the new false-fronted shako. Ironically, the 28th kept their old stove-pipe shakos long after the introduction of the new shako and, in fact, wore them at Waterloo in June 1815. Indeed, a painting by Woollen shows the 28th in square formation during the great battle, complete with stove-pipe shakos. Compare this with Lady Butler's fine but very inaccurate depiction of the same regiment at Quatre Bras where she erroneously painted them wearing the 1812-pattern shako. The men of the 28th, in fact, had the unique distinction of being allowed to wear their regimental badge on the rear of their shakos in recognition of the part played by the regiment at Alexandria in 1801 when the rear rank of the 28th faced about to see off an enemy attack. This was later viewed with some chagrin by the 44th (East Essex) Regiment who performed a similar exploit in 1815 at the battle of Quatre Bras when the rear rank of the regiment also faced about to see off an attack by French cavalry. On this occasion, however, the 44th, which had taken an Imperial 'eagle' at Salamanca in 1812, was denied the distinction of being able to wear its badge on the rear of its shakos.

William Keep's letters provide us with a unique record of one man's uniform throughout the period. As well as the regulation changes to his uniform Keep made other alterations to suit himself, and had non-regulation items of clothing made up, such as a forage cap in the style of a 'Westminster scholar.' He also left us valuable comments as regards the cleaning of his uniform and the effects that certain cleansing materials had upon it. We are fortunate that one of Keep's comrades in the 28th, Charles Cadell, also made observations on his uniform, particularly his trousers. Prior to leaving for duty on the Walcheren campaign of 1809, in which Keep saw action, Colonel Wynch, commanding the 4th, Colonel Ross of the 20th, and Colonel Belson, commanding the 28th, agreed to try grey trousers made in different ways. The 4th had them made tight, with black gaiters, the 20th as overalls, with buttons down the sides, and the 28th loose, with half boots. When the three regiments returned to England after the campaign, the three commanding officers compared results. The trousers worn by the 4th were all torn at the legs, the buttons were off the overalls of the 20th, while those of the 28th were nearly as good as when they started. Naturally enough, the rigours of campaign life took their toll on every soldier's uniform but it is most interesting to be able to read one man's experience of this most studied area of military history and for this we must thank William Keep.

There are other aspects of the life of an officer in the Peninsula and at home to which we are indebted to William Keep. On the training side, it is most interesting to read of some of the methods used in England. We often assume that an officer needed to be a gentleman and little else besides, able to pick up his craft in the field in a kind of 'hands-on' manner. Well, of course, an officer did indeed need to be a gentleman but he also needed to be pretty fit if he was going to march 'over the hills and far away.' Keep's account of having to undergo a great deal of swimming and running and, most intriguing of all, lifting of cannon balls, is very enlightening. He certainly would have felt the benefit in the passes of the Pyrenees where some of the most arduous marching country in the Peninsula is to be found. Keep also makes much of the ability of officers to be able to handle, and shoot accurately with, that most famous of infantry weapons, the 'Brown Bess' musket. The popular image of the British officer in the Peninsula is that of the sword-wielding gentleman leading and directing his troops in action, and yet on more than one occasion we find Keep's brother officers fighting with muskets themselves, at Maya and St Pierre, for instance. On this latter occasion we find private soldiers loading their muskets and passing them forward to an officer who was engaged with French skirmishers. This sort of thing is usually confined to Hollywood but here we have it, and why not? If an officer had a reputation for being a good marksman, gained on a country estate in England perhaps, then it made sense for the private soldiers to keep him well-armed.

Much of what we know about William Thornton Keep comes from two sources, his surviving daughter Julia, named after his sister, and who was still alive in 1914 aged 88, and Mr Robert Macleod, nephew of Henry Alexander's daughter Vittoria. Alexander was a comrade of Keep's in the 28th in the Peninsula. According to Keep's daughter, Keep copied the letters himself in 1830 from the originals, which his mother would not part with. These originals finally went to Keep's sister, also named Julia, and nothing was known of them until after her death. We do know, however, that from correspondence between Julia Keep and Robert Macleod there was an attempt by Macleod to have the letters published and in January 1913 Julia wrote to him saying, 'I fear that you are having much trouble in your kind endeavour to have my father's letters published.' Well, some 84 years on, the letters of William Thornton Keep have at last arrived before us. Let us hope that Keep, his daughter and Robert Macleod are looking down from the heavens, satisfied that Keep's story has finally been told, the story of a soldier in the service of the King.

Chapter One
Gone for a Soldier

When William Thornton Keep joined the 77th (East Middlesex) Foot in 1808 he did so when the events that were to lead to Britain's involvement in the Peninsular War, after having been simmering away rather nicely, were about to boil over into full scale war. Napoleon's troops, some 30,000 in all under Marshal Andoche Junot, crossed the Pyrenees in October 1807, the object of their march being Portugal and its capital city, Lisbon. Much to her credit Portugal had refused to be intimidated by Napoleon and would not be a party to his so-called 'Continental System', by which he hoped to starve Britain into submission by forbidding the rest of Europe to trade with her. Junot's exhausted army arrived in Lisbon too late, however, for when they entered the capital on November 30th they learnt with dismay that the Portuguese Royal Family had sailed for Brazil the day before.

The following year a further 100,000 French troops marched into Spain and in March 1808 occupied the capital, Madrid. Outraged by this and by the ineptitude of both King Charles IV and the so-called 'Prince of Peace', the corrupt Manuel Godoy, the Spanish people rose up on May 2nd and attacked the French troops, killing around 130 of them in what was known as the 'Dos de Mayo'. Sadly, this provoked savage reprisals by the French troops which was to set the tone of the war between these two nations.

The War of Independence, as it became known in Spain, was a brutal war, fought initially between the disorganised, incompetent Spanish army and the fearsome, savage guerrillas on one side, and the French veterans on the other, the invaders always handicapped by interference from Paris, by internal bickering between various jealous commanders and by the constant harassment of the Spanish guerrillas who made life as impossible as they could for the French troops. Initial French successes were matched by setbacks in Valencia and Saragossa and before long the British government was drawing up plans for an expedition to the Peninsula to aid the two Iberian nations. The surrender of Dupont's 18,000 French troops at Baylen — the greatest Spanish success of the war — only served to increase Britain's determination to act, and on August 1st 1808 a British army of 15,000 men under the command of Sir Arthur Wellesley landed at Figueiras in Portugal. The Peninsular War had begun.

There was to be no share in the forthcoming glory for William Keep and the 77th Regiment, however, not, at least, until 1811 when the 77th embarked for Portugal, fighting its first action at El Bodon in September of that year. By then, however, Keep had resigned from the regiment on the grounds of ill-health. But we are jumping ahead of ourselves. Let us return to the winter of 1808. The British army, now under the command of Sir John Moore, has just begun its ill-fated advance into Spain whilst on the French-Spanish border Napoleon himself is poised to enter Spain with 100,000 men to chase the 'hideous leopard' into the sea. Meanwhile, back in the relative quiet of an English garrison town, William Keep is just about to meet his new comrades of His Majesty's 77th Regiment of Foot.

Winchester
7th November 1808

My dearest Mother,

Ever since I arrived here I have been anxious to begin to recount to you what has occurred since our separation — that distressing moment when I left in sorrow and tears your tender embraces to encounter the world and scenes so entirely new to me — quitting a home endeared to me by so many fond recollections. The only consolation now left is to write to you, to impart my feelings and everything that happens in the eventful career Destiny has marked out for me. My Father and I arrived in good time at the Golden Cross, nor did he leave me until he saw the stage in full trot, and all things arranged for my comfort on the journey. I took my place in one corner of the coach, where I sat pensive and sad enough while departing from the spot that had been the scene of all my past joys in this world, and where I was leaving all that was dear to me.

We pursued our route for the first two hours in darkness and silence until we reached the barren heaths of Bagshot and Hounslow, when the grey tints of morn began to appear in the horizon, and discovered to me the countenances of my fellow travellers — two elderly gents and a prim lady. They looked from the window on a house by the roadside where the terrible murder was lately committed on the old gentleman and his housekeeper and began to converse upon the mysterious circumstances of that transaction. But my heart was too full of sorrowful reflections to pay much attention to them; I saw likewise on the heath the Gibbet where Abershaw was hung in chains and thought of those days as described in Roderick Random and other novels, when the roads were infested with Highwaymen, a danger there is luckily now no apprehension of. We breakfasted in an antique parlour at a comfortable inn and resumed our seats in the coach, taking care to make the necessary arrangements for our comfort during the remaining part of the journey by putting our parcels in order. My cocked hat box and sword shifting positions suited to circumstances and announcing my profession to my companions, who were very agreeable people. The green baize bag with the gingerbread nuts and other etcs you had prepared for me reminding me every moment of your tender solicitude was untouched, for I had no inclination to eat anything, and so the nuts were squeezed as flat as a pancake by the time we reached Winchester. As I had never been further from London before than Windsor, when we had passed that place I began to look around me, a new world as it were presenting itself to my observation. By 4 o'clock in the afternoon we arrived at our destination. The glorious sun shone forth on our arrival, and gave Winchester a very inviting aspect, and I took up my abode at the Black

Swan[1], from whence I am writing to you. They accommodated me with a front parlour and you may easily imagine my eyes were soon fully engaged in surveying my new associates as they passed up and down the street. The first objects that struck my attention were some members of the Band in their fanciful apparel, and the officers and soldiers passing about, reciprocally saluting as they met, their uniforms corresponding with my own made me feel as if I already belonged to them. And after tea I uncorded my boxes to prepare myself for their parade next morning. I took from the wrappers my scarlet coat and beautiful epaulette and attached it to the shoulder in readiness[2], proceeding to discompose the various things you so carefully packed for me, in doing which I shed abundance of tears at these proofs of your affection, and as the thoughts of home occurred to me. In the morning I rose in better spirits, and after partaking of a good breakfast dressed myself and walked up the street to the Barracks, which are on a declivity overlooking the city and surrounding country, and consist of a vast pile of building intended for a palace, and erected in the reign of Charles the Second[3]. Under one of the porches of this stupendous abode I met a young officer whom I accosted and acquainted with my name, and he behaved most affably and directly introduced me to two other gents of the Regiment. One of these was the Adjutant, a Lieut. Baird, who invited me to breakfast with him next morning. From him I understood that Col. Whitelocke was at Southampton but expected to return on the following day, having therefore no more to do I returned to the Inn and resumed my plain clothes, intending to take a walk round Winchester and its vicinity before dinner.

I extended my rambles further than I intended, attracted by the beauty of the hills and dales amongst which Winchester is situated and went early to bed on my return. In the morning I went to fulfil my engagement, and was ushered into the room occupied by the Adjutant in the Barracks, and he received me very politely, and began to chat upon military affairs. His employments were so pressing that the serjeants came for orders during our repast, and I was much struck with the soldierlike aspect of everything around me. I felt, as I can imagine a recruit to feel upon his enlistment, somewhat awed by the display of the implements of war and the discipline prevailing among those to be engaged in it. But this was soon relieved by my prepossession for the individuals themselves, to whom I assure you I feel already attached. After breakfast I went with the Adjutant to Col. Whitelocke's quarters, and did not fail to deliver Colonel Pritzler's kind letter of

---

[1] On the corner of High Street and Southgate Street, Winchester. Sadly demolished to make way for shops which, however, still retain the old wooden carving of a swan with a bunch of grapes.
[2] A reminder that at the time the officers of the British army were still wearing the long-tailed coats. The shorter jackets had yet to appear and would not until the introduction of the 1812 Dress Regulations. Ensigns of battalion or centre companies wore just a single epaulette on their right shoulder. This is just one of many fine references to Keep's uniform and, indeed, through them we may trace not only the history of an officer's service but also that of his uniform, as we shall see.
[3] Peninsular Barracks, destroyed by fire in the 1870s and rebuilt on a smaller scale in similar style.

introduction. He received me in a very friendly manner and asked me to luncheon with him. The Colonel looks very sun burnt after his long services in the East Indies, and is much distressed with a weakness in his eyes, that occasions them to flow with water, which gives him the odd appearance of looking as if he was constantly weeping; he is a middle aged man of pleasing manners. The next in command is a Colonel Maddison, who is much older, and so remarkably old fashioned in his habiliments that he might be mistaken for one of the stiff old warriors of past times, such as we see represented on sign boards, or in old pictures, but he is a most social kind hearted man and lives in lodgings in the town, being married. The other field officer is a Col. Spry — a fine military looking officer, whose very appearance seems to indicate all that could be described as a commander in the field of battle.

With this I shall close for the present the description of my new friends in the 77th. I am dearest mother, your grateful and affectionate son, W.T. Keep.

Winchester
20th November 1808

My dearest Mother,

The formalities of an introduction to the Society of Strangers being now at an end, by my becoming one of the Regiment in propria persona, I write to inform you that I am very happily established in an apartment assigned to my use at the very top of this old palace, and from the loftiness of my habitation it commands a fine view of the country as well as of a courtyard beneath, where the evolutions of the soldiers are performed, besides which, as the practising room of the band is not far off, I have plenty of music to entertain me. I must now inform you that I have been making wonderful progress since I wrote last in becoming acquainted not only with the routine of my duties, but with my brother officers as I may now call them, and I really think, though I suppose I am not permitted to say so, that the 77th is a very fine Regiment. This old city is greatly indebted to their presence here, which produces the greatest gaiety, otherwise it would be a very dull place to reside in, and of course bears no comparison with London. I need not tell you how very ancient it is, and the vestiges of that antiquity are very numerous and striking; the gate of entrance near our barracks might make a stranger laugh, or prepare him to fall asleep for a yawning mask has been carved on it by some old wag of a sculptor, but its turreted top and other decorations make it look chivalric, and I can even fancy it might have given admittance to warriors in armour in times past, which I daresay was the case, as this part of the country has been the scene of great events, but they could not have excelled in some particulars what is going on here in our present war with Bonaparte.

Every day adds to the numbers of our Regiment, so that we shall (especially by the volunteering of the Militia) soon have what is called a full muster. Among the antiquities of Winchester, the Cathedral is most worthy of notice, but what

would please you most would be to see us there on Sunday attending Divine
Service, when no one else is admitted. The interior is so spacious that we form a
square, and the Clergyman places himself in the midst of us. The architectural
beauties of the magnificent Building are in the finest state of preservation, and the
snowy whiteness of the fretted walls and arches and tombs with gilt ornaments
added to the great expanse of the place give a fine effect to it. It is encompassed on
the outside by trees and gravelled walks and here in the evening our band plays for
the entertainment of the townspeople, if not engaged at our Mess, which is another
scene I must describe to you. The room appropriated for that purpose is of the
largest dimensions, with passages of great width in which our musicians are sealed.
One long table accommodates us all, with about 15 officers on each side with a
President at one end, and a Deputy at the other. The furniture of the table is
entirely (like the band instruments) the property of the officers, and by continual
contributions is very sumptuous (the Paymaster has deducted from my pay for this
purpose £6.10.0). Grand silver chandeliers and choice plate with all the other things
necessary are provided by this means. When the cloth is removed and the wine
circulating and band in full play it would please the eyes of many ladies to
contemplate the scene it presents, and I am sure you would be delighted with it.
We pay 2/3d each for our dinner, which consists of 3 courses well supplied, but no
dessert except when we have company. It is the only meal we take together; each
officer provides himself with his own breakfast things and bedding, both of them
are therefore required to be as portable as possible. Tables and chairs and coals and
candles are supplied by the Barrack Master. Each Saturday night we give a card
party and supper to the married officers and their ladies, and on other occasions
the Mess room with newspapers is always open. Whist is very much played, at
sixpenny points only. With one of the Surgeons (we have 3) I play a good deal at
this game, with another at Quoits. The former is called by courtesy Doctor
Grieve, who has been many years with the Regiment in the East Indies. The latter
Dr Rudkin, a handsome young man married to a very pretty woman. Among the
officers of my own rank is a Lieut. Leonard Smelt, son of the Lieut. Governor of
the Isle of Man. He is a fashionable friend already of mine. And Ensn Hanwell the
son of a Captain in the Navy I am becoming very intimate with. An Ensign
Abbott is a young and handsome Quaker, and of so volatile and gay a disposition
that he has quitted the fraternity to which he belongs for the pleasure of wearing a
red coat and certainly he is the neatest dressed officer in the Regiment with a fine
slim figure. Next is an Ensign Lemon, a son of Sir Chas Lemon, who is just from
school and a very pleasant youth, and an Ensign Cameron, a Scotchman, a very
simple kind hearted little man, about 35 years of age or perhaps older, for he is
bald, yet of all the officers in the Regiment there is perhaps not one that is more to
be respected, though he is very poor. And a Lieut. Bradshaw has lately joined us
whose tastes correspond very much with my own. He is a very accomplished
scholar and of a literary turn, and is well connected and rich, but derives his
parentage I suspect on the maternal side from a Hindoo. And then there is Captain
Bowes, a most excellent character to form a friendship with. The rest of the
officers are less known to me yet, but many are very gentlemanlike among them.

Assemblies take place frequently twice a week at one of the principal Inns, where the Belles of Winchester congregate. The price of admission is 3/6 for tea, dancing and cards. The Dowagers chiefly amuse themselves with the latter. I attend once a week. The brilliancy of the scene is greatly enhanced by the red coats, I can assure you, and when the country dances are forming a line of them has a splendid effect by candlelight. The Gentry come most of them from their country seats in their own carriages, but chairs are in use, to which we have to escort them and generally those we wish to stay are gone before 12 o'clock, entreaties being too often fruitless with Papa and Mama to remain longer. I do not play at cards there, but perceive to my surprise a strange custom among those that do, which is the quantity of money they place under the candlesticks, which seem to be provided for that purpose, being of silver and hollow. The dresses of the ladies are sometimes superb and their waving feathers when in movement in the dance is very dashing. I will not say a word about the beauty of their persons, nor of the impression made, but leave you to conceive it, and am, my dear mother, your affectionate son,
William Thornton Keep.

Winchester
19th January 1809

My dear Mother,

I have not fulfilled the promise I made of writing to you the beginning of this week, as I have waited to give you positive information respecting my going to Southampton, and I have been put in doubt of it from the Adjutant's having said that I possibly might not go there, although he thinks it very improbable that should be the case and has promised me from day to day that he would question Col. Whitelocke on the subject. But he has not done so as yet, and perhaps I may not know for a certainty till it appears in orders, which it must do on Monday as the detachment marches from hence on Wednesday January 25th. I have not been three months with my Regiment yet, and therefore Col. W. may consider me too inexperienced for the duty, but it is extremely unlikely as Ensign Brown was ordered there, when he had not been with the Regiment much longer. The detachment is stationed at Southampton for the purpose of escorting deserters to the Isle of Wight, and about £60 or £80 is put into the officer's hands (to pay the men and defray incidental charges) who is not at all under the directions of Col. Whitelocke while there, but under the orders of Major Foster, one of the Staff Officers attached to Lord Cavan.

I went to Col. W. the other morning with the main guard to report on coming off duty, and he was mentioning that he had just received a letter from the Major aforesaid, so tauntingly worded that he had some intention of forwarding it to Lord Cavan. For some reason or other Major F. is much disliked by the 77th officers. I am unsettled in my determinations on the most economical plan to be adopted if I go. Ensign Lynch who last returned from duty there tells me that he paid 16s per week for his lodgings, exclusive of coals and candles. Now I think provided I go the most advisable way for me will be to accept my billet and avoid that expense altogether.

There is a house kept by a man named Harland who gives to respectable people bed, breakfast and dinner for 7/6 a day. Now may it not be accommodating myself, without injury to him, if I was to give 3/6 for my dinner only, as I cannot consistently breakfast at any other house than that which I am quartered; and tea and supper I can do without. However this can only be decided when I get there. I spent a very pleasant evening at Col. Maddison's, and I must not forget to tell you that Mrs Maddison is a most delightful woman. I wish it was possible that you could become acquainted with her. She enquired after you with the greatest solicitude (I told her of your confinement) and Miss M. I am very much pleased with. Mrs Barlow has quite retrieved herself in my estimation. The old lady received me with such satisfaction and unfeigned pleasure that the impressions of a former interview faded in my memory. I can now only regret that I should so prematurely have censured the cheerful old widow. We played at Loo, and I had therefore full scope to exercise prudence to avoid great losses. But the evening's diversion ended greatly to my advantage, as it was proposed to finish with Fright, at which I won 19s. One of Mrs Barlow's daughters is a very pleasant young woman, about 32, very fair and rather corpulent. They live in a quiet, retired street with everything handsome about them, but old fashioned.

I shall undoubtedly obtain a fortnight's leave of absence in March, from the 1st to the 14th, if we are not previously removed to any distant station, and I assure you I am all anxiety to see you again, as I have a thousand occurrences to talk over. I am most happy in my Father's and your professions of affection towards me, but I must assure you that there is not a single thing that I would wish to have sent me. I suppose you must have seen Lady Cavan by this time. I am still longing to know where you will obtain a house. How astonished and delighted I was with Samuel's letter; he has indeed improved amazingly and the diction is very good which does him great credit. You must tell him in reply to his letter that I have not seen the "Young Stranger" since I left him after alighting from the coach on my arrival at Winchester, giving my kind love to him at the same time. I am happy to hear my Aunt has safely arrived at Santa Cruz. I have got a cold in my head, the plaguey band monopolized half my coals this week and I have been too neglectful in keeping my room warm with a good fire this cold weather, therefore I hope you will excuse my concluding this letter sooner than usual, but believe me to be. Yours etc. William Thornton Keep.

Winchester
15th April 1809

My dear Mother,

I wish you could think that the receipt of my letter has been retarded by some probable obstacle, but you have been blaming me no doubt as an idle dog, who amidst the pleasures which surround him allows himself to be forgetful of home, pray therefore my dear Mother alter your opinion, and attribute my silence to the little time my present duties enable me to devote to you. General Dyatt is exerting every nerve to get the Regiment disciplined and equipped, that we may be prepared to take the field as speedily as possible, and the success which attends the volunteering from the Militia to the 77th justifies my hopes of immediate promotion. We are now fully employed by the continual drills our long idleness has rendered so necessary, and in order to make a tolerable appearance at the ensuing Review which takes place on the 3rd of May.

I hope to receive my new coat by that time as I shall be desirous of cutting a respectable figure on the occasion (by the bye, my dear Mother, so extremely out of uniform is the colour of my new facings as I before observed that I shall be greatly obliged to you to compare the facings of the new coat with the small pattern I will contrive to conceal beneath the seal of this letter). I admit that the stuff used in cleaning it materially changes the original hue, but as there has not yet been any occasion to make use of it, it is easily seen that the fault is in the cloth[1]. I am plaguing you sadly with this nicety of mine, but I would not do it were it not absolutely necessary.

I suppose you have heard of Lady Honora Woodgate's marriage. It is said the bridegroom has obtained a prize under false pretension and that the famed possessor of a large fortune has nothing but his pay to depend upon as Captain in the 18th Dragoons. So much for report, which circulates with great rapidity, when it is ill naturedly marvellous. Lord Cavan will I dare say come over to the Review. I shall be very proud to be noticed by his Lordship in the presence of my brother officers. I cannot find out whether Lady Cavan is at Southampton. You shall know if I hear.

I find no ill effects from my night duties, you will think it no wonder when I tell you (entre nous) that I sleep as sound almost as in my own room! And I blush to add (but you will laugh to hear it) that we have fallen into a very unsoldier like practise of removing our mattresses to the Guard Room to make this severe duty come as easy to us as possible, my only reason for disliking an officer's Guard is because I see no absolute utility in it, unless indeed it is to make us youngsters acquainted with these duties betimes, that we may be better prepared to campaign.

I went to a Party the other night to Col. Maddison's, and spent a very pleasant evening. They behave to me with the most affectionate kindness. I think it is not improbable that the lady you correspond with of a similar name may be a relation, as they have a large family resident in England. But who is this incognita you write to? Mrs Maddison's Mother died whilst I was in town. I have not seen Miss Barlow since my return. It would not be amiss for me to call on them, and I will if you are of the same opinion. I find Winton but little enlivened by the

---

[1] The facings of the 77th (East Middlesex) Regiment were yellow, which had obviously faded. This is an interesting comment, coming as it does from an officer at home on garrison duty. If the colour so faded at home one can easily imagine the effects that the Iberian climate, for those officers serving in the Peninsula, had upon uniforms.

presence of the Militia Volunteers, they are a great annoyance to the sober Inhabitants, and a great trouble to our Guard, to secure the drunken and riotous.

The Winchester Races took place last Thursday, most of our gents were there on horseback (the race course is on a Down about 5 miles from this); Captain Bowes and I choosing a less expensive way of going, proposed to walk there, but on our arrival you may imagine how surprised and awkward we felt to perceive that there was scarcely a dozen people on foot, even the farmers servants and others being à cheval. The best of the fun was the shifts we were put to to conceal ourselves from fashionable friends (making no great figure besides in our plain clothes) among others the Nunis's, who were driving round the course in their Barouche. The race was ended by an excellent run, and we returned to Winchester well pleased with the day's diversion.

I hope my dear Grandmother is well, and dear little Julia and Alfred. With kind love to Samuel. Believe me to be, etc., William Thornton Keep.

Winchester
28th April 1809

My dear Mother,

With a sad weight upon my heart and spirits I sit down to the painful task of relating an event, by which I have been deprived of the chief friend that endeared me to my profession. That amiable and fine fellow Captain Bowes is dead (and buried). Your own imagination can best paint my feelings at the loss I have sustained in a companion with whom my happiness was so closely interwoven, and on whose friendship I had so pleasing a reliance. Your last kind letter has remained many days unnoticed, for which I need not I am sure apologise now that you know the melancholy occasion of it. Poor fellow, he caught the scarlet fever with which he only lingered six days. I was not aware of his extreme danger until within a few hours of his death. It is out of my power to sufficiently commend so excellent a character. How gratified I was in such an Associate! How many hours of the day did I spend in his company. I never expect to meet with a young man so truly estimable and good, and I am convinced he is gone to Heaven.

I shall turn from this distressing subject, as I dare say you desire to learn some better news from me. All our officers are recalled from the recruiting duty for the purpose of being present at the Review; yet you need not hurry yourself in sending my new coat as I do not expect to want it before the middle of next month. I will not fail to write to the Miss Pilfolds shortly, and hope they are well. I am in very low spirits as I before mentioned, and in addition to which I have a torturing head ache, which may in a great measure account for this wretched scrawl. My time is now completely devoted to duty. General Dyatt is determined to annoy us as much as he can. We must be removed from this dismal spot shortly as we have now become an effective Regiment and I care not how soon, for I can find little enjoyment here after the loss of poor dear Bowes.

On looking over his papers I had to witness a last evidence of his virtues in the many charities which they proved, but although I was in such confidence with him he never spoke of the good he did at the expense of his purse. How worthily is the motive of his economy explained! He caught fever in attending the Hospital (a duty we have very frequently to perform, to ask the sick if they have any reason to disapprove of their treatment, a very useless form, not at all complimentary to the Medical Gentlemen under whose special care they are placed). For this purpose we have to enter the Infection Wards, as well as others, when on duty. Both our Surgeons paid him the strictest attention. They are of the opinion that his system was bad previously to his taking the fever, the infection was very great. The Assistant Surgeon and his Wife have taken it, and poor Cameron has been once or twice on the point of death. I commenced with this melancholy subject, and I must close with it, but I know you will excuse it.

I expect to hear that you are again in Scotland Yard by the next letter. With affectionate remembrances to my Father and Grandmother, kindest love to Samuel (to whom by the bye I shall enclose a letter in my parcel) and to Julia and little Alfred, not forgetting other friends whom haste does not allow me to enumerate. I remain yr affectionate. son, William Thornton Keep.

P.S. I have particularly to request you will oblige me by the acceptance of a relic of my departed friend, that will be mentioned in my next, and with it I shall enclose some lines to his memory I am writing on this melancholy occasion, which I trust will not only make you better acquainted with him, but merit your approbation.

Winchester
24th May 1809

My dear Mother,

There has been so much bustle at Headquarters these last few days that I have not till now found time to say how grateful I feel to my Father and yourself for the present which I received by the Coach on Friday last. The Coat fits extremely well, and the facings are quite regimental, but I am delighted to tell you that it came most opportunely for the Review, which took place on Monday before Lord Cavan. A beautiful day encouraged me to put it on, and if I required improvement to my appearance neither art nor ornament could have effected it. The epaulette looked beautifully brilliant on the new scarlet, and I believe I must altogether have been very stylish.

I told you in one of my former letters that Genl Dyatt had commenced a warfare with Col. Whitelocke, and I must now let you know how it has terminated. It happened that Col. W. had obtained leave to go to Southampton and on the morning that he had intended to avail himself of it Genl D. was with the Regiment at drill. The General desired to see the regimental Order Book (probably with an idea that it had not been mentioned therein that he was expected to visit us) and he found that an order had been inserted with the word "regimental" affixed to it, instead of "District" (and it ought to have been the latter). He immediately called the Adjutant, and told him to desire Colonel Whitelocke to come to him instantly. Col. W. received this message just as he was stepping into his Chaise, and anxious that the Genl should not have to wait he appeared on parade in plain clothes. He pull'd off his hat and bow'd respectfully to the Genl, but Dyatt with the greatest rudeness darted with his horse to the farthest end of the Battalion, there calling out to the Colonel (who was following him) "To go and dress himself", which he spoke in a manner much too harsh to be used to a private soldier.

Col. Whitelocke approached him, and offered an apology, alleging in the most respectful way as an excuse that the General's desire to see him immediately induced him to come in the clothes he then wore. Instead of receiving this as an apology, the Genl became more violent, and after using the most ungentlemanlike language, he added with a taunting wave of the hand "You shan't go to Southampton", repeating these words several times. You may imagine how distressing it was to hear the Col. of the Regiment talked to in this manner before the men. He then proceeded in the inspection of the Regt and went on in a great rage with everything and everybody. After he left us, Col. Whitelocke called a meeting of the officers and stated to them that he believed they must have been sensible of the ill treatment he had that morning met with from Genl Dyatt, to which we replied that we were ready to repeat the words Genl D. had used. A sort of quarrel then ensued between Col. W. and Col. Maddison, and Col. W. asked him whether he had ever given him any displeasure, either in his official capacity or private character, to which the other answer'd "No" he had not. (On the first day Genl Dyatt saw the Regiment, Col. M. pointed out to him some circumstances that tended to the disadvantage of Col. W., which was the cause of this.) Col. W. told him it was no business of his to do so, and added that he did not know what brought him there, as he was not wanted.

It then appeared that Col. M. was displeased because Whitelocke had omitted to tell him that he should be absent from parade at the Genl's Inspection (which for the reasons above, it is plain to see Col. W. had good reasons for not doing). The Colonel told him he did not conceive it was necessary, he (Col. W.) being Commanding Officer of the Regiment.

This sort of jealousy frequently exists in Regiments, so much so that sometimes the officers are divided into parties and won't speak to each other. A good deal exists here, some officers being adherents to Whitelocke, some to Maddison, and others again to Spry. Col. W. wrote a letter to Lord Cavan immediately after this event (which he shewed me) for I have been drawn into this fracas with others, as you shall presently know. It was strongly expressive of his feelings, which you may think when I tell you that he could not refrain from tears at the time. The consequence was that Lord Cavan came over to enquire into it, as Col. W. expressed a desire to lay it before the Duke of York. I cannot conclude this subject at present, being anxious to avail myself of an offer made by a Captn Campbell to deliver this in town, as he is leaving the Regiment on leave of absence (and I am happy to tell you I shall have the payment of his Company which will be an addition to my pay of 2s a day). A very pretty scrawl this! and about what cannot materially interest you. But I shall nevertheless write you further particulars in a day or two, for it is impossible to say yet what may be the result of it, and can only add that Lord Cavan behaved very well to me. Adieu therefore dear mother, & Believe me to be, etc., William Thornton Keep.

P.S. By mistake of Captn Campbell's servant the enclosed letter was not taken with him to town. I am sorry for it, because it may keep you in suspense about me, otherwise it is very lucky as Lord Cavan has sent for me to him to ask where you are at present, and whether the house in Cleveland Court has been let. I told him it had, and that you was in Middle Scotland Yard. His Lordship says that Lady Cavan intends going to town, and that she will of course call upon you. So you can prepare for her ladyship. Lord C. didn't mention when, and I entirely forgot to ask the question, but I imagine in a day or two.

Winchester
22nd June 1809

My dear Mother,

I returned from Eaglehurst on Tuesday last, and being anxious to inform you of it, as well as to describe the kindness I met with there as soon as possible, I had commenced a regular detail, hoping to gratify you with the description of many entertaining scenes in my sojourn amid the Haut Ton, but behold! an old ingenious circulator of news surprised me at the moment I had selected for the purpose, with a somewhat unexpected disclosure of important intelligence! Intelligence that so completely suspended all thoughts of what I had intended to write that I dropped the pen. He informed me of news that we are all in high spirits at receiving, that the Regiment was ordered to prepare to leave immediately to embark for Foreign Service! Until however this report was confirmed I thought it most proper to defer informing you of it, and in consequence did not write until I ascertained that Everything is true as reported. The Regiment was under arms this morning at 5 o'clock, when a selection of the men took place, and the most speedy preparation is now on foot, as the Route to march has been expected this day. We are to form part of the Grand Expedition of 40 thousand men so long talked of, all England and Europe will be interested in our destination, at all events we have the satisfaction of knowing that we are about to be sent somewhere on actual service, as no women or children may accompany us. Nor are we to take our heavy baggage, our absence therefore from England will be much shorter.

The great bustle and confusion prevailing prevents my replying to your long letters just now in any other way than to express how much I am indebted to you for the patience you evinced in writing them, when they can remain thus unacknowledged. I am now about to enter upon a new series of events. I look with some surprise at the changes time has already produced, but who can conceive what is yet to come! I shall write a dozen letters before I go to you, and hope you will not give way to unnecessary despondency. I shall do well in the reliance I have on my good fortune, be assured.

I can only add that I spent a delightful time at Eaglehurst. Lord and Lady C. did everything to render my stay with them agreeable. I slept as before in Lady Alicia's chamber. I need not describe to you the enchanting situation of it, opening with glass doors upon the sea and the lawn, and I much admire the custom in this part of the world of having the bedroom on the ground floor. I thought myself in fairyland there, it was all so elegant and beautiful.

I think I saw a neat little basket directed to Scotland Yard. I can't pretend to say what it contained. Heaven sent it was filled with something more valuable than eatables are to you. I enclose the half of a note from what I received as you expected. I intended to send you the whole of it, for that purpose, and have to regret I have just purchased poor Bowe's camp bedstead, as that is one of the things I do not now require. I shall write to my Father a long letter before I leave England of course, in the interim remember me most kindly to him and to my grandmother, Saml and Julia, not forgetting my good little friends the Pilfolds, and Mr and Mrs Willis, & believe me, etc. etc., William Thornton Keep.

                                                                    Winchester
                                                                    27th June 1809

My dear Mother,

I am happy to be able to tell you that we are entirely out of suspense, as the route is received for us to march to Portsmouth to embark on Thursday week. The Regiment proceeds in 2 divisions, one on the 6th, the other 7th July. This delay will no doubt afford you much delight, it gives us an opportunity of preparing ourselves and is occasioned by the time required to collect so large a force. The whole of the troops will be at Portsmouth by the 8th. We understand that some part of the Expedition will be encamped for a short time, but I believe we are to embark immediately on our arrival. We are allowed to stay here till the latest, as it is only 2 days' march from hence to Portsmouth. Conjectures are still various respecting our Destination, of course on that subject I can give you no certain information. Many are of opinion that we are to act on the coast of France.[1] This is certainly an eventful period. Bonaparte is now to fall or never. The combined efforts of his enemies are destined to crush him. But if he escapes, the

---

[1] Keep was not far out here, as his destination was to be the island of Walcheren. This gives an indication of just how little the officers knew themselves of their destination when a new campaign was embarked upon. If it was Spain, they undoubtedly knew but quite often they were completely in the dark. When the British army embarked upon its ill-fated campaign in the Rio de la Plata in 1806-07, many officers had no idea of their destination and, in fact, several memoirs appeared afterwards with references to the 'secret' or 'remote' campaign. (See Fletcher's *The Waters of Oblivion*, p.59.)

consequences will be dreadful to England and the other nations of Europe, who resist him.[1]

Your kind letters must now be noticed. I am extremely sorry that you are so uncomfortable about me, as I feel every confidence in your receiving the news without relaxing from that Trust, which is established in the best Hope, and that you have always possessed in your sufferings. This is but one among the many cares you have to contend with, yet that it should be most oppressive distresses me and occasions me regret I feel ashamed to own, as I am conscious of being an additional weight of anxiety to you.

Could I forget your troubles I might be much more in spirits leaving you. Rest assured no small obstacle shall deprive me of the consolation of writing to you, and as often as possible. I am sorry my forgetfulness in not mentioning in time my Bedstead was the means of giving you such trouble in procuring me one. We are not allowed to take anything more than a portmanteau. Some of the officers intended to take a mattress, but I am apprehensive in case I took mine I might find it objected to, and have to send it back again when we come to embark. Do you recommend that I run the chance? It certainly might be required particularly in a transport ship, where there may be poor accommodation of that sort. I don't know which of my boxes to take, the one being too large and the other too weak to stand much buffeting. I shall provide myself with half a dozen shirts only, 1 pair of boots, pantaloons, and great coat, 4 pairs of cotton stockings and 3 of worsted. I bought these by the advice of old soldiers who vouch for the benefit I shall derive from them with wet feet. I hardly think it worth the while sending all my clothes etc. to you, the expense of carriage would be so great, but of course if you like it I will. I should wish to send my writing desk, papers and linen, which I can do in the little deal box. My bedstead and heavy trunk would remain very secure here, as a place will be appointed to hold our heavy baggage. Tell me what you would have me do. You very kindly mention the blankets you have put together for me, most of the officers have what are called Boat Cloaks, made of a kind of plaid and lined with green baize, they are very serviceable as they enable one to do duty at night with them. If you could have time to put such a thing together I should like it very much. The Bolster you have sent me I shall hope to lay my head upon on my return to quarters at home from the campaign, and the waistcoat shall not remain unnoticed when I can find myself in a situation to wear it.[2]

---

[1] Napoleon did indeed escape destruction at the hands of his enemies. He achieved a decisive victory over the Austrians at Wagram on 5-6 July 1809 but this was to be one of the last of his great victories and his story would be one of steady decline until his final fall at Waterloo in 1815.

[2] One of the trials of life for an officer going on campaign was the selection of campaign clothing and equipment. Perhaps the most useful items here were wet weather clothing. It is interesting to see Keep, an officer, taking advice from old soldiers on protection against wet feet. Indeed, one of the features of Keep's letters is the interface between himself and his men, something often missing from officers' memoirs. (See Keep's letter of October 8th 1812 for more detailed comment on campaign equipment.)

I am sure you are very thoughtful of me, and don't know how I shall repay you in this World for all you have done for me. Pray my dear Mother don't desire to trouble Lord and Lady Cavan about me, they are your sincere friends, and will not require to be reminded that I am your Son. I took your advice and spoke to them separately about my promotion, and particularly urged to his Lordship the peculiar hardship which I stated to my Father, respecting the junior officer purchased over me. He asked what sum it required. I begged his Lordship to tell me whether it was worthwhile, as I supposed myself entitled to my Lieutenancy without purchase in consequence of the increased establishment of the Regiment, but his Lordship said that we wanted two hundred men more before I could get it by that means.[1]

We have lost many officers lately one way or another, among others Abbott and Smelt. The former was a Quaker and forced to resign, and the latter got himself involved in a very awkward affair at Southampton with an Inn Keeper's daughter, whose father entered an action against him, that has furnished a subject for the newspapers, and amusement for the gossips all round the County of Hants. Col. Maddison was going to retire from the army when this Order arrived, and his military ardour was revived, and he intends to command us. Mrs Maddison is very much distressed at it. The Col. is almost too aged for active service, but perhaps he will act with more coolness and discretion than one much younger. I wonder Lord Cavan has not a command on such an occasion, but am told his high rank as Genl is the obstacle.

The Barlows have behaved very kindly to me. Pray tell the Miss Pilfolds that they have introduced me to many fine people here, which they have really taken great pains to do. Remember me to Miss Ann Jones. With affectionate regards to my Father and Grandmother, love to Samuel and my dear little Julia, and with anxious hopes for the speedy recovery of Alfred. I subscribe myself dear mother. Your very affectionate Son, etc. William Thornton Keep.

Winchester
29th June 1809

My dear Mother,

I avail myself of every opportunity of writing to you before my departure, altho' the contents of my letters may be hardly worth your perusal. You must not think that I doubt my Father's inclination to assist in my promotion if it laid in his power. No, I am sure he would do his utmost to serve me. Pray prevent his writing to me on this subject, as it would only be the means of increasing his regret. I see by the papers the Guards are ordered to embark, and Mr Lambert's

---

[1] Keep became a lieutenant in the 28th (North Gloucestershire) Regiment in 1813, which regiment he joined after two years convalescence from fever contracted at Walcheren. In 1828 he stated that he obtained his ranks without purchase. (WO.25/764).

Battalion,[1] so that perhaps we may be fortunate enough to go together. I wish we may, as I like him exceedingly, and we became very intimate during my last visit to Eaglehurst. I suppose ultimately he will be made his Lordship's Aide de Camp, as Captain Duncombe I hear is about to leave the army. Hubert Gould is a very agreeable companion, he promises to introduce me to his distinguished relations, the Marchioness of Stafford I believe is one of them, from which family I have heard he will inherit a large fortune. Do you know Lady Sarah de Crespigny, I mentioned before that she is a most friendly charming woman, and the Colonel, a fashionable good natured man. We were much amused at his house, in which was a Billiard table to amuse us, and beautiful pleasure grounds within a short distance of Eaglehurst.

I saw in the papers an accident to a Miss Healy of Northumberland Street; I hope it is not the unfortunate daughter of Mrs Elley whose death you so lately told me of. How considerate you are of my wants. I was hurt nevertheless at your returning the £5 and leaving you at the expense of all you have provided me with.

We shall receive the allowance granted on the embarkation of Regiments (£12.10.0 to me as Ensign) besides which we may probably get 2 months' pay in advance. Government finds us provisions on board of ship but it may be necessary for us to subscribe for a sea stock of our own notwithstanding that. But do not be apprehensive of my wanting money, as I could at any time procure an advance from the Paymaster although I trust I shall be able to avoid that necessity. I look forward to spending a happy Christmas with you, when our toils are over. I have no presentiment of danger, and shall take every care of myself. I intend to write to my Aunt before I go. I shall do as you recommend with respect to her letters. A detachment of 200 men will remain here in the charge of 3 officers, and I will get them to forward them. I don't recommend Samuel's going to the West Indies, and think he may do better in the army. I have a friend in an officer of the name of Bradshaw (the clever young Gent I was speaking to you of when in town). He comes nearer in my estimation to poor Bowes than anyone else. The hurry of the moment prevents my mentioning many to whom I must be remembered, particularly the Davis's. Don't let me appear forgetful of a family from whom I have experienced so much kindness. Pray write soon, it will be delightful to hear from you all the news you are in possession of, of every kind before I go. I wish to God I could see you, but time won't admit of it. You must excuse this oddly written letter and in so small a hand that I hope you will use an eye glass in reading it. Once more Adieu, etc. William Thornton Keep.

---

[1] Lieutenant Colonel John Lambert commanded the five companies which formed the Light Infantry battalion. It consisted of 5 captains and lieutenant colonels, 13 lieutenants and captains, 1 adjutant, 1 quartermaster, 1 surgeon, 1 assistant surgeon, 35 sergeants, 35 corporals, 10 buglers and 545 privates. (Mackinnon, *Origin and Services of the Coldstream Guards*, II, pp123-124.)

Bishop's Waltham (on the march to Portsmouth)
8th July 1809

My dearest Mother,

At length we have bidden a final adieu to Winchester, to enter upon a more extensive field of improvement in the military science. The 2nd division of the 77th (with which I am at present) left the old City at 6 this morning, amidst the lamentations of the soldiers' wives, and a numerous concourse of Inhabitants. The weather wore a very unfavourable aspect on starting, but it cleared up, and we concluded our day's march without experiencing the effects it threatened. I must say that I felt rather touched at leaving a place where I had spent so many happy hours, and the recollection of the unfortunate Bowes struck my heart forcibly as we were quitting the spot which received his remains. It made me coincide with your opinion and just observations on the instability of all earthly enjoyments and led to a weakness of feeling I couldn't easily divest myself of or overcome so well as conceal. But this is not a time to indulge in such a retrospect of the past! The influence of example ought to obliterate the remembrance of troubles gone by, and the army is certainly a school to enable one to do so most expeditiously. Yet I am wretched when I think of the many unpleasant tasks you undergo. Your embarrassments must create continual anxiety. Heaven grant you every enjoyment during my absence, let no thought of me occasion an extra pang to your heart! I shall put up with patience and resignation to every thing I may meet with. No rash imprudence or intemperate zeal shall lead me beyond what my duty requires. The ways of providence are so ambiguous that if it is my fate to encounter dangers I may still escape and surmount them. I don't know how sufficiently to express my thanks for the portmanteau and Boat Cloak, and think you ought to have made use of the money I sent to pay for them, but you delight in being generous, and no obstacle do you consider above your capacity in obtaining that which you think will afford me comfort. I am much indebted to Mrs Willis for the fur cap, as it will prove very useful to me on a night watch. I hope Mr Willis is well.

This obscure little town is quite alive with us. It is otherwise a melancholy out of the way place, selected as a station for the French officers who are prisoners of war, and you may imagine with what curious downcast eyes they look upon us. We march tomorrow morning at half past 5 to Gosport (for the Route has been altered) and we are to be encamped there for a few days. It is just the same as Portsmouth as to distance, from which it is only divided by the harbour, so that you can go from one place to another with the same facility almost that you cross the Thames. I have packed up the small black box with the linen etc (a good deal of which I had not time to get washed) and will send it off so as to arrive next week. In the large box I have put several small things, and my regimental coat, but I found they would not contain all I had, and therefore lent them (such things as I couldn't cram in) to Lieut. Smelt, the fashionable young man and friend of mine, who has been involved in that affair I described to you. He remains at Winchester. Merely a morning gown, boot legs, camp chair, and a few little things. In case a letter comes from my Aunt it will be forwarded to you by him (I shall dine with him at Portsmouth next Monday, and will give him further directions). Col. Whitelocke is still at Winchester. He has purchased a farm and intends residing in that neighbourhood for a continuance. Lieut. Baird has joined us from the Military College, also Major McGregor. We shall muster about 40 Officers when we embark. Edward Lambert is in the 1st Guards, and Lord Kilcoursie in the Coldstream. (Lord K. is in Spain at present.) I hope Samuel will be a comfort to you now I am away, and that he will pay attention to his Grandmother (to whom you must remember me most affectionately). I like Samuel's letters extremely, they are so funny, and admire his odd description of the astonishment excited in the Heroines of Scotland Yard! of whom I imagine he must have made a conquest by this time. Their Barouche will now dwindle away into insignificance by the side of the Carriages at your own door. I should like to get another letter from him before I go, explaining particulars. Remember me kindly to my father and believe me to be my dear Mother. Your affectionate Son, etc. William Thornton Keep.

Chapter Two
The Walcheren Campaign

After spending the first nine months of his military career in England, learning to be both an officer and a gentleman, William Thornton Keep finally got his chance to put the months of theory, drill and training into practice. Unfortunately, his first campaign, Walcheren, also proved to be one of the most ill-fated ever fought by the British army. Indeed, the very word Walcheren conjures up images of sickness, of misery and of farcical mismanagement by those upon whom the fate of the campaign was entrusted. 'A cocked pistol pointing at the head of Britain' was Bonaparte's own appreciation of the strategic situation of the island of Walcheren, which lay just off the coast of the Netherlands. In March 1809, reports indicating French naval activity in the Scheldt, involving, amongst other things, the presence of a French squadron in the port of Flushing and the building of new docks at Antwerp, led to the decision by the British government to send an expedition to capture Walcheren and to destroy the docks. The expedition was a combined army and navy operation, the former being commanded by the Earl of Chatham and the latter by Sir Richard Strachan. The British fleet set sail on July 28th 1809 — the very day that Sir Arthur Wellesley defeated the French at Talavera — transporting almost 40,000 men, and began landing two days later. Unfortunately, foul weather had prevented the landing for 36 hours and when the troops did eventually begin to land they did so at the on the northern coast of the island of Walcheren, the farthest point from Flushing. On July 31st Middleburg surrendered and on the same day the fortified town of Veere was invested. After a short but fairly intense bombardment, Veere surrendered on August 1st. The march south continued and on August 13 the British batteries opened fire on Flushing itself. The following day Denis Pack's force stormed one of the town's outworks and Flushing was duly summoned to surrender the same day. However, it was not until August 15th that the town capitulated, the British taking some 5,800 prisoners.

The capture of Flushing was about as good as it got for the British and Antwerp was never seriously threatened. This was due, not to any intervention on the part of French troops, but by the outbreak, on August 21st, of miasmatic fever which broke out on South Beveland. By the end of the following week there were some 3,400 British troops sick on the island and as the fever spread hundreds began to die. Bodies were buried on the low, flat land, only for high water and rain to wash the bodies to the surface, and the effluvia which rose was as disgusting as it was deadly. The whole operation lurched to its inevitable conclusion on December 1st when the last British troops were evacuated. Even then the full impact of the fever had yet to be appreciated. However, figures later showed that by February 1st 1810 some 4000 British troops had died of the fever against just 100 killed in action.

Many a good soldier, whilst not actually dying, was never to see active service again owing to the fever contracted at Walcheren. Probably the most famous was Benjamin Harris, the famous diarist of the 95th Rifles who, having served throughout the Corunna campaign, went to Walcheren, contracted the fever and returned home sick, his army days at an end. Many more Walcheren men did see service, particularly in the Peninsula, but their constitution was severely weakened and the rigours of the campaign in Spain brought about other forms of sickness partially induced by the fever contracted during the Walcheren campaign.

William Keep could be said to be one of the lucky ones, in that he contracted the fever, survived and lived on to fight in the Peninsula. Of course, he would have considered himself far luckier if he had not contracted the fever at all. Had he not done so Keep would have found himself in the Peninsula in July 1811, which is when the 77th made its debut on the great Iberian stage, taking part in both of the sieges of Ciudad Rodrigo and Badajoz, after which the battalion was sent back to Lisbon on garrison duty. However, those particular episodes were yet to come. For now, we must turn to July 1809, as William Keep once more puts pen to paper aboard HMS Illustrious, bobbing about in the channel at Spithead.

On board His Majesty's Ship 'Illustrious'
Spithead
17th July 1809

My dearest Mother,

After receiving so many letters from you, containing such proofs of your anxiety about me, I am quite ashamed to think that I was unkind enough to allow them to remain unreplied to but never did time fly more swiftly, nor did I ever regret so much the loss of it, as I am sure I can never adequately express my gratitude and affection for your kindness as it deserves. As soon as we arrived in camp, we were brigaded and reviewed constantly with the other Regiments we found there, and had no leisure to do for ourselves what was required, being kept in practise of ball firing etc. etc. General Picton commands the Brigade in which the 77th is to serve, and it is composed of the following Regiments, 1st Battalion 82nd, 1st Battalion 36th, 77th, and two flank companies of the 8th Regiment, a very fine body of men.[1] General Picton is the man whose character suffered so much by the public statements of his conduct in Trinidad, represented in the print shops with the poor girl who was said to have been most inhumanely treated by him.[2] He is extremely

---

[1] Picton's brigade consisted of the 1/36th, 2 coys 2/8th, 77th and 1/82nd, some 2,500 men. It was part of Mackenzie Frazer's 4th Division, which formed part of the left wing of the army at Walcheren. (Fortescue, *History of the British Army*, VII, p.56).

[2] Thomas Picton (1758-1815) was one of the toughest characters of the British army. In 1801 he was promoted to the rank of brigadier-general and was appointed governor of Trinidad. Unfortunately, he was charged with torturing a black woman suspected of theft

polite to us, and appears to be a shrewd clever General, he does not stand upon the minutiae of drill but displays a very comprehensive mind in his military character.

We had very bad weather on our arrival in camp, but although our tents were the same as the soldiers, and afforded only indifferent shelter, we did not feel the injury to be expected from such a change of situation. After the rain ceased and fine weather commenced, it was truly charming. We were encamped near the beach at Stoke's Bay with a beautiful view of the sea, and of the numerous ships of war laying at anchor. I was delighted with the novelty of the scene, and the variety of new objects to be met with in an encampment. I was particularly pleased with the sight of so many troops brought together, most of them Regiments I had never seen before, some Regiments of Highlanders with their martial costume I thought very elegant and when in movement or close column their black plumes and tartans had a very picturesque effect, and even their bagpipes had charm. My first introduction to these warlike North Britons inspired me with a great respect for them. Bugles and Bands of music constantly playing, with the white tents extending over hill and dale formed altogether a very animating scene. We were generally up at the break of day (which may be considered as a treat at this season of the year when the invigorating breezes are blowing) for the purpose of manoeuvring together with the different Regiments of the other Brigades, who met us on an extensive plain on the sea shore. There we usually stayed several hours, but notwithstanding our close application to duty, I never found employment more agreeable. We contrived to mess as we could in small parties, 3 or 4 of us occupying one tent, and I really enjoyed cold meat and a bottle of porter on the grass under these canvas canopies much better than the finest dinner I ever sat down to elsewhere.[1] The week we were there passed so rapidly that I was quite astonished at the short time it appeared since we left Winchester, when it had elapsed. The embarkation was one of the finest sights I ever witnessed. We were directed to strike our tents at 2 o'clock in the morning, and to be at the beach by 4. We embarked yesterday accordingly.

The morning was extremely favourable, but it was dark when we were first aroused, and I awoke to a scene that would afford me great scope for description (had I not many things more material to fill my paper with) for on opening my eyes I was surprised to see the tent appear as if it was enveloped in flames, the canvass of a bright red. I ran out and perceived innumerable fires blazing over a

---

and was tried in 1806. The judgement went against him although at a new trial in 1808 the original verdict was overturned. The Duke of Queensbury, 'Old Q' offered to pay much of his legal costs for the latter trial, an offer which a very flattered Picton generously declined. Picton was to go on to be one of Wellington's most able subordinates in the Peninsula, where he commanded the 'Fighting' 3rd Division with great distinction. He was knighted in 1813 and promoted to lieutenant general. His career ended at Waterloo where he was killed by a French bullet. (See Robinson's *Memoirs and Correspondence*, Myatt's *Peninsular General*, and Havard's *Wellington's Welsh General*).

[1] Keep was fortunate in being able to enjoy the pleasures of campaign life in England under canvas. Tents did not become standard issue to the British army in the Peninsula until 1813, by which time hundreds, if not thousands, of British soldiers had fallen by the wayside owing to ill-health. Until the introduction of tents, Wellington's men were billeted in towns and villages or simply bivouacked in camps beneath the stars.

wide range of country and different grounds of encampment, so that the sky was illuminated, and as day broke the whole camp seemed to have vanished as if by enchantment, and nothing but the troops in marching order left on the ground. I never saw a camp break up before, and was not prepared for the strange effect it produced. The fires were occasioned by the quantities of straw etc. that the men threw out of their mattresses, to which they had set fire as a feu de joie. As soon as the tents were packed, we marched off in high glee to the inspiring national air of the "British Grenadiers", the two Brigades of our Division assembled at the same point lining the shore to a considerable extent, comprising about 6 thousand men. The men-of-war's boats arrived almost as soon as ourselves, and we were put on board with astonishing expedition. We left the shore amidst loud shouts from the spectators cheering, and huzzas from the soldiers. We finally arrived safe to the ship that is to convey us, which is a fine 74 that has a most majestic appearance in the water, and deserves to be called the "Illustrious". Here I find enough amusement in admiring the interior of so large a ship of war, where everything is new and surprising to me. I suppose there is about 14 hundred on board now we are embarked, as she carries the whole of our Regiment in addition to her own complement of seamen, and I leave you to judge what an animating scene it is, to see so many red coats and blue, thus assembled together, with a large body of officers of both services, and from the deck to behold on the surrounding ocean the largest fleet that ever was seen on the coast of Old England! The shores appear deserted, except by spectators, and the soldiers all afloat on the waters, which seem to be animated and in motion proud of the noble freight, with gay pennants flying from the crowd of ships, each of which seems a citadel in itself, with cannon peering through its battlements, and while gracefully undulating in the waves, ports open, and garrisons on board, with bands playing, they look impatient of restraint and ready to start from their anchors. Beautiful weather, the picturesque coast of the Isle of Wight and Hampshire completes the picture!

We gave the officers of the Illustrious a grand dinner at Gosport last Friday which cost us a pound a piece. Government is very indulgent to us, for we are to live entirely free of expense here (and we have a famous table much superior to Winchester). We have claret, port and sherry as much as we choose to drink. The men are allowed half a pint of wine every day. Our sleeping is only tolerable, being much crowded, however, I am very comfortable altogether, and never in my life felt in better spirits and health. My portmanteau is extremely serviceable to me, and as we are situated, I don't know what I would do without it, having no other place to deposit combs, towels, brushes and all the etceteras in. They have allowed our mattresses to come on board. I placed mine in a cot last night and never slept better in the World. I know that if circumstances had not prevented I should have taken my farewell of you in the way your affection points out. It would have been a gratification to me to see you, but it would have been a painful thing to me to put you to the fatigue of a journey in addition to the parting. I am happy that you have declined it as it might have done you much harm. You ask me what I think of Samuel's being sent to Delapierres. I think that as to the treatment no school could be better, but as to his improvement I cannot judge, as the teachers are I dare say different to those who were there with me. French he will necessarily acquire, but they paid too little attention to Latin (I find myself deficient in a knowledge of the principles of pronunciation) a great point in education, which I attribute to the little care paid to my instruction in Latin, as that is the great use of that language and Greek. However I would recommend his being sent there half a year to try. I was much pleased with his letter, and think he will become an excellent scholar soon, at least according to the improvement he has made lately.

The general opinion is that we are going to Flushing, if so, we may be back in a fortnight.[1] I think it very probable as the men are ordered to take a great deal less with them than they brought from Winchester. It is perhaps some place intended to be taken by a Coup de Main. I shall look forward to seeing you very shortly, leave of absence can be obtained easily on our return. Lieut. Baird commands the Company I belong to, which I am glad of. I am much obliged for the newspaper, it afforded me amusement at such times as I could peep into it.

I imagine you have not yet received the box from Winchester as Mr Smelt has only left a day or two, you will get it at all events this week. I think I put a toy in it for Alfred. I hope he is well. The mistake did not take place which you apprehended with respect to the letters sent to Mr Bankes to be franked. The equipment for Mr Lambert is very well considering his rank, but otherwise I don't see that he wants half what you mention. Canteens are superfluous upon the kind of service we are going. The only advantage of the Bear skin is, that it is more portable than the mattress, but that does not signify much as we are not likely to have long marches. The pistols are good things to be provided with because circumstances may occur to render them particularly useful. However I dare say I shall be able to get pistols without purchasing them.[2] In short there is nothing that I wish for that I can absolutely do without, and there is nothing I do wish for (except it is that you may have plenty of money, and be happy). I hope I shall obtain a few hundred pounds to contribute to that object. I remember that Ensigns got £800 each on the first attack of Buenos Aires.[3]

---

[1] A wonderfully over-optimistic statement from Keep. As he was about to discover, it would take much longer than a fortnight for the Walcheren campaign to come to a conclusion, and not a very satisfactory one at that. Nonetheless, it does give us an indication of the high morale of the British troops on the eve of embarkation.

[2] Pistols were privately purchased by officers at their own discretion and expense as they were not a regulation army item. Pistols were only issued officially to cavalry regiments although many infantry officers took them as part of their campaigning equipment. When John Kincaid, the famous diarist of the 95th Rifles, marched to Deal with his battalion prior to embarkation for Walcheren he did so 'carrying a donkey-load of pistols', designed to impress the natives. (Kincaid, *Adventures in the Rifle Brigade*, p.3).

[3] When Beresford captured Buenos Aires in June 1806 the Spanish viceroy sent into the interior a vast store of treasure which was subsequently taken by the British and brought back to England. Altogether, over one million and a quarter dollars were captured by the British in Buenos Aires. Sir David Baird, although not part of the invading force (he remained in South Africa at the time, from whence the expedition began), received £23,990 5s 8d prize money, and Beresford £11,995 2s 10d. Each soldier and sailor received £18 6s. It is unlikely that ensigns received as much as £800 each. (See Fletcher's *The Waters of Oblivion*, p.30, for an account of the capture of the treasure and prize money).

I am afraid I shall be sick on the voyage, and I have no desire to be, from the description I have heard of it. I have no symptoms that way yet. We are in expectation of sailing tomorrow. It is not known yet whether we proceed direct to the place of destination, or whether we shall stop in the Downs. Some of the naval officers think we shall shift our ground to St Helens, and not sail before Wednesday, but we are certain to be off on that day at all events. I am afraid I must be deprived of the pleasure of hearing from you more than once again, as you won't know where to direct. I shall have better opportunities of writing to you. I shall write to my Father tomorrow morning. I am rather drowsy and giddy this afternoon with the motion of the ship, as the sea is rather rough. Pray remember me most affectionately to him, and particularly to my Grandmother. I would write to Samuel but I have not time. Tell him I am much obliged to him for his amusing letter. I can only now add. God bless you, my dear mother, and believe me to be, etc. William Thornton Keep.

On board H.M.S. 'Illustrious'
St Helens Roads, Spithead
20th July 1809

My dear Mother,

I hope you received my long letter which I wrote a few days ago, by which I dare say you have thought it useless to write to me, as you may have imagined we are not in this spot still. We can not tell what detains us here so long, as our Commandants are all with us, and we begin to wish ourselves off. We are very comfortable however in this ship, and have nothing to complain of with respect to our accommodation. I suppose you have got the box by this time, unfortunately I left all the towels behind me, but it is now too late to have them sent to me. I must therefore contrive the best way I can. We are badly off with regard to washing, as our servants are the only people we can get it done by. I long to hear from you and am apprehensive I shall not get your letters before I go, in case you write. We are certainly kept in a most unpleasant state of suspense, as we hourly expect the order to sail, and yet we may not get it for some days.

The orders are issued with regard to our landing etc. The officers are recommended to take no more on shore with them than what they can carry. We in consequence intend taking our boat cloaks rolled up and fastened to our backs like the soldier's knapsacks, and carrying our eatables in haversacks etc. I do not wish it (although it is so honourable a duty) because I have no great faith in my own personal strength, and don't desire to be encumbered too much lest we should have to scale walls, etc. etc., and I shall be loaded enough without it. There is a long detail of orders out, respecting our landing; each boat is to contain 40 men, what baggage we have is to remain on board for a few days, so that we shall probably bivouac (that is, remain in the open field, in such cover as we can form for ourselves with the boughs of trees etc.). It is certain from all this that we are not going to assist our friends in Spain or elsewhere (otherwise we should take the field at once with our camp equipage, or be put into houses on our first landing). Petersburgh is among the number of places surmised at, but Flushing is more generally talked of. We shall be allowed 8 guineas each on landing, in addition to the £12. 10. already received, but this I suppose only in case of need to purchase animals for conveyance of baggage, if it is a protracted campaign. But we must first make good our landing. I don't care about anything so long as we effect that in safety, for I cannot bear the water, there being no room to act, and to be assailed under such circumstances must be very annoying. I think it must be an amazing strong place to resist such an enormous armament. Our force is certainly sufficient to attack something more than common. I have a most excellent friend in a young man of the name of Hanwell. He is the son of a Captain in the Navy. In case of need, I can commission him to do anything for me. I made a very pleasant trip with him to dine with the Midshipmen on board of a Ship of 120 guns called the Caledonia. We went in style, had a boat manned for us with a coxswain, and if my admiration and respect for our Navy could be increased, this visit tended to complete it! I was highly amused with these Gents in their Cockpit (a part of the Ship that never sees daylight) and certainly a merrier banquet I never was present at. My learned friend Bradshaw is also a young man whose friendship I much value. Poor Cameron goes with us, he is a truly excellent Character. His wife is in Scotland with a Mrs Macpherson, in a bad state of health, and he frets very much about her.

The weather continues delightful, and we are anchored within a stone's throw of the Isle of Wight, at a part of it beautifully wooded but wild in appearance, with few inhabitants. We are like a hive of bees in this floating habitation. We may be considered to have 2 rooms for general use (the officers I mean of the 77th) both of the largest dimensions. One is called the Gun, the other the Ward Room. The first is our sleeping place, extending the whole width of the ship (we swing on wooden frames erected for us, in hammocks at night). By day they are taken down and put away, leaving sufficient space to move about in, and our boxes, portmanteaus, etc. are arranged round the windows (or portholes) of which there are several, on both sides of this extensive apartment. This is open to us at all times, and here if you desire it you may even enjoy retirement, for by the aid of a greatcoat, or blankets suspended from the beams, each porthole (the cannon having been all removed purposely to thus accommodate us) may be converted into a separate chamber. Here during mid-day you may take a nap even, or sheltered from the rays of the sun watch its beams playing on the green sea, from the open and commodious window. Here I often come to inhale the breeze, and peruse your letters, or an odd volume. The apartment above has other attractions. That has real windows of glass, giving a handsome finish to the stern of the vessel, or the exterior. In other respects, it resembles a large coffee room in an hotel, particularly when filled with groups of officers chatting and perusing newspapers, etc. A long table is fixed in the centre of it, and the sides panelled off into little chambers for the naval officers, to which there is access by small doors, that have a pretty effect, being opposite each other, and neatly painted. One flight of steps higher leads to the deck, which in ships of this description is a place of great ceremony, so much so that it is necessary to take off your hat on appearing there, with as much form as you would enter a Ballroom. The discipline in the Navy is much more severe than the Army, perhaps rendered necessary owing to their proximity chiefly, and their constant intercourse with each other; the two services agree very well, and I believe they lay aside a good many of their ordinary forms in compliment to us. At all events this part of the ship is always open to us. I this moment hear that we shall not sail till Saturday. It is very strange what can detain us thus long. I fear Bonaparte will have received information of our intentions.

Pray tell my Grandmother I hope to see her well, and in her usual spirits on my return. I have put a necklace in my writing desk for little Julia. She will doubtless understand that it comes from me. By this time I suppose she can talk pretty well. I long to see her. What do you think of my being employed on the Recruiting Service in London on my return? It will be my turn for that duty, and if I don't go there I shall be sent somewhere else. At all events I must look forward to spending my Christmas with you. I wonder what time we shall be absent. Perhaps only a month, and perhaps 4 or 6. If the Regiment distinguishes itself on this occasion, as it has ever done on similar ones in the East, we shall not be stationed abroad in the Colonies but kept at home for services like the present in Europe, as many other distinguished Regiments are. God send we may succeed. You must not forget to remember me to the Davis's. They have been very kind, and have a right to expect it from me. I hope Miss Ann Jones is well. I wonder if she is in the Island just now. If she is she probably does not know that I am so near her. From one of those little windows before mentioned, I see the waves rippling on the sand with the overhanging woods above it. I might easily distinguish her, if there, we are so close to it, but it seems the abode of solitude and quite deserted. I shall write to my father by this day's post, in the meanwhile remember me to him, to my grandmother and Samuel, and all kind enquiring friends, etc. etc. William Thornton Keep.

On board the 'Illustrious'
in the Downs
28th July 1809

My dear Mother,

We have just arrived here, and I embrace the first moment I can command to write you a few lines, a few it can only be as we are in expectation of an immediate order to sail! If I thought the fleet numerous at Spithead, here they appear to be quadrupled, and the sea quite covered with vessels of all kinds. I received your letter of the 22nd with the newspapers which accompanied it. The last I got from you, if you wrote since it has been returned I dare say to the Adjutant General's office. We left Spithead on Tuesday morning at 5 o'clock and we have had such good weather that I have not been in the least sick, and I make no doubt I shall be a tolerable sailor in case of a gale. Some part of the expedition has already sailed, but I do not know whether the ship in which Mr Lambert is embarked has gone. We have not yet learnt much of what has been doing on this part of the coast.

A signal is this moment made from Sir Richard Strachan[1] that we are to put to sea in one hour's time! We are all bustle and hurry. Conceive about twenty of us all writing at once in the Ward Room, all anxious to have our letters conveyed on shore by finishing them as early as possible. There does not appear to be any doubt of our going to Flushing. How we are destined to act is not yet known. We have some reason to suppose that our brigade with General Sir Eyre Coote's will be employed in the first instance in making a false attack, for the purpose of drawing the enemy's forces to a distant point from that which will be attacked by our troops. God knows how we may be employed, but I hope conspicuously. Perhaps ere this reaches you we shall have commenced operations as they say we shall (with the wind prevailing) be near the coast of Holland in the course of this night.

I have everything I can possibly want, and nothing left to wish for, unless in looking forward to something advantageous being derived from going on this service. Heaven send you every earthly comfort during my absence, for to be assured that you are in the enjoyment of health and happiness is what would give me the greatest gratification in the world. So God bless you my dear Mother. I shall ever remain, etc. etc. William Thornton Keep.

On board the 'Illustrious'
in the Downs
28th July 1809

My dear Father,

I cannot leave my native shore without addressing a letter to you, although I have just written to my dear Mother. We have arrived here after three days sail from Spithead. Our progress has been slow, and in our eagerness to hasten it we met with an accident in the channel that might have had fatal consequences. Our ship ran foul of the Ganges of 74 guns, as crowded with troops as we are. She did not hear the signal from the Admiral to weigh, and we came in contact with her at anchor, in consequence of a thick fog, although we had drums beating on the forecastle, and used every other precaution. When from the attraction of the vessels our junction became inevitable, I never witnessed a more critical period of intense anxiety, both Ships becoming visible to each other suddenly as it were, and the decks crowded with so many anxious faces, there being hundreds of soldiers as well as Mariners and Sailors on board of her. The seamen were provided with

[1] Rear Admiral Sir Richard Strachan, 49 year-old commander-in-chief of the naval element of the expedition, joined the navy in 1772. Fortescue described him as, 'a brave and energetic officer, but eccentric in his conduct, very irregular in his hours on board ship, and of greater zeal than ability.' (Fortescue, *History of the British Army*, VII, p.57). He was also known as 'Mad Dick'. He made the rank of Admiral in 1821.

hatchets ready to strike, with arms uplifted on all parts of the rigging as we closed (to prevent ill consequences from its entanglement) and when the hulls came in collision the concussion made them both heel over on their sides, and everything that was cut away fell into the sea between the two ships, besides which anchors cast down a head were forced to be cut loose at the expense of several hundred pounds. But it was well it was no worse, had it blown hard one or both of us must have gone down. There is a great number of vessels here, although a great part of the Expedition has already sailed. We are ourselves preparing to be off, which will account for the hurried manner you may perceive I am writing in. Flushing is undoubtedly our destination. There is a report that Bonaparte is marching 100,000 men in that direction. If so we may expect a pretty warm reception.[1] It is judged to be about 9 hours sail from this to Flushing, tomorrow or following day. We hear that the plan of operations is materially changed. Our Division was to have been the first to land, but other parts of the Army seem now to have the start of us.

I hope we shall make a conspicuous figure. The 77th was ever a most gallant Regiment and I trust will maintain its character. I could not have received anything more acceptable than the newspaper you was good enough to send. I can assure you it was a treat to the whole Ship. The complimentary paragraph you pointed out did not escape the observation of our Naval associates with whom we are extremely united. Our supplies are ad libitum, Claret included, and other choice wines. I have an invitation to dine with the Captain today in the State Cabin. Captains in the Navy rank much higher than in our service, being equal to Lieut.Colonels, and the distinctions of all grades in this Service more strictly preserved than in ours, and the regularity and arrangements that exist in a man-of-war are truly admirable.

We have a good deal of card playing, gambling, and conviviality, a pound at lansquenet on the turn of a card! I look on with wonder at such stakes. This and vingt et un are the usual games, as the time is too busy a one for slow calculating Whist. You may suppose it is impossible to be otherwise than amused among such a large Party. Our dinners are sumptuous, and the festive board furnishes a high treat to the Bon Vivant, of which we have several among our Gents. I know how anxious both you and my Mother will be about me during my absence, and shall take every opportunity to write, so that you may expect a detail of the particulars of what may occur, as soon after our arrival as possible.

There is nothing I wish for that I am unprovided with, and am well assured you would do everything for me within your power. I trust in Heaven that my dear Mother may be spared any more sufferings, and have confidence in my hopes that she will. I must now conclude, so God bless you my dear Father. And believe that I am, your very dutiful and affectate son. William Thornton Keep.

---

[1] Napoleon Bonaparte was far too busy dealing with the Austrians at Wagram and Aspern-Essling to be concerned with the threat to Walcheren and Antwerp. However, it is clear from his correspondence that Napoleon was more than a little anxious for the safety of Walcheren and, indeed, in 1810 made further provision for the defence of the Scheldt following the island's recapture by Bessieres. (See Fortescue, *History of the British Army*, VII, p.96.)

Zouburgh, near Flushing
6th August 1809

My dearest Mother,

Thank God I have an opportunity of writing to you, it is more than I expected to be enabled to do, so soon. I suppose your Anxiety has been somewhat relieved by hearing of our having landed safely, through the public Dispatches. The perils of the Sea are over — they chiefly arose from the shallowness of the water in these parts which kept us constantly heaving the lead to ascertain the depths as we approached — injury being apprehended to the ships from running aground — though we had no boisterous weather to contend with. One of our fleet (the Eagle, a fine 74) was not so fortunate as the rest, having run upon one of these sand banks, and it is reported broke her back. I don't know what the nature of this injury is to ships, but believe it was sufficiently great to oblige the troops on board to be removed to other vessels. The officers of the Illustrious behaved to us in the most handsome manner from the time of our going on board until we left them, on doing which we were only at the expense of half a guinea as a recompense to the servants.

A division of the army quitted the ships for the shore soon after we came in sight of it (the coast of Holland lies so low that it is scarcely visible until you are quite close to it). Imagine us at that moment full of anxiety to watch the appearance and movements of the enemy. It was a beautiful evening, the sea hushed to a perfect calm, and our little flotilla crowded with troops proceeded in good order to one point, at which they were directed to make a descent (these troops consisted chiefly of what are termed Light Companies, who generally lead in these affairs supported by others when necessary). The beach upon which they had to disembark was exceedingly low and sandy, and for a long way out to sea very shallow, yet we could not see into the interior of the country in consequence of not being at a sufficient elevation ourselves to overlook a range of sand hills running parallel with the coast.[1] Behind these hills we imagined the enemy to lay concealed, and all our glasses were employed expecting to behold them spring up when our men came within a range of their shot. You will naturally feel for the perilous situation of these brave fellows crowded together in the boats and thus exposed to danger without any means of helping themselves, particularly where cannon is brought against them, but these perils are considered so imminent that

---

[1] The original location chosen for the landings was on the western coast of Walcheren but heavy surfs, and the prospect of coming under fire from enemy guns on the Kadzand side of the West Scheldt, meant that the plan was changed. Instead, the fleet sailed round to the Roompot, on the northern coast of Walcheren, where the landings took place. From here, it was sixteen miles to Flushing. The delay, whilst not proving fatal to the campaign, certainly allowed the French to prepare for the assault on the town and for King Louis Bonaparte to organise the defence of Antwerp.

they have an especial protection provided for them in another branch of the Service, the Navy, who are furnished with boats carrying mortars and cannon, and called Gun Boats on that account. These little vessels have one or more guns on board, with a few brave men and are so admirably constructed that they swim on the water like a sort of wild ducks, called Eaves Dappers, that are often immersed but constantly rising again on the crest of the billows. They accompany the troops, and this service is termed covering the landing. When our men had approached within some hundred yards of the beach, several shells were fired by the enemy. (These are very large iron balls, hollow in the inside to receive gunpowder, with a small perforation stuffed with a sort of flax that is ignited. They are levelled upwards to descend and explode at a certain distance, and are very destructive.) They came from a masked battery, and our Gun Boats returned the salute in fine style. The shells were the only means the enemy took to oppose the landing, and fortunately the little army escaped the risks they were exposed to, and received no hurt from them. They then marched into the country, and the boats returned to receive more troops, but the battery being soon taken, there was no more opposition.

At 11 at night the 77th quitted the Illustrious and I believe at about 12 we stepped out of the boats. A good natured Tar took me on his back some little distance, which prevented my getting up to my middle in water. It was dark, though the moon appeared at times from behind the clouds that encompassed her. I never saw anything more beautiful than the sea washing on the shore, or I should rather say it presented an extraordinary phenomenon for the rolling waves were quite illuminated, and appeared exactly like phosphorus, so that our feet and legs when we reached the beach were luminous and seemed covered with it. Before we arrived there we thought our troops were destroying some place in the interior, as in that direction the sky was of a deep red, but on reaching the tops of the sandy hillocks we supposed it to be the light of fires the troops in advance that way had made to cheer themselves, particularly as we heard no distant sound of cannon or anything to indicate hostilities. The darkness of night now increased so that it was deemed prudent to remain in position on the sandhills till the day broke, nor should we have been allowed to light fires if we could have done so, being for security obliged to remain in complete silence and darkness. The men piled their arms however, and laid themselves down on the sloping sandhills, in their great coats, and now the rain began to descend very heavily, which it continued to do with little intermission during the six hours we reposed there. Here I found my boat cloak of the greatest service, as I remained coiled up in it with my fur cap[1] on under the hood, as snugly as if I had been under a gilded canopy. I pronounced the camlet to be waterproof, the thick green baize lining being scarcely damp protected by it. We heard a heavy and continued cannonade in the morning, and commenced our march to Veere, a garrisoned town, which we were to be

---

[1] The reference here to a fur cap is rather curious as it obviously implies that Keep served in the grenadier company of the 77th. However, as he goes on to say shortly afterwards, he carried the colour, something which a grenadier officer would not do. Was the fur cap simply a non-regulation item?

employed against. We had taken a most bountiful farewell supper before we left the ship, and our friends at parting had crammed our haversacks, so that we were at no loss for a breakfast. Our canteens besides were well filled with brandy and wines (these are little wooden barrels suspended across the body like shooting belts. They hold about 3 pints, the haversack contains two pockets, a clean shirt, a pair of shoes and stockings in one, and provisions in the other, and is slung across the canteen cord like a cross belt. Having adjusted these things, and folded my boat cloak, and strapped it to my back over my shoulders, I took the Colours and fell in,[1] and we moved forwards in the best spirits, towards Fort der Haak[2] (the battery from which the enemy fired the shells during the landing). It had been taken by our light troops at the point of the bayonet over night and the guns spiked. After a fatiguing march of several hours through deep sands we halted on the dike to refresh the men and wait for orders. We were soon however in movement again, and towards evening reached Veere, which we found to be a strongly fortified place on the margin of the sea. We were moved up quite close to it, to take it by assault, some artillery in the Gun Boats having been employed in effecting a breach. This was not yet deemed practicable, and we were withdrawn for the night, retiring to Zandik, a small village at a short distance. Here we piled our arms, and had large quantities of straw put down on both sides of the street or road running through this place, and after fixing sentries and outposts laid ourselves down to sleep. And here you must fancy you behold us, locked up in slumber in this pretty Dutch village, the moon unclouded shining down upon us, and the sentinels alone being in watchfulness on the outskirts.

The next day we were to storm the defences and take the place. At daylight we were awoke by the renewed firing of the Gun Boats, a division of which had arrived in front of Veere in the night under the command of Lord Beauclerc, but we didn't move out of the village for some hours afterwards, and then advanced inland to secure the approaches on the opposite side. The most remarkable feature as we proceeded was that the ground we had been marching over the preceding day was the highest to be seen (the whole Island as afterwards proved lying considerably below the level of the sea) but the cultivation when we had left this ridge of sand continued improving, and the character of the Inhabitants to develop itself, beautiful orchards and farm houses presenting themselves, which we had plenty of leisure to look at en passant, as difficulties and uncertainties in our front occasioned us to be continually halting.

The sun peeped out and began to shine upon us very powerfully. Several of the peasantry we accosted gave friendly indications, but seemed indifferent to what was going forward. The most remarkable thing I saw was a gigantic horse grazing in a meadow. It was as tall as an elephant, and the largest I ever beheld, and would have been a fine show at an English fair. But here it is not considered surprising. Our columns as we advanced continued closing up, and the country became more

---

[1] See previous note.
[2] This was the fort of Den Haak, on the Veere Gat. It was taken by the 71st under Denis Pack who found the fort abandoned, save for a few prisoners. It was then used by Chatham as his headquarters for the night.

intricate. In the meanwhile the cannonade proceeded and we found ourselves approaching the scene of action, the first evidence of which was from a shell that descended in a field adjoining us, had it been projected with a little more force it must have fallen in the midst of us at the centre of the battalion where I was carrying the Colours, instead of which it fell about 20 yards short of us on the other side of a bank or hedgerow.

This was my first affray, and Ensign Cameron who was carrying the other Colour, looked at me and laughed to see my face somewhat paler than usual. I was taken by surprise, but soon recovered. We had now arrived at an angle of the road, to move forward from which was to be in the fire of several pieces of artillery planted on the walls to command it. The 71st Regiment had already passed, and we had enough to do to receive their killed and wounded thrown back upon us, among the rest a poor Surgeon met with a dreadful laceration. At this critical moment the enemy perceiving us in such force and dreading the assault, displayed a white flag, and the firing was discontinued, and our advance countermanded. The men then left the road open by falling back upon both sides of it, and our General Officers and others rode forward. The capitulation was finally agreed to, but we did not see the French garrison march out, being ordered immediately to proceed on the great advance to Middleburgh.[1] I was sorry time did not admit of our seeing the fortress we had been led up to the gates of. The garrison consisted of five hundred men only, and the Gun Boats I believe may claim the chief merit of its capture, for although we threatened and were upon the point of storming it, the fire from that force became insupportable. If this was a separate branch entirely of the Naval Service (which I wonder if it is not) they would especially deserve to have Veere inscribed upon their Colours. The 63rd Regiment was left there and we marched from it at 6 o'clock in the evening. The French disputed our advance, and there was some skirmishing, but we arrived at Middleburgh by sunset. This is a very considerable town in the centre of the island, and from the high banks around it we expected it would have been defended, having no regular garrison. However, it surrendered and our entrance into this place was as fine a sight as you can imagine. I understand it is built upon the plan of most Dutch towns, and is very handsome. The houses of considerable height, and canals for the shipping (of which there was none there then) running through the street with several small bridges, and broad walks on both sides, ornamented with rows of trees, giving it a very fine effect, particularly with so large a body of troops seen defiling through it, lining the walks in dense columns and crossing with their Colours over the different bridges. The Inhabitants were all at the doors and windows, but received us in profound silence. I suppose there was not less than 10 or 12 thousand men passed through the place in this silent procession (for not a drum was beating) to the siege of Flushing. The sun was setting in great splendour and tingeing the Heavens with crimson, added to the grand but somewhat dark and sombre aspect of it. I observed marble floors to the halls and entrances of houses here (level with the street) set out in diamond fashion, black and white. Many wealthy merchants

---

[1] Veere surrendered on August 1st after a very brief but spirited resistance during which the French guns sank two British gunboats which were bombarding the place.

reside there I believe. We halted for an hour when we had passed through it, and then proceeded forward by a noble broad paved road enclosed with trees planted at regular distances the whole extent of it. In our front in this grand avenue a few shots were exchanged from time to time by our advanced guard and the enemy's pickets, and we pushed on so near to Flushing that a fire was opened upon us which kept us on the alert, and we continued in movement in one direction or other until 2 in the morning. Our loss has been 260 killed and wounded at Veere and on the advance to this place. Before we left the former three Companies of the 77th were detached to attack a fort called Ramakins (but neither of them being the Company I belong to, I remained with the Battalion). Our men handled their arms so successfully from a commanding point they obtained against it, that the enemy could not stand to their guns, and were forced to surrender. Lieut. Bradshaw was the bearer of a flag of France (perhaps you may see in the Dispatches some honourable mention of it, and of the two Sevens). The siege of Flushing has now regularly commenced and we are in full employment raising batteries against it and have just been sent to relieve another Regiment which has suffered a good deal, having imprudently been led too close to the walls, so that we are at a more respectful distance and can hardly be said to be within shot of it.

There is a rumour that Antwerp has been taken by Sir John Hope's army,[1] if that is the case it will materially expedite our return, in the delightful anticipation of which I remain. My dear Mother. Your affectionate Son, etc. etc.
William Thornton Keep.

Remember me kindly to my Father, Grandmother and Samuel and to every friend, so God bless you my dear Mother, rest assured that by every opportunity that offers you shall hear from me.

On the Lines before Flushing
13th August 1809

My dear Mother,

I trust that you have 'ere this received my letter informing you of our landing, and subsequent events until we reached Flushing. This will afford you equal satisfaction, as I well know that the good news which will accompany it will occasion much anxiety about me.

The town has surrendered after a heavy bombardment that has continued since Sunday.[2] The delay that took place in our preparations had put us into a

---

[1] This was a false rumour. According to Fortescue (*History of the British Army*, VII, p.86), Sir John Hope had been in South Beveland for just a few days before he perceived the impossibility of ever taking Antwerp.

[2] Governor Monet surrendered the town of Flushing on August 15th 1809, after a bombardment which began on August 13th. The British barrage included rockets which set fire to several building in the town, causing large fires. The surrender was hastened by

dread of being obliged to leave the island without completing our object, as the enemy had it in their power, by opening the sluices to lay the whole place under water, which they had commenced doing. We however continued our labours in erecting batteries, and completed them before any material interruption was sustained, although we were obliged to be continually measuring the depth of the inundation, in a panic every inch as it increased. As you cannot be expected dear Mother to know much about sieges, I must be a little more descriptive than usual, and inform you that at first we approached this formidable place (to construct our fortifications against it) in the night, provided with canvass bags which were filled with all possible dispatch to provide cover for ourselves from the cannon shot to be expected to be levelled at us when discovered by the enemy at daylight. Great numbers of these were accordingly filled with sand and earth and piled upon each other, and then beat down into solid masses with heavy mallets. This occupation was afterwards continued by day, and at which we have been working incessantly for the last fortnight, until they increased to the size of little castles, in defiance of the shot we were still exposed to while erecting them, being then quite prepared, and the cannon mounted in them. Our task was over, and the soldiers of the artillery took possession, leaving us little more to do than to observe the effect their fire produced upon the town, and singular and terrific indeed it was! especially at night when the shells sent an immense height aloft into the air appeared like falling stars, producing on their descent into the town a distinct reverberation, and the Congreve Rockets with their trains of fire crossing each other illuminated the Heavens,[1] the whole of which was reflected in the waters around us, then rapidly increasing on the ground we occupied, so that to keep our feet dry we climbed the trees, watching with anxiety the result of our operations. The batteries being opened on other parts of the lines in succession as completed, our fire kept increasing, until showers of rockets and shells ensuing at last set the town in flames! making the steeples and highest buildings clearly visible to us, so that we saw them set fire to and hurled down, one after another. It became at length appalling to witness, and a sudden cessation was ordered by the Commander in Chief, and a summons sent in to General Monet to surrender. This lasted only a short time and led to no other result than some protection for the sick and wounded, granted on our part (a conspicuous flag being hoisted on their hospital, our firing to be withheld in that direction) and then presently our batteries opened again with redoubled fury, and now the flames increased all sides

---

Denis Pack, whose men stormed one of the town's advanced works on August 15th. Nearly 6,000 French prisoners were taken when the town fell, whilst the entire operation is reckoned to have cost them close to 9,000 men. (Fortescue, *History of the British Army*, VII, p.80).

[1] Congreve Rockets, invented by Sir William Congreve, were notoriously unreliable and were prone to change direction in mid-air and fall back upon their firers. Wellington considered them rather more a hindrance than an advantage. Nevertheless, rockets were used with some success at Copenhagen, at Walcheren (sparingly) and in the Peninsula, notably at the crossing of the Adour in February 1814. They were also used extensively during the Waterloo campaign. A troop was also present with the Allied army at Leipzig in October 1813.

of the town, and we heard drums beating to drown the cries (as we have since heard) of the terrified women and children. Again a cessation was commanded, and a very urgent letter sent in stating the deplorable consequences that would ensue by their non compliance with the terms offered, but General Monet only returned a fierce and laconic answer, to the effect it is said that they would be "knee deep in blood" before they would surrender. Lord Gardner then passed with the Fleet in front of the sea defences, and the cannonade became more terrible than ever, for as the men-of-war advanced in rotation to pour forth volumes of flame and destruction, another battery of very heavy cannon erected on the shore by the seamen opened its fire which soon brought General Monet to a different decision, and a flag of truce appearing terminated hostilities. So far we have been successful. It is now thought that the army will cross to the continent and join the forces under Sir John Hope, and that we shall first be employed against Fort Lillo in the river, where our fleet are assembled. There will be a force of 10 thousand men left on this Island to keep possession of it (these are the prevailing reports for we know very little officially).

The force that is here only consists of 16,000 men so that it is probable our Brigade may remain behind. I hope not for I have a great desire to see the continent independent of wishing my Regiment to be actively employed.

Antwerp is mentioned as the ultimate destination, which is a fortified place like Flushing, and will be taken I suppose by similar means. I wonder that the usage of war permits of such a barbarous mode of attack. It is said not less than 4 or 5 hundred of the poor hamlets' inhabitants have been killed or wounded here! General Monet did well (if as reported) he ordered the drums to beat to prevent their cries ringing in his ears if he wished to be able much longer to hold out. He requested to send the women and children to Middleburgh and I was much surprised to find (being so young in these matters) that it could not be admitted. We have inhabited a ploughed field for the last week, beat down by so many feet into a parade ground, in huts we have raised for ourselves of the boughs of trees by the hedge rows, and you would be surprised at our ingenuity in providing accommodation. Here we reposed on hay and dried leaves very snugly when things permitted but we have been shifted about a good deal, and in consequence of the inundation obliged to retreat into barns, which are very commodious. We live extremely well considering circumstances, and very cheap. The Dutch people are very fond of us, and draw some very favourable comparisons between the French and ourselves. They say the English give them good money and protection for their goods, while the French steal and plunder them like savages. Our portmanteaus have been sent on shore, and you can't conceive how delightful a clean shirt is, now that we are so much confined to our clothes. Washing ourselves has been a luxury enjoyed about once in three days. The more I see of this Country the better I am pleased with it, and think the industry and cleanliness of the Dutch can be equalled by few other nations. We have plenty of fruit here, of which the inhabitants are very bountiful. The orchards are delightful. Here we frequently spread our table under the shade of luxuriant fruit trees, and enjoy all the pleasures of rustic life, surrounded by farms and gardens, little prepared for such visitors, but which are beautiful to the eye and agreeable in a thousand ways.

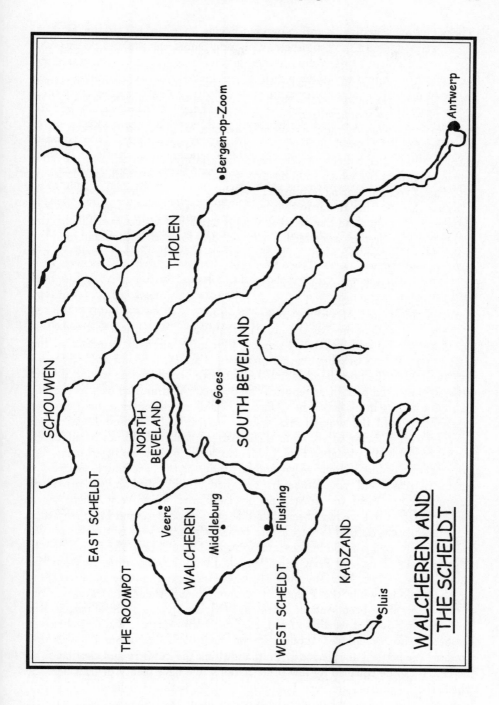

Antwerp

Bergen-op-Zoom

THOLEN

SCHOUWEN

NORTH BEVELAND

SOUTH BEVELAND

Goes

EAST SCHELDT

THE ROOMPOT

Veere

WALCHEREN

Middleburg

Flushing

WEST SCHELDT

KADZAND

Sluis

WALCHEREN AND THE SCHELDT

The people are resuming their occupations, having no fear of molestation from us, and to secure it almost spoil us officers with indulgences. But the men do very well (being well supplied by the Commissaries) and we have little occasion to interfere for them. You should see a Dutch farm to be able to conceive its beauties. Their dairies and household arrangements are so neat that you might suppose every thing about them to be brand new, and the exterior of their houses tastefully gilt and painted, look as if just out of the hands of workmen. They have recesses in the walls instead of bedsteads, concealed in the day by green glazed calico curtains running on brass rods which leaves the room disencumbered, the floors of small bright red bricks closely united and arranged very prettily. Caps are greatly in fashion among all classes of females to the exclusion of bonnets. My Grandmother I dare say would take great exception to them on account of their altitude, vying in that respect with the caps of our Grenadiers. I observe too that the borders are all of one material, which I suppose she would likewise object to, and indeed I think it somewhat extraordinary as they make fine lace in these parts, perhaps so fine however that they are reserved for Holidays to be worn as veils and tuckers. They have large silver buckles in their shoes and coloured stockings, with fine large clocks to them, and ponderous Ear rings, either of a bright metal or gold. But their petticoats are hideous, being so Wadgy, and composed of a coarse stuff as thick as baize. They stick out amazingly and are so short that I wonder how they can stoop (never having yet seen them without showing their bottoms). Wives are called Frows, and the Gentlemen Mynheers, and it is Yar Mynheer (Yes Sir) to all our demands. We have heard that a shell fell into an apartment of the Stadt Holder, or Governor's house, where some Gentlemen were conversing with General Monet, and that the General himself was severely injured, some say killed.

General Houston's Brigade is ordered to march into Flushing at 4 o'clock this afternoon. I feel quite anxious to see the place. There is a report that Austria has not made peace with France. This is very excellent news just now, as Bonaparte will then have less opportunity of sending troops to oppose us. We are terribly annoyed with mosquitoes here (I did not expect to find them in this part of the World). They disfigure us frightfully, some of our faces are so swelled that we can hardly see out of our eyes, nor the men put their caps on at Parade. For my own part I have escaped this annoyance pretty well, but only by binding both hands and face up in silk handkerchiefs at night in the barns where we sleep.[1] In other respects we repose there in great comfort (with the large doors open, the weather is so fine) upon clean straw.

I am becoming very anxious to hear from you. I know it is not from forgetfulness of me that you have not written but from not knowing how to direct. I think you may now write to me in this island ('with the army at Walcheren', or 'to be forwarded') and it will be sent here, or to whatever place the

---

[1] The island of Walcheren abounded with stagnant pools and dykes which swarmed with mosquitoes, the great fever carriers on the island. The fever was thought to be a combination of typhus and dysentery, although several other unpleasant characteristics began to emerge. See Richard Blanco's *Wellington's Surgeon General* for a very fine treatment of the medical problems during the expedition to the Scheldt.

77th moves. We were for a day or two close to the sea and had excellent bathing there on the dikes as they are called; these are barriers provided by these industrious people against the inroads of the salt water, that would otherwise render the island uninhabitable. They are kept up at prodigious expense of labour and money, and display considerable ingenuity. At this pleasant spot they had put down (to protect the beach and prevent its being washed away) a strong matting, formed of ropes of straw, pinned tight down to the shore. This formed a charming soft platform for tender feet, while indulging in this wholesome recreation there. By various contrivances of this kind they manage to keep Neptune at bay and very necessary it is or they might all be drowned. They say it is twice my height below the sea in the centre of this isle. We are throwing the water off again now, as fast as we can, and repairing the dikes the French General destroyed. The plan of defence is reported to have been written by Bonaparte himself for the instruction of his Generals, on a recent visit here.

We have not been able to ascertain whether Monet was restrained from carrying his orders into complete effect or not, at the solicitation of the inhabitants, or whether it was impracticable (he being shut up in Flushing) to open sufficient number of floodgates. At all events it was fruitless, only forcing us to make more expedition, and he might as well have left it alone, he might as well too I should think have surrendered as soon as our works were completed, laughed at our labours and had the supreme satisfaction of preserving the town and people from destruction. At least he paid dreadfully dear after our batteries were opened for every hour of the time he purchased in protracting the surrender. The Eclat of the thing, and the compliment of all Europe's eyes upon him, perhaps cost many a poor soul his life.

I scrape acquaintance here among the little folks wherever I go, if I walk up the road that is near this I am sure to meet a cluster of little Dutch children, and very comic is the meeting and survey of each other, they with their large hats and wooden shoes. On my approach they leave their play and run and gather flowers and fruits for me with which they crowd round me, full of glee and curiosity to examine me close and to admire the buttons of my scarlet coat and the prince's feathers on the tails of it. I wish you could have witnessed their delight at my giving them a scramble for an English sixpence. I suppose Samuel has left home for Hackney, and trust he will improve there. Pray remember me affectionately to him when you write. If he is at home I shall expect an account from him of all amusing occurrences that may have taken place in my absence.

I shall write to my Father in the course of a day or two. Remember me most dutifully and affectionately to him, also to my Grandmother. I suppose Julia has become quite a little woman by this time, you must give her a kiss from me, and I hope Alfred is recovering fast after inoculation and growing a fine boy. We hear that our army in Spain has gained a brilliant victory at Talavera, and I suppose Lady C. is in great alarm about Lord Kilcoursie, as the Guards are said to have suffered severely in the contest.[1]

---

[1] George Frederick Augustus, Lord Kilcoursie, fought at Talavera as an ensign with the 1st Battalion Coldstream Guards. The Guards suffered fairly heavy casualties during

It is now rumoured that the attack upon Antwerp will be given up in order that a reinforcement may be sent from this army to join Sir Arthur Wellesley. The Hon. Ed Lambert's Regiment you may tell Lady C. has not been employed with us but is in South Beveland, opposite us, with Sir John Hope's Army, and they have had very little to do except with some small towns on the way to Antwerp.

You will smile when I tell you that I have been engaged in picking currants (fine ripe red ones in a garden) with my Messmates as we intend today to give a party, to dinner, which is to consist of beef, boiled fowls and currant pudding. Having no oysters here for the sauce, we thought of getting parsley for the fowls, but what is very strange to us, although the gardens here are so delightfully prolific in every thing else parsley is not to be found, so that our visitors must content themselves with plain melted butter.[1] We always make the most of every opportunity for such jollifications, being uncertain how long they may last.

I have nothing more to say at present my dear Mother than that I am very well and want for nothing, and remain, etc. etc. William Thornton Keep.

Flushing
28th August 1809

My dear Father,

You should have heard from me before this, had I been able to get a letter forwarded to England but owing to some new arrangement which has been adopted for the conveyance of letters we have been directed to discontinue to send them to the usual place, I have hitherto heard of no officer being appointed to receive them. I am but this moment awakened by the Orderly Corporal with orders, by which I see that a vessel will sail in the course of an hour to England. Of course I value the opportunity too much to allow it to slip.

As we conjectured, so it has occurred. Our Brigade is left in this island, and we are deprived of the laurels we were in anticipation of reaping by being otherwise employed. The surrender of this place has occupied a good deal of valuable time, and our loss has been considerable considering it as a bombardment, although a breach was opened and we should have stormed it had not the French General (a brave man too) prudently resolved to avoid it, not hoping I suppose to be able to resist us with the garrison under his orders. They consisted of very

---

the battle owing to their eagerness in pursuing a defeated French column. Kilcoursie came through unscathed however. He left the Peninsula in September 1810 and was promoted to lieutenant in the 2nd Battalion on December 13th 1810. He retired from the army on March 24th 1813. (Mackinnon, Origin and *History of the Coldstream Guards*, II, p.509).

[1] Keep appears to have been finding it relatively easy to supplement his army rations at Walcheren, judging from this description. However, it is not surprising that he was about to come down with the dreaded Walcheren Fever, given that he was spending his time picking wild fruit and, even more dangerously, wildfowl that presumably drank from the pestilent pools of stagnant water, one of the great causes of the fever.

inferior troops and were in a state of intoxication when they made their sortie, as it is said they could not be otherwise induced to come out, which is very probable considering the ample means in our power to drive them back again. The sortie took place not in our part of the lines, but we moved up as a reserve and had our bayonets fixed, but with no great expectation of being engaged. All I saw of this affair was comical enough. We were halted on the bivouacking ground of one of the Regiments engaged in front, and their camp kettles were left in their hurry on the fires in Gypsy fashion, which of course were held sacred by us. However it was curious to see with what sang froid the wounded returned to look after their grog. One man made us laugh exceedingly to see with what dexterity he handled a hot potato although he had a finger knocked off, and displayed the bleeding stump.

The business being finished without our aid, we marched back to the position we had proceeded from, and everything went on as before. As soon as the flag of truce announced the surrender we were active enough, and certainly we made preparation enough to receive our foes. Plenty of pipe clay was used and oak leaves ornamented the men's caps, and we formed an avenue of great extent for them to march out with all the Honours of War.

Our Regiment formed one side of the square at the extremity of it, where they were to lay down their arms, the 36th, 79th Highlanders and 82nd, the other faces, and here we awaited their arrival with all the ceremonies of a Grand Review, and indeed they had all the honour of this to themselves for such a set of miserable Banditti looking fellows were never seen. Their uniforms and accoutrements of the most motley kind, the officers with top boots drawn over rusty pantaloons that livery stable grooms might have been ashamed of, and making a truly shabby appearance. I believe the few decent French among them disowned the rest and said they were Poles and Jews. We were not backward however in snatching some trophy or other in the Wreck of things around us, and some of our musical Gents interested in the welfare of the 77th Band took no small delight in seizing a trombone, or bassoon etc. As for the little rascally drummers they wouldn't give in to ours, but with the greatest effrontery thrust their feet through their drumheads. It was almost farcical to see these men received by their captors with the ceremonies performed, and I believe our Generals and Staff Officers (of which there was a great number splendidly attired) felt somewhat ashamed of the ostentation displayed when they discovered for whom it was done, for it was found that Flushing is looked upon as a condemned hole and the receptacle for deserters and all the refuse of the French army. The place is however very strong, the industry and neat habits of the Dutch being conspicuous in its construction. The ramparts towards the sea are particularly fine, displaying beautiful masonry, and the works are mounted with splendid brass guns. I was surprised to find this part of the fortifications had sustained so little injury, as the whole fleet passed in line in front of them saluting them with a broadside. On looking over the parapet I observed however several cannon shot in the basement of the walls so that it is probable our seamen could not sufficiently elevate their guns, being obliged perhaps in obtaining deep water to pass too near the walls. At all events it was a bold act, and had expert artillerymen been here not a few of our ships would have been destroyed in attempting it.

I perceived the enemy were provided with furnaces for red hot balls, their wickets open, with the iron pincers, cinders, etc. in a state as if just used. The front it presents here must look very formidable from the sea, the fortifications extending (at a considerable elevation) for some hundred yards in a straight line. We have had enough to do, strange to say, since we took possession in collecting with wheelbarrows our own Shot. These arranged in a pile would make a pretty sized pyramid, and great destruction they have done. There was one battery of ours served by seamen, and the houses in that quarter are as full of holes as a rabbit warren, or a nutmeg grater. It is curious to observe how the shells have ploughed up the pavement (which is like that in the centre of our streets in London, but without the convenience of the flat stones on the sides). Our troops are all busy now doing duty as scavengers to the great satisfaction of the Dutch, who are the very opposite of their old masters, the French, in cleanliness. This is one reason for the disagreeable effect produced by this place, which was their abode, for being in ruins and filth it forms the greatest contrast imaginable to the country places around. Its very atmosphere is felt to be tainted, like that experienced on coming out of the fresh air into a close room. The shipping in the basins in the streets gives it a confined look, and the deposit of mud at the fall of tides must throw up some very prejudicial vapours. I don't know for what reason, but we have been ordered to take all the fire arms we can find here from the Inhabitants, and I made a seizure (as Custom House officers would say) of a small truck full, at least I reported my having seen them, which prevented their being carried away. There are a few good coffee houses here. On entering one, of three stories or more, I was surprised on looking up, to observe a large perforation through the centre of the ceiling, one of our shells having descended as from the skies entirely through the house to the ground floor. This will give you some idea of the miseries of a bombardment. The unfortunate Inmates must have been in great terror. I hear that numbers of the town's people have been killed and wounded, but have not myself seen one of them to confirm the sad report. Poor Captain Brown of ours (whom I heard you had seen when in town) has been most unfortunate. He has lost his leg very high up and two fingers. It is a great pity that so brave and valuable an officer should have met with such a misfortune in the way he did. He received the shot in a battery in the construction of which a party of our Regiment consisting of 200 men were employed, and he was the only one touched. I was on the same duty, though not at the time the accident happened. A private of the 36th Regiment had his head and one arm shot away within 10 yards of me; so that I may consider myself tolerably fortunate to have escaped. The 77th have only had 1 man killed and 1 wounded during the siege, besides poor Brown.

This is a most diabolical place to remain in now you may suppose. Indeed there is scarcely a house uninjured, such a heap of ruins I could not have imagined. Whole streets are destroyed, the sick and wounded of our troops as well as the enemy's are everywhere to be seen. I am quartered in the second floor of a Chandler's shop with little more convenience or comfort than what I could expect in a workhouse in England. I wish we had been lucky enough to remain in Middleburgh, as that is a very fine town and truly Dutch; the people here seem to be half French, or rather a mixture of all nations, Smugglers, Jews, etc. We know less perhaps of what the other parts of the army are doing than you do in England, but Antwerp undoubtedly is the grand object. If we remain here, our army will be almost annihilated. It is wretchedly unwholesome and our Regiment increase in sick not less than 30 every day.

Remember me most affectionately to my dear Mother and Grandmother. I hope to see them well on return; with every other remembrance due to kind relations and friends, I remain. William Thornton Keep.

I am extremely well and do not want for anything which can be afforded me in this country. I shall look forward to my return to England for every pleasure.

Flushing
11th September 1809

My dear Father,

I can in no better way expect to relieve your anxiety about me than by referring you to Captain Smith for an account of my recovery from an attack of the fever. It will afford you great pleasure to know that his attentions to me deserve him the name of your friend most truly. Every kind of assistance that I could have required I might have derived from him. How miserably uncomfortable is everything here. The increase of sick is beyond all precedent. We have 22 officers of the 77th at this moment ill.

I have to thank God for being on my legs again. I trust that I shall not have a relapse. We are kept alive by the hope of evacuating the Island shortly. To remain here a Winter would be purgatory complete. If it were possible you could spend half an hour in this place, you might have some conception of its horrors, but it is impossible otherwise. We hear of a change of the Ministry. It is to be expected after so disastrous a result of things. I should imagine that this will be the last time the British will be employed in Holland. At least long experience will prove it now to be desirable. What a state of dissatisfaction the people of England must be in! and what can at all quiet them? Surely not the possession of the island of Walcheren, where we are losing more men than in half a dozen campaigns. Had the Ministers been informed of the unhealthiness of this place, different measures would doubtless have been adopted. It seems extraordinary that they were not, as it is proverbially the place of transport for the Military Delinquents of France, and they sent us here at the very time of the year in which the fever prevails. Not having secretly dispatched some intelligent individual to ascertain these things appears to be a most shameful piece of neglect. Lord Chatham bears the blame for it all, but considering his operations as confined to Walcheren to be equally efficient (the best informed upon these subjects seem to think) they could not have been carried out with greater dispatch, unless it had been determined to take the place by Coup de main or storm. In that case all the artillery possible would have been directed to one point, to effect a breach only, for the entrance of the troops; instead of which batteries were raised all round it, and combustibles and cannon balls etc. thrown into all parts of the town. These were however so ably constructed that the annals of war do not present another instance in which the effect was so complete, destruction greater, and consequently work better performed. But the garrison as I observed before were the very refuse of the French army, and didn't deserve the honours they received. (These unfortunates have suffered with ourselves, dying by dozens in our transports, before they could be conveyed away.) Antwerp would have fallen, if we could have got there as easily as to Flushing with our field train. Altogether it is a grievous thing that the operations of so grand an army should have terminated in so poor an exploit, whereas the capture of the enemy's fleet would have been a splendid achievement and worthy of the forces employed.

I see little chance of promotion, indeed none, for we have 18 Lieuts and the senior Ensign, Green, will not succeed to any vacancy until the number is reduced to 12. We hear that Cols. Maddison and Sprye will quit the army immediately on going home. Col.M. will sell out from old age and incapacity, and Col. Sprye because he conceives himself ill treated in not succeeding to Whitelocke's Lt. Colonelcy. We hear that Col.Bromhead with the detachment is ordered to join us. God send we may reverse the report by joining him. Poor Captain Brown has sailed for England. I wonder whether he will obtain promotion in a Garrison Battalion or sell out. He has great interest and is related to the Marquis of Sligo. He has been singularly unfortunate, and a strange fatality has attended him. You already know how precipitate his journey was from Ireland, to obtain leave from the Duke of York to join us, instead of being left on the recruiting service. The rebuke he received for leaving his station so precipitately, his earnest request to have the duty allotted to him changed, his final success, and departure with all speed to follow us, notwithstanding which we had sailed when he reached Portsmouth. But at great expense he hired a boat to follow us, and when out at sea we were surprised to be hailed by it, and find it was Brown on board. We took him in and he accompanied us. When on the surrender of Fort Ramakins, by the Adjutant's roster, he was appointed to remain behind in the command of it, this he objected to, and still determined to go on with us he prevailed upon Captain Heriot to take that duty off his hands, and was volunteering his services in the trenches when he was struck. I was the first who saw a Soldier running into the lines, breathless and without his coat, exclaiming 'Captain Brown is dreadfully wounded, and I am sent for a Surgeon!' He was removed to Middleburgh and had the best attendance from the principal surgeons of the army. We heard that he could move the toes of the wounded leg, but the injury was so great that he was obliged to suffer amputation in the thigh. He was hit by a cannon ball on the left leg, to which was suspended an elegant sabre, which was shivered to pieces, by which he lost two fingers of the hand resting on the guard and had his gold repeater in the other hand at the instant, noting the time between each shot. It is usual to employ a man for this purpose, whose business it is upon perceiving the flash to cry out Shot!. The men who are employed with their shovels digging the earth, upon hearing this, fall flat upon their faces until the shot has passed, which it does with a rushing noise, particularly a shell, and where it falls it makes a terrific excavation, throwing up the mud and sand yards into the air. Luckily it is impossible to fire these missiles with exact precision, or the destruction would be immense, but you must stand your chance of it, fixed in one spot from sun rise to sun set. That is the nature of this duty. The battery we were employed upon was on the extreme margin of the sea and I was only twice upon this duty during the siege. In the course of so many hours not more than one or two shots did any execution, but those the worst. One man stooping to scoop some clear water in his tin canteen had both legs and one or both arms carried off, and singular to say the trunk was thrown upright and he cried out 'Good bye Jack' to a comrade by the side of him. Another man was struck on the hind part of his head and the face fell like a mask on his back, very little discomposed, but a small quantity of blood issuing from his eyes, forming a horrible spectacle. The Honble Basil Cochrane of the 36th coming into the trenches and seeing him cried out 'Bury that man immediately', so that in less than ten minutes we witnessed life, death and burial (for the men had shovels in hand, ready to prepare the grave). Col. Cochrane is a fine dashing gallant fellow, but Col. Pack of the 71st has acquired the most renown of any. He has been remarkably indefatigable with his Regiment, clearing all before him. (Col. Sprye would have done the same with us, if he had had the Command.) Col. Pack came close to me to reconnoitre with his telescope in the trenches, while I was reposing (having nothing better to do) at his feet, protected by a pile of cannon balls. Poor Captain Bowes always advised me never to volunteer, thinking there was a fatality in it, and certainly there is something singular in the only two individuals out of 3 injured in the 77th, having no business where they were. Captain Brown was one instance. The other perhaps was more remarkable. His name was Burke (a tall man formerly of the Grenadiers, but employed at home to beat the big drum). This man just as we had received the Order for foreign service at Winchester came suddenly into possession of a handsome independence, which enabled him to purchase his discharge. But he would accompany the Regiment, saying he had seen many a hard fought battle with the 77th and would have another turn — and he was the only man of the 77th we had killed! He was very active and one of the enemy fell dead under his hand, in a very singular manner, so much so that at first it could not be discovered what injury he had received. Burke was pursuing him with his bayonet, but being outstripped he gave the chase up, cursing the Frenchman's speed, with a plunge at arm's length of his musket, and the fugitive fell forward instantaneously dead on the ground. On examining him, he had no external wound, but stripping his clothes off a small cut appeared, such as a penknife might have made in a particular part of his loins. The extreme point of the bayonet must have touched this vital part; his own fate it seemed hung upon as slender a threat, for he was himself killed in the trenches. If I knew the case of the wounded men you would have a full account of all the slaughter I have heard of that has taken place in the 77th. But we have a worse enemy to contend with now, in the dreadful disease that is so rapidly and fatally thinning our ranks, from which we know not how to shield ourselves, or where to look for relief. We can only trust to those who have our destiny in hand at home! How ill timed and cruel it appears when we look into the papers at the debates upon this subject, to find 'great laughter' 'much laughter' so frequently in Italics in the same column. If the same merriment prevails in the Cabinet council chamber, we are undone! And what is worse, the Enemy must be laughing at us too. I think if some of these merry members of the lower house were here they wouldn't laugh long. We have been losing lately 200-250 and more men per week so that now we are employed constantly in digging trenches for our own dead.

I received my Mother's letter of the 23rd August (the only one I have received) on the 2nd Sept. and shall write to her in a few days in reply to it. I can't write now because I have no time, as I am in instant expectation of Captain Smith's coming, and it is quite uncertain whether he may not be required to go directly on board. In case a contrary wind should prevail to occasion him to stay another day, I will trouble him with another letter, and shall rejoice in the opportunity of writing to my Mother, as I have much to say to her. In remembering me most affectionately to her, say now how much delight I anticipate and that I rely upon seeing home before Christmas. I am not forgetful of my Grandmother. Next to my mother and yourself she holds a place in my heart. It seems that she is ignorant of my absence from England. You will not mention therefore but in the usual way my regards to her. I shall not return myself for duty this week, as I have much weakness yet left from my last attack, as you will perceive by my writing. This disease usually comes on with a cold shivering, so great that the patient feels no benefit from the clothes piled upon him in bed, but continues to shiver still, as if enclosed in ice, the teeth chattering and cheeks blanched. This lasts some time, and is followed by the opposite extremes of heat, so that the pulse often rises to 100 in a short space. The face is then flushed and eyes dilated, but with little thirst. It subsides, and then is succeeded by another paroxysm, or cold fit, and so on until the patient's strength is quite reduced, and he sinks into the arms of death. I have hitherto escaped the third paroxysm, and have thus kept up. I did not starve myself according to the rule of treatment prescribed by the medical officers here, but on the contrary took all the nourishment I could, and kept my mind as much amused as possible.[1] As I shall have much leisure on my hands, I intend to perfect myself in the French language, and am desirous likewise to be acquainted with the Dutch. I have many of Kotzebue's plays in that language at my command but with the mortification of not being able to read them, and French books are more scarce. I was rather surprised to see Sur's Winter in London translated into Dutch when I called into a bookseller's the other day. Pray send me a newspaper when you write, which I hope you will gratify me by doing shortly. You may conceive how very desirable news of any kind must be to us. If we don't quit this place voluntarily we shall be driven out of it. Colonel

---

[1] There was, in fact, little that the British army medical officers could prescribe for the fever. 'The medical department was helpless. Regimental surgeons distributed Peruvian Bark and antimonial powder to their patients; they warned the healthy not to sleep in the open air, to avoid wading in the ditches, to wear flannel clothing, and to shun unripened fruit. Troops were given extra rations of rum and were urged to smoke cigars in order to purify the air.' (Blanco, *Wellington's Surgeon General*, p.100).

D'Arcy, Commandant of Engineers, has reported that the island is entirely defenceless in its present state, and an officer of the artillery with whom I am acquainted told me that he went the day before yesterday on duty to Veere or Tervere to try the distance they could send a shell from a mortar, and they found they could send one quite into the interior of the country on the opposite coast, from which he says the Engineers are of the opinion that the enemy can destroy the town (that is, what we have left undestroyed) in a very short time if so disposed, for they are protected by a dike behind which they can plant (or have planted) thirteen mortars, and that our vessels can't come at all near them. This officer likewise informs me that in case of an attack now there is not more than two men to a gun, so large a proportion of the artillery are sick, and that we are embarking the brass guns, and consequently no preparations making for a defence! If this is true, we shall soon be afloat again on our return.

You will remember me to Mr Cooper and Mr Perry. I hope Colonel Pritzler and Major Pilkington are well. You will give my respects to them both. My Mother does not mention anything in her letter of Alfred. I trust it was from mere forgetfulness, and that he is quite well.

Captain Smith (who has arrived) prevents my saying more as he thinks I must have said enough from the appearance of my letter, and I dressy you begin to think so too. I only wish that I had been well, that I might have received him in a different way, but he knows that it is in consequence of my illness he is so shabbily entertained, and will excuse it.

I can now only add that I feel every hope and confidence in retaining my health during our stay here, as I shall take every necessary precaution, and further to say that I feel happy to think this letter will be put into your hands by one who is so capable of telling you anything you may want to know respecting me, and from whom I must again repeat that I have met with every kindness, so God bless you my dear Father, And believe me to remain, etc. William Thornton Keep.

Flushing
18th September, 1809

My dear Mother,

Delighted indeed I was by the receipt of yours dated the 23rd August and it was brought to me at a moment when I most required it, at a time when I was in the full contemplation of the wretchedness and distressed appearance of the place of which we had so recently become possessors. What a contrast it formed to the happy spot from which your letter was directed, and it set my fancy at work in picturing you seated at the cheerful window, with the balsams, and the balmy breezes you was literally inhaling, compared with the vapours that hang over this unfortunate island, and doom its Invaders to destruction.

By a letter which I put into the hands of Captain Smith for my Father dated September 11th you will have heard that we are still at this, no longer to be called a town, but pile of ruins, where alas there is so little left to contemplate except each other's rueful countenances. Every individual amongst us wakes with anxiety in the morning, hoping to learn something favourable ere night returns of our departure hence. Day after day thus passes in eager enquiry and expectation. In the meanwhile our friends and companions are falling sick one after another and dying, I may say by hundreds. Under these circumstances you will not be surprised that I write in such a tone of despondency and that my spirits are depressed, yet you must not suppose me unproperly weak or childish. No, I do not forget that I am a soldier, and that it is my duty to bear with fortitude every hardship of my profession in every situation, and that the good must inevitably be mingled with the bitter in every path of life, but in the ardent hope of being in England before Christmas, and with you at that time, I derive my greatest pleasure for all that. What I wonder will be the result of this unfortunate expedition. Lord Chatham is to be tried most undoubtedly they seem to think. If Antwerp had been attacked we should not have been there as it would have been necessary to leave a large force for the defence of Walcheren, in which our Brigade would have been included. Setting aside the dreadful unhealthiness of this island, I should like it very much. That which is most pernicious to us is perhaps the most conducive to vegetation, and the country wears an aspect of what might otherwise be termed beautiful fertility. But I must withdraw your attention from this luxuriance of nature to the description of my present abode. I have been removed from the lofty garret of a Chandler's Shop to the first floor of a Baker's in an adjoining street. 'Brood te koop' is the inscription over the door which signifies "Bread sold here". I have one neat little room, the bed very good, and floor covered with a fine Indian matting. There is one very singular ornament in it. It is a figure as large as life, standing erect near the entrance of the door, and is a clever painting on board, cut out to the form, which it represents, that of a buxom ruddy faced female holding a tea kettle. If it wasn't too weighty a toy, I should like to bring it home with me. It would make you laugh finely to see a stranger's surprise on coming suddenly into the room, in dread of its contents.

You must know that the Dutch housewives even greatly excel the English in (I may say the astonishing) cleanliness of their houses and domestic furniture, and are extremely fond of setting them off to the best advantages, both inside and out.

I have seen gold on the fans of their windmills, and fine lace ornamenting the edges of their crockery shelves. My hostess has below in her shop a fine glass closet containing a very pretty assortment of curiosities of this kind, among the rest a pair of very small but admirably executed Chinese Images which are (without assistance) constantly nodding their heads. I intend to purchase them for you, with some other things when we leave this, if I can hope to get them conveyed to you without injury to their mechanism.

Lieut. Bradshaw is my chief associate. He is employed in the Engineer Department at present (having taken some lessons at the Military College in that science in his youth) but he comes to me whenever his duties will permit, and we spend the time in friendly chat, full of conjectures as to the future, with a sad retrospect of the past, for the pleasures of Winton are indeed no more! Scarcely dare we think of them. He seldom leaves me until late at night, being billeted about in this large place the officers are very much divided from each other, and a visit's a treat. So many are unable to leave their beds. English books are in great request but exceedingly scarce. I obtained 4 for ten shillings, and Bradshaw and I make the most of them, sending them backwards and forwards to each other when prevented meeting, with our remarks (very shrewd ones you may suppose) in the margin. Employment for the mind is more necessary on a bed of sickness than anywhere else, and we are glad to be amused in this way. I live according to your prescription and as well as circumstances will permit, and on that subject I must let you know that I often wish you was my guest! for I could furnish you with a more delicate morning repast than you can get in London itself.

My breakfast table is spread, and if incredulous let me convince you of it. That bright polished brass urn contains a delicious cocoa, mixed with a milk as rich as cream. Those buns with plums are excellent in themselves, but the butter intended for them is an incomparable treat! No British dairies can supply the like. The china cups are of the finest fabrication and worthy to receive what may be so readily conveyed into them by turning that little spicket of the urn. Could you taste, you would confess how much my cocoa surpasses your best Bohea, and the buns with their exquisite accompaniment your English smoking rolls or greasy buttered toast. Certain I am you would be proud to give your most fashionable friends such a treat. My dinners I cannot boast of. They come from our own Commissaries, and I generally content myself with John Bull's delight — a beef steak. As we are over our cocoa I must gossip a little, and make you the confidante of our Regimental secrets, by touching on what we call parish news! Our labours may now be considered over, in as much as we have done with marching, fighting, trench digging, and the place has surrendered. But we have had some rubs in the prosecution of our services. General Picton (though no parade General like Dyatt) has more than once given us a wiggling. (This funny term is of our own coining and means a smart reprimand.) I must tell you that the 77th were brought home from the East in a very enervated condition, and had been so long accustomed to a sort of easy mercantile tactics with the Company's servants that they were little prepared for the modern system of European warfare. After our successful feats at Ramakins and Veere, we were marching to Middleburgh with as much nonchalance almost (as you may remember) we proceeded with from Winchester to Southampton, when the General overtook us on the march and halted us instantly, and here we thought we saw plain enough the Governor of Trinidad. He peppered us finely with his tongue and that was torture enough, but would you believe it he sent us to the right about, making us do the day's march which was half over, all over again! Conceive how ridiculous we appeared! Luckily other Regiments had as much to mourn, or we should never have recovered from the effects of it. He told us he would teach us how "to march in an Enemy's Country", and truly he rode back with us for that purpose, while we were doing penance and dare not speak a single word the whole way, a great honour to the ragamuffin troops we were opposed to, as it afterwards proved. But the General did not know that, and was vexed probably that he could not get a peep at them even, behind their stone walls! or they would have paid for it, as I believe he would have challenged them to combat with his single Brigade (if they would have come out) much as he was displeased with us, for he is a very enterprising man, and above vexing the soldier about trifles if he can avoid it.

Pray let me know in your next how my Aunt is and do not shorten your letters by omission of what you may mistake to be uninteresting to me. I have read those I am in possession of until I know them by heart. I husband them too well as I can, only allowing myself a perusal now and then. I think you acted very properly in writing to Mr Smelt. He is a careless character and omitted sending the box entirely I dare say from forgetfulness. Admiral and Mrs Gould being with you I hope is the means of affording you some relaxation and cheerful company. Of dear little Julia I cannot say too much, and am glad to find she is such a favourite with your visitors. Pray give those kisses to her, she is so deserving of for her recollection of me. I must now conclude, having no time to spare as the packet sails at 3 o'clock. I am rejoiced that my Grandmother is in ignorance of my being here. You won't fail to remember me to her. I had intended to have written to my Father, as it looks so odd now we are so far separated to address a letter in his name, without one for himself. However you will remember me most kindly to him, and to everyone whom time does not allow me to name. Remaining with every sincere prayer for your happiness, my dear Mother, your dutiful and affectionate Son, etc.
William Thornton Keep.

Flushing
24th September 1809

My dear Father,

I trust that you received my letter of the 18th sent under cover to the Adjutant General. I do not fail to write by every opportunity that occurs. Judge then my vexation, at your having been in uncertainty about me from the 6th of last month to the 13th inst. Col. Maddison yesterday brought me the enclosed letter, which he has written to you, and read to me, to my utmost surprise. He acknowledges yours dated the 13th, and I felt much pleased when I considered that you would be so soon relieved from suspense about me, by the arrival of Captain Smith, as I remembered that he left the Island on the 12th. Strange indeed, you must have thought it, not hearing from me for such a length of time.

The day after Captain S sailed I had a serious relapse, from which however I had in a great measure recovered, when by imprudently going out too soon, the attack came on. From this I have been taught the necessity of caution, and by the effect of care I have at this moment to thank God for being in a tolerable good way of shortly enjoying my normal health.

I am aware that fever is not favourable to getting fat, so that I have nothing uncommon to complain of in saying that I am half a skeleton. Of course I am considerably reduced, and very weak. Col. Maddison advises me not to put myself too forward, and I have learnt enough to attend to his kind recommendation. The mind has so great an influence on the body that unless a person's occupied in some manner or other in this place everything is to be apprehended. We have lost two officers within this week, and a considerable number of men. How many hundred brave fellows have resigned their breath in this destructive island. The French may very well call it The Tomb, for to such of that nation as have been sent here the grave was prepared. Nothing in the East or West Indies can equal the sickness that has prevailed here. We have only 60 men out of Hospital, and I suppose we brought at least 600 into Flushing, so that you may imagine how little the army is ready to take the field in case of necessity. We understand that Sir Eyre Coote has sent his aide de camp to England with dispatches to Government representing his situation and stating that the Island cannot be retained without some considerable reinforcements.[1] With what impatience we shall await the arrival of the next packet as it will contain instructions for Sir Eyre either to evacuate the Island, or put it into a state of defence. The bare idea of remaining a Winter in Flushing is horrible. I hope we shall hear the talk of a change of Ministry confirmed by the next arrivals, and that Lord Chatham's trial has commenced, but his acquittal seems certain, and although he is much laughed at he is not blamed. We hear that the Caricatures on His Lordship have been drawn from some very comic scenes, and that they occupy a good deal of glass in the print shops. Pray give me all the news when you write.

I am afraid your eyes will be much tried in reading this letter to make out many words, but you will excuse it as my wrist and fingers are so weak. It's terrible small too. This letter will come to you by the two penny post, as Ensign Hanwell who has obtained a sick certificate will pass through London on his way to Sheerness, where his family reside, though I very much fear he will not reach England alive.

The officers of our Regiment who have died all obtained leave of absence, but it was granted too late. Pray remember me most affectionately to my Mother, to whom I would write by this opportunity but that my head won't allow me to write too much at one time. I shall however certainly write to her this week, as another Packet will sail in a few days which will give me an opportunity. God bless you my dear Father. I remain, etc. William Thornton Keep.

---

[1] Sir Eyre Coote, commanding at Walcheren, was left in desperate straits by the situation. With the fever at its height and hundreds sick and dying, he could barely muster half of the garrison available to him. On September 29th he wrote to Chatham, 'Something must be done, or the British nation will lose the British army — far more valuable than the island of Walcheren.' (Coote, quoted in Fortescue, *History of the British Army*, VII, 89).

Harwich
8th October 1809

My dear Mother,

I have obtained a sick certificate to return from Walcheren, and I have just arrived here with the fleet in the Princess Royal Transport. Anxious to be in London as soon as possible, I was desirous of procuring a seat in the Mail of tonight, but owing to the many officers who have come over, and have the same intention, I have been disappointed. However I shall get to Colchester to sleep, in order to secure a place in the daily coach of tomorrow. I believe they stop in Gracechurch St, and get there about 4 in the afternoon. I shall take a coach immediately I alight and come on to Scotland Yard, where I trust I shall find you all well.

Conceive my surprise immediately on arriving here at receiving a message to wait upon two ladies at an Hotel. I followed my conductor, puzzled at such a circumstance, and had a most melancholy duty to perform, being ushered into a room by a waiter I found two fine women in travelling dresses who I soon learnt were Relatives of a Captain MacIntosh of the 77th, their anxiety about him having brought them to this port to embark to him at all risqué. This gentleman who was a Scotchman and Captain of Grenadiers had died only two days before I left Flushing. I had to impart this melancholy intelligence, and their grief was so great you would have cried yourself at beholding it. Let me defer particulars until I have the pleasure of throwing myself into your arms, only assuring you I am at present, though' a spectre, labouring under no other complaint, than debility, so that you must not apprehend that I am so bad as might be imagined. Adieu my dear mother until tomorrow. William Thornton Keep.

Chapter Three
With 'the Slashers' at Berry Head

The effects of Walcheren fever bit hard into the human resources of the British army and William Thornton Keep was not alone when he resigned suffering from its effects. Others, like Rifleman Benjamin Harris, the famous diarist of the 95th Rifles, never served in the army again having already endured the rigours of the retreat to Corunna in the winter of 1808-09. Between them, the Corunna and Walcheren campaigns consigned many a good soldier to the back pages of history whilst others, apparently recovered from the fever contracted during this latter campaign, returned to the Peninsula only to have the sickness return. It is little wonder that Wellington fought long and hard to retain those Peninsular veterans whose battalions had been decimated by actions, in the so-called Provisional Battalions, even when convention dictated that they should return home to recruit. One good veteran was worth two or three fresh soldiers in Wellington's eyes.

When William Keep resigned from the 77th Regiment in late 1809 he spent some of his time at home recovering and some at the home of an aunt of his father's who was married to the King's Huntsman and who lived at King's Kennel, Ascot. He later took part as an amateur in dramatic productions at the Theatre Royal, Richmond, acting under the name of Mr Thornton.[1]

The lure of smoke and powder proved to be too strong for him, however, and on August 29th 1811 he joined the 28th Regiment as ensign. It was here that he met Henry Alexander who was to be a friend for many years to come. Keep was No.657 on the Roll and Alexander No.658. The two men joined the 28th at a time when the war in the Peninsula appeared to be taking a turn for the better after the anxieties of the previous year. 1811 had seen Graham's victory at Barrosa on March 5th and the first capture by the British army in the Peninsula of one of Napoleon's much prized Imperial eagles, carried into battle on this occasion by the French 8th Line Regiment. Wellington himself had finally thwarted Massena at the battle of Fuentes de Onoro on May 3rd-5th, whilst at Albuera, on May 16th, the British infantry had staged an astonishing comeback to snatch what appeared to be a French victory from beneath the nose of an infuriated Marshal Soult, and thus saved the day for the inept Allied commander, William Beresford, whose handling of the battle left much to be desired. There had been setbacks too, none more so than the failure of the Allied attempts to take the fortress of Badajoz, although success would come here in 1812. The 28th had both battalions serving in the Peninsula in 1811 and suffered heavy casualties at both Barrosa and Albuera. The accounts of these battles, and the war in general, would have been circulating in the

---

[1] This theatre was demolished in 1884. The archivist at the Richmond Theatre on the Green actually has a playbill with Keep's name on it.

mess of the officers of the 28th at Berry Head, most of whom would have been kicking their heels in frustration, longing to get to the Peninsula. William Keep and Henry Alexander would have to wait, however, until late 1812. In this chapter we find Keep getting back into the routine of army life with his new comrades of the 28th in their barracks at Berry Head.

Brixham, Devon
near Berry Head
Sunday Morning, October 27th, 1811

My dearest Mother,

I am happy in the first place to assure you that I have safely arrived here, without fracture or bruise, except indeed that I have felt a stiffness and pain in my neck, about the joints of the bone which usually assist in bending the head. I believe I may say I am as staunch a traveller as ever sat on the top of a stage coach. Multum in parvo I intend small to be applicable to this sheet of paper, being resolved to fill every corner of it. For me to be too concise on this occasion would be both unpolite and ungallant, since I can so well conceive you to be attending with all eagerness and pleasure to what I have to communicate.

Were it possible to arrest the flight of time I might first expend a few words in the retrospective survey of things passed, but as that cannot be done, like young Rapid in the "Cure for the heartache" in the elevated position from which I started on my departure from the Great Metropolis "I will push on, and keep moving".

Outside the coach with the flaming lamp at my heels we rolled on to Knightsbridge, when the horses getting into a long trot on the soft road our journey fairly commenced. Some little sickness prevailed in my stomach, with a good deal of heaviness of heart. I kept my mind intent and fixed however upon the bright side of human events, resisting with success despondent thoughts from assailing it.

As we increased our distance from London, the air blew keen and refreshing, but the heavens were overcast and threatened a bad day. We rattled on through long narrow dirty Brentford, and by that time I was tolerably well jolted, so as afterwards to bear with great composure the rapid movement of our vehicle.

When we came in view of the lofty towers of Windsor, I met with many objects familiar to me, and my old companion Waxy. The creaking sign posts, with "Entertainment for man and horse" caused a smile for some of these inn yards had often been contestable points between us. "Ah, that's right, give him the spur — hold the bridle tight — he can't throw you" from the bystanders. But Waxy could have told a different tale, when he chose to be obstinate in going into these well remembered places, and would rear up determined to pitch me a somersault in the dust rather than baulk his inclination.

We vacated the coach at a very pretty inn at Salt Hill to breakfast, the company consisting of one female, a Portuguese, two Ensigns of a Militia Regt, and two merchant travellers. I felt rather unwell here with sickness and a slight headache, which I attributed to the late hour I went to bed the night before, and getting up so early. With a relief of horses and a little warm tea in my stomach we again started. Within a few miles of Newbury we first enjoyed the enlivening beams of the sun, shining with warmth and animation upon a part of the country wooded and hilly, and very beautiful to behold, and at this town we dined. I still felt qualmish and disinclined to eat, yet I contrived to pull to pieces the best part of a fowl. A fat Militia Ensign and rapacious consumer squared the act however, emptying most of the dishes at table with surprising speed and dexterity. "Pray Sir," said a droll looking Porter coming into the room and addressing this gorgeous son of Mars, "Aren't you the Ensign William Thornton Keep, because as how there's gand two pence to pay for your luggage." This was a signal for me to draw my purse strings and I accordingly went out to see it weighed, and settle for it. We next proceeded to Marlborough and from thence to Devizes, which latter place we reached at the close of evening, and here there was a grand fair. Finding myself chilly and agueish with the bleakness of the breeze I treated myself to another glass of negus, having taken one before dinner, and now it was that I began to be sleepy. No weary traveller could ever have found the path more tedious, first uphill, and then down a deep descent. So powerful was the disposition to sleep that it required the painful exercise of all my energies to keep myself awake (as I must in dozing have fallen from the coach).

I never suffered so much in my life from this cause, being obliged to bite my lips, pinch my fingers, and practise all the acts I could think of to resist it. I would have given 5 guineas for 40 winks, for my safety depended upon it. We were obliged for a long time to proceed (most luckily) at a very slow pace for the night was uncommonly dark, and the coachman was afraid of running over the country people who crowded the road, returning (many tipsy) from the fair. My drowsiness continued thus increasing accompanied with a giddiness from combating it, added to the effects of the wine upon an empty stomach, and the dazzling objects passing under my eyes from the shadows of the coach lamps, for I dared not venture to keep them shut an instant; in addition to which the whiteness of the chalky roads in the neighbourhood of Bath, gave a strange and painful sensation to the sight.

All these causes combined must have kept me tottering on my seat. At this critical moment of my fate, the sash of the coach window was suddenly let down, and the fat Militia Ensign popped forth his head, and cried out to his companion on the top of the coach, in a most comic broad Irish accent, as if no time was to be lost, "Michael, don't you see the Carmet, oh look at her tail!"[1] There was something so droll, so squeaking, and unexpected in the sound of his voice that the coachman and everyone who heard him fell into a loud laugh. This was a seasonable alarm for me, my eyes being blind almost with the effort to support

---

[1] This comet was seen in Portugal by Captain William Bragge, of the 3rd Dragoons, on September 20th 1811. 'I have seen newspapers as late as the 20th Sept. in which they speak of a comet, to be seen between such and such hours. At that time the animal was conspicuous for the whole night in this country [Portugal] and had a most brilliant tail.' (Cassels, *Peninsular Portrait*, p.22).

their heavy lids, so that the drowsy God had nearly overpowered me. Not until it was approaching to half past eleven did we enter the emporium of fashion. What kind of place it appears by daylight I cannot say, but to me at that dark hour, owing to the whiteness of the houses, it appeared like a huge mass of buildings laying under a deep snow.

We alighted at the Lamb Inn, and I need not say how rejoiced I was. I was shown into a room where at that late hour of the night I found two very fashionable Bucks sipping coffee and playing at chess. With great good manners however they rose, and made room for me at the fire, but the waiter coming in and apprising me that the chambermaid was in attendance I declined their civility and followed her with the warming pan up stairs. The bed was a mountain of down, and the sheets lovely and sweet, and I laughed with hysteric joy as I leapt into it, for surely never was "Nature's restorer, balmy sleep" more acceptable to me!

The appointed hour too soon arrived, and a thundering knock at the door awoke me from my slumbers. I sprang from the bed of soft repose, and admitted a man in a smock frock and lantern in his hand. "What's o'clock?" said I. "Why Zur it be close on to 5. Shall I take the portmantel down to Coachee Zur?" "Ay do," said I, "and put it in the boot my good fellow." "I fears as zow the boot's full Zur, howzumever I'll see it stow'd right." And saying this he was taking his departure with the lanthorn, but recollecting himself, "God it ud been funny enow, to have left you in the dark your honour — he! he!"

I was soon dressed, and took a small quantity of Brandy (that excellent cordial my Father had provided me with) for drawing the window curtains aside I perceived that much rain had fallen in the night, and that the dawn was overcast "and heavily in clouds was bringing on the day". Not very well pleased at this discovery I descended the stairs, and took my old station on the new coach, and we left Bath just as daylight began to appear.

We continued on the descent for miles as we proceeded into Somersetshire, and I sat exposed to heavy showers until we reached Wells, a distance of 25 miles, where we breakfasted. Here I was seized with a shivering, and determined to go the remainder of the way inside, if the coachman could accommodate me, which he did; in the inside was Col. Griffiths, the inspecting field officer of the Recruiting Service at Wells, a Barrister, and a country gentleman with a Lieut of the Navy and his wife. The Barrister was so corpulent a man that I was squeezed like a collar of brawn between his fat sides and the panel of the coach. However to compensate for this inconvenience, which was a great subject of mirth on the moment of my entering (as the perplexity to find room for me was proportionably great), the driver swearing his coach was licensed to carry six inside, and the lawyer grumbling to be so incommoded, he proved to be a remarkably pleasant man, full of anecdote and fun, and kept us in a continued round of laughter. He was an extraordinary character, and we left him to explore the ruins of Glastonbury Abbey. This antiquated place is on an eminence by the road side, looked exceedingly picturesque, and I could have enjoyed some hours ramble there myself.

We dined at Taunton, where we arrived about 4 o'clock, and then started for Exeter, by which time the characteristic features of Devonshire began to unfold themselves in luxuriant verdure and enclosures, apple orchards lining the roads, from which they produce their excellent cider. We passed through the village of Wellington, and from this place our great commander derives his title[1]. It consists of a long street of poor and small cottages, with turf growing on the roofs of many of them a span high. By 10 o'clock we reached the City of Exeter, and stopped at the London Inn. I supped with the Navy hero and his lady off oysters and cold beef. I must now tell you that my luggage to this hour is not arrived. I lost a day at Exeter in my enquiries about it, detained not only from this cause but because I found there was no mode of finishing my journey without hiring a Post Chaise, and Berry Head still distant 32 miles!

At length I heard that as my luggage was directed to Berry Head it would certainly arrive there by the usual conveyance on Friday at the furthest, and learnt besides that I might get on 16 miles of the distance by the Plymouth Coach going that road the next morning. This was a relief of my anxiety, as it was the Mail from London (if they should have room for me). I went to bed this the second night in this expectation, and was not disappointed, the coach arriving at six the following morning and taking me up accordingly.

Fortunately I met with an officer of the 88th Regiment, which is in Garrison with the 28th at Berry Head, an Ensign Edgar going to join them there, and of course we agreed to take a Post Chaise between us on our arrival at Totness, where the Mail was to put us down. My day's rest at Exeter had recruited me famously, and I made as hearty a breakfast as could be desired when we alighted, after which we hired the Chaise and finally arrived at Brixham, within one mile of our destination by 2 o'clock in the day. My things not having arrived, it was impossible to appear in Regimentals. I therefore discharged my overalls and put on clean boots, blue pantaloons, round hat and clean cravat, and marched up to the Barracks.

Brixham is a small dirty town in a valley on the sea shore in Torbay (which is a fine but open Harbour 3 or 4 miles broad). The inhabitants of this place are chiefly fishermen. Leaving this delectable spot by a gradual ascent over cliffs, rugged pathways and briery tracks along the edge of the sea, and proceeding onward about three quarters of a mile you may espy (if you have taken the right direction) upon a platform of naked rocks, a low range of Battlements[2] with cannon on the walls, and this is Berry Head. Climbing up the steep eminence to level ground, you enter this fortification by a drawbridge over a dry ditch, and then you are struck with the insignificance of the Interior, it containing only rows of mean diminutive wooden sheds, not at all corresponding with the exterior walls which might very well prepare you to enter some noble Castle!

Here it was I appeared to report my arrival, and to take up my abode, among men I had never beheld yet, my boots concealed by mud and dirt, in my approach

---

[1] Sir Arthur Wellesley, commanding the British army in Spain, was created Viscount Wellington of Talavera on September 4th 1809, some five weeks after his victory there on July 27th-28th. He first signed his name 'Wellington' on September 16th 1809.

[2] The battlements remain today in a good state of preservation. It is thought that Keep was in Fort 3 of the two forts at Berry Head (Nos 1 & 2).

to it, and my spirits dejected, which my entrance there did not tend to dissipate, it appearing to me like a prison, and all the severity of military discipline I had witnessed in my first career, recurring to me from objects around.

I soon understood that a Colonel Ross was in command of the Battalion, and enquiring for him was directed to a door marked 22. I paused a moment to collect my thoughts and then gave a respectable tap with my knuckles (the doors and houses being composed of thin planks, no other knockers are supplied). Hearing a voice say "Come in", I entered, and beheld a lean and taper man, quite close to me (the room being about three paces wide only) seated at a table covered with a bit of green baize and overspread with letters and papers. He had a small grey flannel jacket on, and kept his seat, a somewhat time-worn military countenance, and his mind was evidently engaged in the business of the Regiment which imparted a sort of austerity to his otherwise pleasing features. I bowed and told him my name. "You have come to report yourself," said he. "Pray have you heard anything respecting our removal (to which I could only reply in the negative). I have applied to be sent from this place. We have a Mess here and dine at 5 o'clock. Have you got a room?" "No Sir, but I intend to apply to the Quartermaster for one." "Yes," said he, and then added after a moment's pause, "You should see the Paymaster too." (Yes, thought I, I must indeed. But he of course did not mean to recruit my finances, but that he might certify, which he is required to do in conjunction with the commanding officer that I was present, in returns sent up to the War Office.)

I accordingly made my bow, and left him to seek that worried man. I was presently shewn into an apartment where I found him with a gentleman whose name he informed me is Teulon, a Captain of Grenadiers. Captn T. very politely invited me to breakfast with him the following morning and I went and was introduced to the Quartermaster who gave me possession of a room, but the misfortune is that I can neither dine at the Mess or sleep in barracks, for the most obvious reason, because my bedding and things are still on the road only.

I cannot give you a very favourable description of my new companions, for my first impressions here are none of them very promising. One half of the Regiment bound hither in a Sloop of War from the Mediterranean are not yet arrived, and have been I hear so long on their homeward voyage that great fears are entertained for their safety. I am apprehensive their Mess is expensive, but do not like just yet to ask too many questions on that head. I have dined with them once, but cannot venture again as I nearly fell over the cliffs on my return by night, to sleep at this place and we have had such incessant rain that there is no stirring out.

I think I have now given you a full history of my journey, and present situation, and must bid you adieu again for the present my dear Mother, promising to resume this pleasing employment shortly, when I have more to relate to you, And remaining, your very affectionate son, William Thornton Keep.

Berry Head
30th November 1811

My dearest Mother,

You have I dare say been anxiously awaiting a letter announcing my return to this place from Bristol, and I should have written before, but as you may conceive have been so very fully occupied.

I write this from the Guard House fronting the wide ocean, where I am today on duty, which affords me the opportunity. Thus you will see at once that I have resumed my professional employments, and am again prepared to follow the drum and fife. I am surrounded by fortifications and cannon, and the ramparts are on the edge of rocks, from which it would turn you giddy to look down on the foaming deep "where the choughs and crows, that wing the midway air seem scarce as large as beetles". But let me pass over the description of the scenery, to what more materially concerns my happiness, as I well know, and gratefully remember that that is essentially to your comfort. I made my approaches with a heavy heart, but soon were the clouds dispersed! Colonel Ross behaved in the kindest manner to me, gently reprimanding me for my conduct, as it appeared to him extraordinary, and a disrespectful step to a commanding officer, for he would he told me, have procured me leave by nine the next morning, had I applied to him properly. I did not tell him how pleasant a fortnight I had spent at Bristol, or how essential it was to my recovery from my nervous depression of spirits, on arriving here. Many alterations have taken place during my absence to brighten the aspect of this gloomy place, and several young officers come to join the Regiment. Among the latter is an Ensign Maxwell, a youth about 17, and friend of Col. Ross's. The habitations constructed for the accommodation of the troops here are insufficient for the numbers assembled in the two Regiments forming the Garrison, and we are so crowded that two officers of the junior ranks are forced to divide one room between them, yet this room, with another for servants' use, forms a separate cottage! Great inconvenience arises from this arrangement — two bedsteads to be put up, dressing tables, writing tables, breakfast apparatus etc, and it is necessary that the inmates should act in thorough good accordance with each other's wishes, and be thorough good friends, to go on comfortably, in such close approximation together. Maxwell is my associate, in this house keeping system. We breakfast together therefore, and are becoming very intimate. He has just left his father and mother in London, and I think him generous and good hearted, and he is very merry and most excellent tempered, so that I hope we shall agree very well; for if we do not it can only be my fault. We both breakfasted with the Colonel yesterday, and went to the play the night before. The performances were "Douglas" and "The Devil to Pay", performed by a strolling company from Plymouth in a Warehouse for Marine Stores.

It is an agreeable novelty to me to see soldiers marched from their barracks to an amusement of this kind. I believe I omitted to tell you that I went to the Theatre at Bristol with a party during my stay there, and saw Elliston play Lothario and the "Deaf Lover" in his usual admirable style. The party alluded to me, and with whom I became very intimate, and experienced every kindness from, as I did from another family there, under whose roof I spent many happy hours. The expenses of my journey exceeded what I had calculated, although I walked sixteen miles from Exeter on the road to Brixham, and would have walked the whole distance had I not been pressed for time, nor was it until 8 o'clock on Sunday night that I arrived as it was.

I know you will be pleased to think that acting in compliance with your desires I shall be reconciled soon to the path marked out for me. In this comfortable anticipation I must conclude for the present, remaining my dear Mother, you very affectionate son. William Thornton Keep.

Berry Head
24th December 1811

My dear Mother,

A day has escaped me, or I intended you should have heard from me ere you partook of your Christmas Dinner. Not that I could have sent up any of the feathered race to grace your table with, but "my fair wishes" and the news of my good health, I know, would have gone some way to increase your felicity. I am at all times anxious about your health my dear mother, and I am sorry to think your last letter gave cause for great uneasiness in that particular. I trust in Heaven that blessing has been restored to you, and that you are now better; and while I hope it, cannot but wonder at the fortitude with which you have borne up against the evils of life, thinking no Eulogism can be paid to you equal to your merits and desert. I wish I could impart to you any very gratifying indications of my own feelings since my return here, but I am not quite at home yet, although a good deal more reconciled to my abode in this sea-girt fortress than at first. My friendships are never very suddenly formed, and I am so exclusively engrossed by them when they do take place that those not so familiarly acquainted with me, are perhaps too frequently altogether neglected. In this way I find an apology for the behaviour of others, and must attribute the rest to my short residence here.

I fear I should make but a poor soldier, were it not for the companionship in peril of those I am attached to. At all events without friends in whom I could find a relief from the peculiar evils of the profession, it would have few attractions for me. Hitherto I have found them and have always considered that the friendships formed in it constituted one of its greatest charms. I should be fixed in any Regiment, as soon as my affections are fixed in it, but while they continued strangers, and if they proved disagreeable to me, could not be otherwise than miserable, so distasteful to me is the mere training for the dire purposes of war. You will perceive that I am expatiating upon an imaginary case, and I am happy to think so. My chief companion is Maxwell, who improves greatly in my estimation, and a Captn Kelly, a somewhat old soldier, and very agreeable man, who is very kind to me, and whom I like exceedingly, but I must tell you that great apprehensions are entertained of the Regiment being reduced, for we can get no recruits nor men from the Militia. If this does not take place, I expect to become effective in the first Battalion in the Spring, as I have already four Ensigns junior to me. They are eleven hundred strong, and we are so composed of nothing but Sergeants and Corporals[1], and cannot muster two hundred. I shall be very anxious to hear from you again, to learn what has occurred. Heaven send your prayers may be propitiously fulfilled. You do not say anything concerning the family at Eaglehurst. How did you act about Lady Honora's commission? What discoveries you have made I cannot possibly guess relating to Lothario (but suppose you allude to me under that name) and how you could have lately seen or heard of the Miss Gs of Winchester is a mystery at present. I suppose you have met with some lady, who having quitted the train of the Graces is content to yield the palm of victory to the young and aspiring of the sisterhood. From the description I have given, you may easily conceive that Winchester is beyond compare with these quarters. You cannot picture a spot more wild and desolate than this. The only diversion has been in the dramatic performances in a barn at Brixham. There I pitied the poor heroes, and blushed for Thalia's Daughters, partly indeed from the fraternal regard I feel for the followers of the Sock and Buskin.

Of all the diabolical walks of a wet and boisterous night, that from Brixham to the Garrison is the very worst. We are not to venture over the cliffs, but are forced to return by a circuitous route of a most breakneck description, to say the best of it.

Col. Ross failed in his application for our removal, but is going to apply again to another authority that we may be sent to Exeter. The expenses of the Mess are nearly the same as in the 77th. Every officer is obliged to take wine once or twice a week. Not much ceremony is used on ordinary occasions, and we do not dress for dinner (not in full dress coats etc). The first bugle sounds a quarter of an hour before the last, to prepare ourselves, merely a change of boots and so forth. We subscribe to the Band which generally repays us with a few martial strains, when the cloth is removed. The usual deductions have been made from my pay for this and the Mess utensils.

Maxwell and I go on very well together. He is a very gentlemanlike youth, not very rich like myself, and is liberally inclined. His equipment is very handsome, the Duke of Sussex being the family friend, and provided it at his own cost. He is Maxwell's Godfather. His own father was a Captain in the Army now on half pay and his mother a sister of General Prescott's (who is Colonel of the 28th) but it seems it was not through the General but the Duke that he obtained his Commission, for Genl P. is more of an enemy to the family than a relative, from an aversion to the choice his sister made and to the Captain. And now my dear mother, as I perhaps may be more intimate with this young Gent, and know your sex are all fond of gossiping, I have been (considering it is not very greatly your peculiarity) abundantly communicative, as I hope you will admit.

---

[1] The 2/28th was reduced to a skeleton, the majority of the men joining the 1/28th on 24th August 1811. The officers and NCOs returned home and were stationed mainly at Berry Head, being used as a draft-finding battalion for the 1st Battalion. William Keep was no 658 on the roll.

I hope to hear in your next letter that dear little Julia, Alfred and Alicia are well, and that your own health is improved, so important to us all. I suppose you have heard from my Aunt in the usual style of her communications, that is so very inconclusive about her return. I trust however that she writes in better spirits on the state of her health. Remember me with all kindness to every one at home, and believe me to be, my dear Mother, your very affectionate son, William Thornton Keep.

Berry Head Banks
14th January, 1812

My dear Mother,

I should have written last week in reply to your long letter and its interesting contents but we were then preparing to receive the Reviewing General, and it kept us out of doors a good deal. Last Friday he paid us a visit and inspected the Regiment, and we afterwards invited him and his Staff to dine with us, where the wine that night flowed so abundantly that several of us were absent from the next day's parade, and on the Doctor's list. I was myself attacked with headache, but small potations have that effect on me. I was delighted to hear of the improvement in your health, and of many of the events you described to me. Col. Ross thought to have prevailed upon General England to remove us to Exeter, but there we deceived ourselves for I saw the Colonel at his lodgings in Brixham yesterday and he told me we shall most probably remain here during the Summer. I called on him from a rumour I heard of being appointed to Chatham to receive volunteers from the Militia, and from what he said think it not improbable.

I should have no objection to it, as my expenses of travelling would be paid by Government. I begin to be much more comfortable here than I was. My prejudices are wearing off like a man with a new life. I must endeavour to forget the attractions of the object lamented, and am making friends very fast of those who were strangers on my first arrival. We have young men from the three Kingdoms and it forms a strange medley (not unconducive however to the pleasures of the service in which we are engaged from the variety of characters it produces).

Maxwell and I are in one room still, an inconvenience we are all subject to, from the 88th Regiment. and detachment of the 11th Regiment being here besides ourselves. I have already four Ensigns junior to me who have recently arrived, Hill, Maxwell, Byrne, from the Militia, and a youth named Colleton (the only one from London in the Regiment). He is the son of Sir James C., who I believe is or was a Banker in Pall Mall. We have several from Ireland and other parts.

These young Gents seem in want of the initiative qualities to be acquired only at Headquarters, as London may be termed, but are interesting from the specimen they give of the people of respectability connected with them elsewhere.

Brixham is crowded with fishermen, and has no other trade, and employs a large number of sailing vessels in it, and those who follow this occupation are called Trawlers. We have no other place to promenade in, and you may suppose do not stand upon the same ceremonies in our equipment for it that we should in Brighton or Bond St, and could you see our Gents perambulating there you would be struck dumb with surprise, or killed with laughter, it being the rage now to wear hats with brims and quarter of a yard wide of white beaver, with red wrappers for cravats and loose great coats — a very suitable undress for such a place, for it is dreadfully dirty and in every respect no better than Billingsgate. It furnishes us with a few books however from a circulating library, and a good billiard table in a bow windowed room overlooking the beautiful bay, where Maxwell and I frequently resort and where I have passed some of the merriest hours of my life here. We laugh incessantly at some odd whim or other, for we have generally the room to ourselves, and can give birth to any witticism we please, caring little about the game, as far as gambling is concerned.

I cannot add more at present, a wild young fellow named Alexander[1] being with me. He is spouting some poetry from a book that is laying open before him, besides which I hear the bugle which calls us to the Evening Parade, so situated I must say farewell for the present my dear Mother, and believe me at all times to be your very affectionate son, William Thornton Keep.

Pray tell Samuel I shall expect him to write me very frequently, as it maybe some time before we meet again. Let his letters come distinctly from yours, and I shall write accordingly to him. I am very anxious to know the result of your interview with General Calvert with regard to him, and what are to be his pursuits. Once more God bless you my dear Mother.

Berry Head
14th February 1812

My dear Mother,

Samuel's letter has indeed surprised me and Heaven be praised that you are tolerably well, which is the most delightful part of the news. I was fretting about Julia, as you left me in anxiety about her, in your last letter, not imagining that my dear little brunette was likely so soon, to have another rival in your affections. It is a long while now since I wrote to you, since which I have been twice away from

---

[1] This was Ensign Henry Alexander, No.657 on the roll. Described as a 'gent'. Gazetted on 13th June 1811 as Ensign. He was awarded the General Service Medal with clasps for Vittoria, Pyrenees, Nivelle, Nive, Orthes and Toulouse. He later transferred to the 12th Light Dragoons with whom he was killed in action in 1847. Thus, he probably never saw the GSM he claimed as it was only issued as late as 1848. He remained a very close friend of William Keep until his death. His daughter, Vittoria, died in July 1914 aged 77.

the Regiment on different duties, of which indeed I intended to have informed you ere this, but one interruption or other has prevented me. I have another officer in the same room with me now (Maxwell having gone to Exeter on leave of absence). One of his relatives, an Ensign in the llth Regt, has been staying with us for the last week, besides which I have been confused these three weeks by a severe scald on my instep occasioned by my Messmate having accidentally spilt some boiling coffee upon it, and it is likely to be a fortnight more, before I shall be able to draw a boot on. The box arrived this morning and I would not defer writing longer, although I am so little enabled to do so with comfort. As to the contents of the box, I never saw so beautiful a coat before, and the pantaloons are excellent, yet every thing happens unfortunately and I have been put to my wits end to find resources for different purposes. The Prince Regent I think is very inconsiderate in ordering such constant deviations in our uniform[1]. Long coats, fringe epaulettes and cocked hats are now to be abolished! A new Cap came down for me yesterday from Bicknell's in Bond St, the price of which is £3.16. Tailors have just arrived from Plymouth to take our measure for the new jacket, the cost of which is £5.16. and the new bullion epaulette will cost £2.4. Next a sabre instead of the present sword[2] will cost 3 or £4 more, and the Colonel has put it into Orders that we are to provide ourselves with grey overalls instead of the present trousers, with patent leather ends and chains which will cost £3.10 a pair[3]. All this is a sad interruption to schemes of economy, and you may suppose what difficulties I shall be under for some time to come. The duties I have been upon cost me £2.15 and this happened

---

[1] The General Order regarding the adoption of the new uniform was issued by Horse Guards on December 24th 1811. Long tailed coats and cocked hats were to be replaced by jackets of the sort already worn by light companies and by the new false-fronted 'Belgic' shako. However, although the jacket was adopted by Wellington's officers the 'Belgic' shako saw relatively little use, if any at all, in the Peninsula, the old stove-pipe shako being worn until the end of the war. This shako was already being worn by the rank and file and by officers of light infantry companies. The introduction of the new uniform caused much anguish amongst many officers, including John Mills, of the Coldstream Guards, who wrote, 'We are all in consternation at the idea of the dress of the army being altered from cocked hats and coats to caps and jackets. Ye heavens, what will become of crooked legs, large heads, and still hinder parts?' (Fletcher (Ed), *For King and Country; The Letters and Diaries of John Mills, Coldstream Guards, 1811-1814.* p.81.)

[2] The majority of British officers, save for flank companies, were equipped with the straight-bladed 1796 pattern infantry officers' sword. In 1803 a new regulation was issued introducing a new sabre with a curved blade. This was subsequently adopted mainly by the light infantry companies and regiments, particularly the 43rd Light Infantry, who loved to ape the cavalry, some officers of which regiment even went so far as to wear pelisses. Keep's reference to having a sabre instead of a sword is somewhat curious as there was no new regulation regarding swords issued in 1812. The only regulation swords for infantry officers at the time were the 1796 and 1803 patterns. Perhaps Keep was thinking of purchasing a non-regulation sword, many types of which existed throughout the army. (See Brian Robson's *Swords of the British Army*, London, 1996, for the best study of the subject.)

[3] The adoption of grey overalls reinforced with leather seams and bottoms became almost universal throughout the officers in Wellington's army in the Peninsula. They proved much stronger than the old white breeches although many officers continued to wear white trousers and even pantaloons with black gaiters.

to schemes of economy, and you may suppose what difficulties I shall be under for some time to come. The duties I have been upon cost me £2.15 and this happened in consequence of the Colonel's selecting me for this duty, for the junior officers were all younger than myself, in experience certainly (the Colonel knew that I had been on service with the 77th).

I was ordered off in pursuit of 13 deserters who decamped (with their fire arms, and property they had stolen) from a Man of War in the bay, the Captain of which sent a request to that effect to Col. R. begging him without delay to send some of the 28th in search of them. I started at eight o'clock at night with a Sergeant and 20 privates (provided with ammunition) on this unpleasant employ. Maxwell volunteered to accompany me, and the Colonel called him a spirited lad and approved of it. However we could not trace them, although we were out the best part of that night and two following days, and the adventure turned out in other respects very agreeably.

Our researches led us about midnight to a cottage on the sea shore. The sailors were supposed to be lurking about this neighbourhood by their Naval Commander, and not to have proceeded inland (but there he was mistaken). We knocked at the door of this lonely abode and were invited in by a genteel woman who was the mistress of it. We accepted the welcome invitation and were shewn into a pleasant apartment where we found a comfortable fire and every other accommodation.

The lady was as young apparently as ourselves, and very pretty, and though she was at first surprised now seemed pleased with our company. Maxwell appearing more the school boy than young man could hardly restrain his merriment, for I must inform you this kind young lady upon whom we had intruded had various snow white garments airing before the fire which she could not in time remove to be in accordance with her ideas of prompt politeness to us. Whilst we were laughing and blushing, between embarrassment and mirth, the tramp of a horse was heard, and presently a Gentleman entered who was the lady's husband. He had just returned from Exeter, and you may imagine his astonishment to see two young red coats, quite strangers to him, in the company of his Cara Sposa, at that late hour of the night. This made our mirth the greater, in which he with great good humour united. We explained to him our situation, and he shook hands very kindly with us and said he could not think of allowing us to seek shelter elsewhere. Accordingly beds were ordered to be prepared, and we gave directions to the Sergeant to conduct the men for the night to a public house about a mile off. Boot jacks and slippers were brought, and we sat down to supper. This kind friend of ours we found to be a Medical Officer of the Navy, holding some situation that enabled or required him to live there. In the morning we rose very early, but found a breakfast prepared for us. We invited this lady and Gentleman to see us at Berry Head, and with many thanks for their hospitality departed. The other duty was equally full of agreeable adventure, when I went

---

proved much stronger than the old white breeches although many officers continued to wear white trousers and even pantaloons with black gaiters.

whether my youngest sister promises to be dark or fair. I think Caroline would be a pretty name for her, but this may perhaps require deliberation. I am very much obliged to Mrs Willis for the fur, which is really superb. To her, and to Miss Ann Jones, I must always be remembered with the warmest affection. Heaven bless you my dear Mother, with all due remembrance, I am yours most affectionately, William Thornton Keep.

Berry Head,
6th April 1812[1]

My dear Mother,

I snatch up the pen with a determination to write to you a few lines, that however short my letter you may the more readily excuse my late neglect, which I am sorry and ashamed to say I cannot satisfactorily account for. But indeed the interruptions we are subject to, from two of us living in one room, and our situations in other respects, may chiefly be considered the cause of it. We cannot be said to reside in a barrack here, as at Winchester, all our habitations being on the ground floor and separate.

In the old palace at Winton we might find retirement at all times, a stillness prevailing in the attics of that lofty building equal to the grave, only interrupted by the twittering of the swallows, rattling of the casements, or rush of wind through its long passages, but here we might as well be living in a booth at a fair, our windows being breast high and sliding back in an invitation to the lounger or wag to pop his nose in at all hours. A range of little cottages extending in lines along this elevated platform and promontory makes it resemble a village, and so many of us so confined to it as we are keeps it constantly alive. Among such a crowd of 'good fellows and merry ones' you may suppose little opportunity occurs for uninterrupted avocations of this kind, besides which I have been in daily expectation of having to communicate news that I fear will not be pleasing to you, for we are in hopes of being sent out to Portugal soon, Col. Abercromby having applied to the Adjutant General for some officers to join the 1st Battalion immediately. Your last letter put my heart at rest entirely about yourself and the dear little girls, and day has passed after day with such agreeable rapidity that I declare I have been insensible of the length of time since I wrote last, having nothing very striking to relate, though we expect now soon further intelligence about our departure. Maxwell has gone up to town to take leave of his parents, and I am now in the same room with an Ensn Hill, an officer who has lately joined the Regiment, a very fine young fellow who has been wasting his time in the Navy, and is now gratifying his more recent penchant for the Army. It is curious to think how inclination varies in the choice of a profession. Many of our Gents are restless to remove from the infantry to cavalry, particularly if at all aristocratically

---

[1] Whilst Keep was writing this letter Wellington's army was storming the fortress of Badajoz in Spain.

inclined, for the latter though expensive is considered much the most dashing service, and is generally selected by young men of good fortune and family. The consequence is that officers of the infantry hold themselves in very low estimation comparatively; but there is another service still held in higher respect, which is called the Staff. Generally young members of the nobility, or Individuals highly connected, are nominated to these employments, as Aides de Camp or Brigade Majors, attached to the services of General Officers. Such appointments as these offer the best, and most certain path to preferment.

I gave you a statement in my last of the unwelcome demands our new equipment was making upon my income, which makes the hopes Samuel gives me of the Walcheren prize money being soon paid most agreeable to me. I imagine Mr Campbell told him that the first payment would amount to no more than ten pounds, for prize money is seldom paid all at once, but as the different things are sold. You say nothing about occurrences that I nevertheless conjecture have taken place, for I hope and conclude you have brought the General to capitulate on such honourable terms that dear Sam has opened the campaign at the Horse Guards. My interview with the General promised well I think from the interest he manifested and enquiries about you. This and many other events I look forward to, as a treat to come, in the next Budget. Colonel Ross told me today at parade that I have grown very fat and stout. I have only to add that the salubrity of the sea breezes has given me as fine an appetite as I have ever enjoyed, and that I am performing my part in the present stage of life in very excellent health and spirits, and remain dear Mother, Yr very affectionate Son, W.T. Keep.

Pray tell Samuel I am most impatient for another of his entertaining letters, and trust if my merits are deserving his Encomiums, he will write soon.

Berry Head
7th August 1812

My dear Samuel,

In this idle time of Military Service I prepare my pen to write again to you, lest by not doing so you should conclude I am unmindful of the agreement between us to keep our correspondence about things however trifling that may nevertheless be conducive to our mutual amusement. This may be the more desirable as I cannot expect it will be of long duration, for we are no holiday soldiers to be kept in perpetual idleness, but must be ready at the first summons to join the ranks of our comrades of the 28th who are now engaged in the stirring scenes of actual warfare.

I wish my dear Sam I could describe so clearly all I witness that you might suppose yourself here among us. It is probable you would then feel inclined to enlist with us and become an aspirant after military fame, and like the countrymen in 'The Recruiting Officer' soon be taught to sing 'Over the hills and across the soldiers to be kept in perpetual idleness, but must be ready at the first summons to join the ranks of our comrades of the 28th who are now engaged in the stirring scenes of actual warfare.

I wish my dear Sam I could describe so clearly all I witness that you might suppose yourself here among us. It is probable you would then feel inclined to enlist with us and become an aspirant after military fame, and like the countrymen in 'The Recruiting Officer' soon be taught to sing 'Over the hills and across the Main, thro' Flanders, Italy and Spain' etc and care little about 'The Cap that dubs a man a Gentleman in the drawing of a trigger, smelling woundily of Gunpowder'; for although we are in the full enjoyment of this interval of leisure we are familiarizing ourselves to the smell of it, in the practise of ball firing at targets, that is not quite bloodless either, for our faces are sometimes specked and stained with the coarse powder used by the men around us, particularly in firing blank cartridge in line.

Our ears too are becoming accustomed to the sound of volleys close to us, and our visual organs to the smoke that envelops us; and then the charge of bayonets, and formation of hollow squares to resist cavalry foes, and rapid movement into close and open columns, and into line again, all very forcibly representing what we may expect to have to do hereafter. Nor is this the only preparative in present practise, for dangers of all kinds are becoming familiar to us in the athletic exercises of swimming, lifting cannon balls, climbing precipices etc. I have twice myself been very nearly drowned, once thrown from a horse by passing a mischievous linker in ambush (a Captain Moriarty) who threw his cocked hat plump into the face of my charger and brought me plump to the ground from where I was taken to our Paymaster's cottage in the Brixham Road, with some doubt about my neck being broken, as well as my Chin, which suffered on this occasion, and from precipices I have had innumerable escapes. In the constant pursuit of these diversions precaution is often of no use. I was one day bathing in deep water close to the rocks, and when tired thought it was easy to leave off, but found the sides of them so perfectly smooth that I could discover no crevice within reach to dart my fingers upon to support my body. At another time swimming out a very short distance, a shoal of weeds completely interrupted my return, my arms entangled with them became powerless, and nothing but the most violent exercise of my legs with my head downwards could have extricated me; but we have all been equally fond of courting dangers of this kind.

One day Mr Taylor and Mr Alexander were so persuaded they could both climb a very steep and dangerous declivity that they commenced their labours in full confidence of succeeding and were very facetious about it as they proceeded, while I was dressing after bathing. Somewhat surprised by their sudden silence I turned round, and perceived they had arrived at a sufficient elevation to break every bone in their bodies if they ceased to employ circumspection. This they appeared fully aware of, for I soon found they were breathing hard with the intensity of their feelings and exertions.

I ascended the cliff by our usual path intending to watch their ascent from above, prepared to laugh as we all do at such trials of skill, but when I got there I saw they were in great peril at the summit of the precipice where the difficulties were almost insurmountable. Alexander was in the most favourable position and with so much reliance in his own exertions that he required no assistance. But looking over the edge of the cliff poor Taylor it seemed had chosen a much less easy mode to ascend by, and his safety was then depending upon the nearly exhausted strength of the muscles of his feet and fingers, which were resting upon the narrow ledges of the jagged rocks supporting them.

Providentially a seaman in charge of the signals at the flagstaff found a rope at hand which he instantly coiled round a cannon to aid in his rescue. Other pleasures you may suppose, not so perilous, please me as well. I like pedestrian excursions, and the further removed from our usual abode the more agreeable. There is a sort of delightful feeling of being at liberty which I am in the full enjoyment of when I find myself alone on open paths and unfrequented roads, with no other guide than a Finger Post, or on top of a hill from whence I can reconnoitre in our military fashion. In these long walks when passing the most pleasant places amidst woods and green sloping banks with the sea glistening in the sunshine between them, or on the shore strolling like Robinson Crusoe, I often wish you was with me, and am not infrequently reminded of you by the milestones marking the distance from London. Agreeable as these things are, you must remember it is not all gold that glitters, and the road to distinction is a hazardous one. Every Gazette shows besides a list of killed and wounded, many retirements and resignations, and poor Hanwell in the 77th found the trenches at Flushing (where he now lies buried) much less inviting than rural occupations, and regretted he was not a farmer, to wield the plough share instead of the truncheon.

In the pursuit of happiness surely one chief essential is security for life and property, yet both are risked in the military profession, and commissions often bought that lead to the destruction of the purchaser; just like fox hunters we have pleasures in the Chase and the dangers attending it are forgotten. One of the best is the intimacies formed, which keep one in heart and cement an attachment to it. We have been so shut up together here that it has been impossible to be otherwise than well acquainted with each other's affairs, even letters from our mothers with Maxwell and myself have been mistaken and intermixed (both our parents writing very much in the same hand) and I've often laughed to think how they would have been amused with a similar interchange of their sons' communications. Mr Hill, a new associate of mine, not being so well acquainted, looked with wonder at my large and constant supplies of intelligence sent under the printed official covers 'Upon His Majesty's Service', until I explained to him that you was in a Military Government Office having that privilege. It occasions surprise no doubt, and perhaps a suspicion, comic enough (as in the 77th) that I am a spy in communication with persons in authority, for conjectures are soon formed, where curiosity is once excited, as you so well know now, by recent events in Masquerading. Hill's family secrets are very singular, and we have liked each other well enough, to be as unreserved as Maxwell and I was. His father is a Cornet in the Royal Horse Guards, and he is himself very anxious to get into the same service, and regrets he has not money enough to accomplish it, as Alexander has, who is a young man of good fortune, and I believe the wealthiest among us. They are both very fine young soldiers with generous dispositions.

Berry Head
12th August 1812

My dear Sam,

It would be difficult to describe the scenes here, to give you a perfect idea of them, and of the impressions they are likely to leave. Imagine so select a family inhabiting such a populous village, thus removed by a vast expanse of high ground from the main land, yet connected with it by up and down path ways lined with briars and bushes on the sea shore, the cliffs upon which our cottages are built rising almost perpendicularly from the deep blue sea beneath, and the turbulent billows often roaring around us. This is enough of itself to excite an interest in the beholder, but when turning attention to the inhabitants, all military heroes employed in such a war as this, and seeking a temporary repose here the mind is filled with curiosity and pleasure, for our pursuits are all the same, Guard mountings and Reviews with drums and trumpets, and banquets at the Mess tables where joyous festivity prevails and time flies imperceptibly in these recreations. Some of these young soldiers would engage your attention from personal attractions in their military equipment and vivacity over their wine in our jovial meetings, and you may suppose there is no want of friendly feelings arising from such intercourse.

We furnish our cottages as if living in poor circumstances, and not at all disconcerted at the poor contrivances provided to show them off, and with a snug fireplace, and a kettle simmering on the hob prepared to welcome tea parties. In the same cot where I now reside another officer is quartered, only separated by a narrow passage between the doors. Fancy an invitation coming to me to take a pipe and glass there, from a Captn Bean, who having lost the use of his limbs by campaigning on damp ground is invalided and goes on crutches, but the fun to you would arise from the odd circumstance of his total ignorance of Theatricals, so that when at a loss for a subject to entertain him with over our grog I accidentally alluded to Archer's adventures and Lord Aimwell's in the Beaux Stratagem, and describing it made it appear a real event in life, his astonishment was great and as I happened to be eloquent in the description it considerably increased the interest of the story, he never dreaming from whence it was borrowed. This he has since been talking about with a great wish that other officers should hear me recount it, but some would soon find it out, particularly Taylor, who is well acquainted with these literary treasures and often talks of our most famous actors and actresses. But many a thought frequently intrudes to give a deeper interest to our conversations, he being undecided about going to the wars, and carrying on a very interesting correspondence with his relations in Liverpool respecting it, his father and mother being both gone, and his brother a cotton merchant there, from whom he receives constant communications that he imparts to me, and he has a sister whose entreaties to forsake his present dangerous profession, often brings tears into his eyes with fond remembrances of her. All the poetical scraps that touch upon the uncertainties of life he can quote with a fine appreciation of their truthfulness, and uncommon talent in giving effect to them. Burns' Tam O'Shanter he recites admirably, fit for any audience to be entertained with. Think therefore how pleasantly the hours fly in his delightful company! At Brixham lately Taylor invited Crisp, the manager of the strolling company to dinner at the London Inn, a strange coincidence with "Hit or Miss" at the Richmond Theatre where the Dramatis Personae opened the Farce at an inn of the same name, and where I sung with other travellers the sprightly ditty, and you was enamoured with one of our pretty actresses on coming down to see our performances. That interesting Company of Players I was acting with only 2 years since, I often think of, under Beverly's management, and of the many rambles you and I have taken in that delightful neighbourhood, and of tea parties visited with female professional associates in rural lodgings with little gardens near the stage door, leading down that pretty avenue to the river, where under the trees with benches I have passed so many agreeable hours frequently meeting our young actresses coming there to read over the plays announced for performance. Do you think sometimes of those days, when Thornton was wanted by the Gods in the gallery to play the ghost of Gaffer Thumb, and no other actor tolerated in it? That was an odd event, producing such an effort of ventriloquy, by the fright it occasioned in having quite forgotten the words he should have uttered to wake the dead from their slumbers. Nothing could occur more laughable, when eyes were opened of the prostrate bodies looking reproachfully at the ghost for not giving the desired signal, and the prompter's anxiety to hear him repeat the words required before they could come to life again, Gaffer Thumb totally unable to oblige them, till at length remembering the concluding lines uttered them in a voice so suited to a ghost that nothing earthly could be compared to them! What fun could equal that, beholding from the wing straddling Watson, with laughter in convulsions! I was then playing a few assiduities to her, as a Romeo. That clever little actress I am glad to see is now at the Coburg, and as my Father said will no doubt become a public favourite, when she has left off (which she may easily do) placing her legs too far apart in the height of her emotions.

Sweet Richmond adieu! It was not without regret I left pleasures so enticing, and business to be done with fair partners to give enchantment to it. I don't think I ever showed you the lines I wrote about the young lady mentioned above — here they are, as well as I can remember:

> Winding down the pathway yonder,
> Who is she my steps arrest?
> All alone thus led to wander,
> And by me by now addressed.
> Can it be Miss Blandford strolling,
> With her eyes cast on the ground?
> Love within her breast controlling,
> Whilst she roves in thought profound?
> Or Miss Wildenham, by pity touch'd,
> In charity to soothe the grief,
> Of him — her Father's Collar clutch'd,
> To give a Mother some relief.

Either would affection win,
As angel sent on errand kind,
But to charm, when both begin,
What refuge can a lover find?
Miss W. has acted well,
In each admir'd for many graces,
And I have felt the tender spell,
Though never seen two different faces.
The last young lady then must be
The magnet that can both unite,
And she it is, I plainly see,
Comes hither to afford delight.

Such were the boyish peaks, the poetic muse was playing with me, but the present scenes are equally interesting to me which I shall continue to describe to you on every opportunity, remaining dear Samuel.
Yours ever affectionately, William Thornton Keep.

(once a Member of the Richmond Company, but now in company with other actors, that obliges me to bid once more adieu to you.)

Berry Head
20th August 1812

My dearest Mother,

I am about to bid adieu to Devonshire, having been ordered by Colonel Ross to hold myself in immediate readiness to embark for Portugal, a letter having reached him this morning communicating directions to that effect. I am very happy that the order has arrived, for I have long desired the opportunity of going there. Pray make up your mind, my dear Mother, to this event in the confidence (mutually felt) that Providence directs all things for the best.

I know that your heart, tender as it is, must exult when you consider that I am going forth in a cause that does honour to the Country and profession to which I belong and in which so many noble characters are engaged. Fate seems to have decreed a separation it is impossible to calculate upon, but as far as I may be removed from Albion's shores all my affections will still concentrate there, and my greatest delight be derived from hearing that you are all well, and in the anticipation of meeting again in more felicitous times. Cheer up therefore, and remember I am not going alone, and shall have those with me that I may hope will prove sincere friends to me.

Every objection I entertained on first joining the 28th has long been banished from my mind. I have found brothers in the officers to whom I have become attached as such, and Colonel Ross's treatment of us has acquired the appellation of a father. The detachmt is to consist of 5 Ensigns, and 10 Corpls, Ensns Parks,

Power, Taylor, Alexander, and myself. Mr Taylor I am most intimate with, he is the son of a Physician of Manchester. Maxwell has left the Regt entirely, and is now at York as a Cornet in a Regiment of Dragoons. He kept us all in total ignorance of the affair, and left us very abruptly.

My regret is increased by such separations when going on service, but I wish I may not have another, that will affect me more deeply. Poor Taylor is unwell, and besides in great dudgeon since our trip to Guernsey. Colonel Ross (owing to our folly in telling the officers we had been there) was obliged to reprimand us in their presence, and he has taken it very much to heart, conceiving that the greatest blame rested with himself. I should have kept the secret, but Taylor unfortunately announced it at once, a most imprudent thing to do, that brought with it its certain punishment.

Yet it is altogether ridiculous, because many officers might have relatives in those places, to which of course they could not be restricted from visiting, as parts of the British Empire. I cannot believe therefore that it has reached the Horse Guards, but Taylor nevertheless fancies that is the reason we have received the mandate to join forthwith our first Battalion, and we cannot persuade him to the contrary, although it is plain it is at the request of Col. Abercromby we are sent out, to complete the numbers under his command, as we see by the Sergeants and Corporals who are to accompany us, and its having been talked of so long since. This has so damped the buoyancy of his spirits that he does not partake in the enthusiasm prevailing among us all on this occasion.

I must now enter upon a subject very painful to my feelings, and that is with regard to the pecuniary aid I absolutely require in consequence of this order. I cannot possibly, my dear Mother, go without £20. My living at Plymouth until we go on board quite alarms me, lest we should be detained any time there, and then there is sea stock to provide for the voyage, which must be sufficient to last a month or more in case of contrary winds, and different things to be bought where we land for the march up the country that may occupy a month or six weeks, General Hill's Army (with which the 28th are serving) being as we understand on the march to form a junction with Lord Wellington's in the heart of Spain, at the distance of 3 or 4 hundred miles from Lisbon where we shall disembark.

From all this you will be enabled to picture my situation, which is really a very perplexing one. I cannot help contrasting the state of feelings of those who have plenty of money with my own. What gladness it diffuses over the countenance to have the pockets well lined, and what joy to the heart it affords, at a moment like the present! So omnipotent is gold in all human undertakings that without it nothing can be done. Ambition is useless without that aid, for those who desire promotion must lodge money for it in the hands of the Agent.

We do not expect to embark before the middle of next week, but we may be ordered to march to Plymouth before we are quite prepared to leave this, however direct as usual, and with kindest remembrances to those ever Dear to me, believe me, Yrs ever affectly, W.T.Keep.

P.S. I am finishing this in a great hurry, being obliged to prepare myself in time to an Invitation to dine at Col. Paterson's, which is two miles distant from this. All I entreat is that you do not flurry yourself, for it is very uncertain whether we may move as soon as expected.

Berry Head
27th August 1812

My dear Sam,

Since the order came to prepare for foreign service we have all been anxious to be in readiness to march at a moment's notice; fortunately some delay has arisen in withdrawing the Sergeants from their recruiting stations, otherwise many of us must have been left in the lurch. As it is I fear I shall be late. The last Sergeant arrived yesterday afternoon, and Col. Ross will in consequence write this day to General England at Plymouth, acquainting him that the Detachment are all at Headquarters and in waiting for his orders, so that next week will certainly bring the route.

You may guess how the aspect of affairs has been changed since I wrote last to you, and must have seen the constant addition to our numbers from the Returns of the Recruiting Service to your office. Meanwhile many new appointments of officers are taking place to supply the vacancies continually occurring, for the Fates are busy in disposing of us all to fulfil the mysterious decrees hanging over our heads, and little do we know at what we ought most to rejoice or most lament, but it is certain our feelings are not the less acutely interested in the event.

Friends are separated perhaps never more to meet, and just as an attachment is formed calculated to continue through life, in which we meet as in a dream, and are as suddenly lost to sight, like the Borealis Race. Burns speaks of 'that flit away 'ere we can point the place'. Among a family of officers united as we have become by association in our daily amusements and pursuits, engaged in the same glorious cause, of the same Regiment and age, dining at one board, and partaking equally in all the vicissitudes incidental to such a precarious life, any changes are severely felt, at least by me, and I look with surprise at my companions who can bear with such a stoical indifference their frequent separations from each other.

But I forget that you will think me a very dull correspondent if I continue in this theme. A young Gentleman named Delmar has lately joined, who promises to become as interesting a companion as Maxwell was, though not so merry a one. He is gentle and amiable, very fair and delicate, and has been carefully brought up and is from Canterbury. Taylor, Alexander, Hill and Colleton are my other chief friends. I hope you have some more companions in your office, and pleasant ones, and that you go on smoothly there.

You are passing over the ground I saw before you, but the situation is improved, the emolument being larger it promises a comfortable support hereafter, and I trust you will lose no opportunity that may offer to bring yourself into notice. Your attention must be principally turned to the dictation of letters in the abundance of correspondence going on. My choice is made and I must abide by it. When abroad in the midst of scenes of trial and exertion, my tranquil hope will be that you will cheer the drooping spirits of our dear Mother, and I know that your heart will always prompt you to do so. Remain with her my dear Samuel, and contribute to her happiness by every means in your power. I need not remind you of the debt of gratitude we owe her, for you have witnessed the same acts that I have, and must feel as I feel.

We have little diversion here, except what I have already described to you that arises from our proximity to the sea. In that way plenty, the coast is beautiful, affording very fine rambles, and such as I am so very fond of, being both solitary and romantic. There is a cavern near this on the beach, almost as large as Westminster Hall. Water perpetually filtrating has formed a fine fretwork roof to it. It is not very easy to approach this spot, except at very low water, but we are always doing venturous feats of this kind.

I went lately to see the Young Roscius, Master Betty that was, at Dartmouth, about 7 miles from this. He played Tancred, but I shouldn't have known him again, and he can hardly be said to be the same person, his astonishing powers having quite forsaken him, and his voice become as hoarse as a Raven's. Had he remained as he was, it would have been worth going 20 times the distance to have seen him. But then we should not have found him at this obscure place and the connoisseurs in London would have been breaking down the boxes as formerly to get a peep at him, and the Royal Family running a race to obtain his company at breakfast the next morning. As soon as we heard of his coming here, we did a similar thing, and a dozen servants were despatched to hire horses for their masters. Six or seven only could be obtained, and when I arrived at Brixham hoping to get one I found them all engaged. Mr Taylor made a great sacrifice of his own comfort to prevent my being disappointed, and very kindly took me up behind him.

We crossed the Ferry at Dartmouth by moonlight, and rode back in company the same night as soon as the play was over, an excursion just adapted to what I like so much, and arriving there by moonlight was a suitable introduction to the playhouse, on passing over the river one of our companions singing the Canadian boat song of "Row brothers row" etc. With kindest love to my dear Mother, believe me to remain, Yrs most affectly, William Keep.

Berry Head
30th August 1812

My dearest Mother,

I have received your very affectionate letter with its valuable enclosures safe, and was deeply moved by the maternal love it assured me you feel for me, and the solicitude expressed so eloquently and with such warmth in my future destiny. I know not how I can repay you for the many anxieties and sufferings I have occasioned you. The wayward moods of my childish days must be controlled to obey the dictates of a heart that beats only for you, and I will cease to think wherein I should be most happy, or give way to caprices that are unreasonable under present circumstances.

The career before me is one I might have chosen had I been born to titles and affluence, though certainly not from ambitious motives, but being the mere soldier of fortune without any other dependence I am now especially urged to pursue it with firmness.

I have obtained leave from the church parade to scribble to you in time to go off by this day's post, the Regiment having gone to Brixham, about a mile and a half from this, to attend Divine Service. No letter has yet arrived from General England at Plymouth. Great anxiety of course prevails among us to know when we shall be on the move, some opinions prevailing that it maybe a fortnight or 3 weeks first, depending upon the arrangements for our embarking, and ships being in readiness to put to sea, as we shall sail in company with other vessels going under the same convoy. Ad interim, tailors, shoemakers, etc are in great requisition, none arriving according to promise and order, and to the accustomary delays in those offices. There is an old fellow who lives in an alley up one pair of stairs in Brixham, who is in my employ, but I fear I shall not see his well known face today. He is in fact what you would call a fine old Jockey, and I believe he is in great demand at this all important crisis. I shall visit his shopboard early tomorrow morning and give him a wigging, for he is very slow in performing my orders lately. My debts I find will not admit of my making any more purchases and I must contrive in the best way I can to do without many things I intended to take. Our stock to be taken on board will cost me I fear £5. (It is very different from the Walcheren Expedition, where everything in that short voyage was provided for us.) We must lay in pigs, poultry, tea, sugar, etc from our own purses, nor can we rough it, as we must unavoidably all mess together, and officers of superior rank of other Regiments perhaps on board with us, who won't confine themselves to short commons, nor sit down to a poor table.

We shall have no use for money after leaving Lisbon, and that is the reason as I observed before of the expense being so great on setting out, there being no prospect of obtaining any thing beyond our rations on the advance up the country. Our baggage animals must therefore convey all that we shall require from that city. In short I understand it is not very different from a journey in caravans over the Deserts of Arabia (the French marshals having overrun the country and reduced it to that state).

Happy England, to be exempt from the ravages of war! thanks to our gallant fleet. But for them it may be presumed Bonaparte would not let us remain thus idle, in hostile array here. We have a magazine and cannon prepared and two Regiments to guard the shore, but nothing but the angry surge approaches us. That dashes with great fury at times over the sea-beat rocks and timeworn base of this fine promontory, but only leaves us in contemplation of the waters of the deep, or in dread of shipwreck for our own vessels.

This is a beautiful morning, and the glorious sun shines with great fervour upon the placid waters of the noble bay opposite our windows. Everything is hushed, and the barracks deserted by their usual tenants denotes the calm repose of the seventh day. I can almost fancy I hear the only interruption to the ordinary stillness of a Sunday morning — the bells from the distant hamlets and village spires across the water. I wish you could enjoy the prospect, and inhale the sweet air that blows over us here.

I shall soon be upon ocean's bosom again with a gay pennant flying, and should be glad if we could flatter ourselves that we shall be conveyed by a ship of war, but that I hear is not at all probable, so many transports now being engaged in the Service.

The silence of the Scene around me, so unusual here, inclines my thoughts to linger over this brief interval of mortal existence and makes me unwilling to close my letter and bid adieu to you. I feel as if I had something yet to say, as before an approaching separation. This is the tranquil hour of prayer throughout all England, and perhaps you are now at church thinking of me. If I had been there today I should have had a companion of your sex in the same pew with me — the Curate's daughter of the little church at Brixham, an interesting young lady who attends there alone with us, and it is strangely pleasing to consider how promiscuously we are often brought together to join in Devotion.

I remember at Winchester, Abbot, who was a Quaker, being on one side of an heiress and myself the other, a pretty little creature that Col. Maddison in his friendly way used to joke with me about as having thirty thousand pounds ready for a husband, but being a true Votary at Cupid's altar, how incompatible I thought it to be allured by the God of Riches. And yet I could have loved, and must have done so, from all that is so affecting yet gratifying to the heart, where such a proof of attachment is given. But that strange concomitant pride stifles feeling, even love, where it exists, under these circumstances, shuns all manifestation of it, and I may say from experience dreads it. How many sensitive hearts undergo this martyrdom. Why then should I desire to mingle with the titled and the rich? And that I find is a question I cannot so easily answer.

Torquay and Sidmouth are at about 10 and 15 miles from this, and are places of fashionable resort. The only means we have had of mixing in good society has been by attending the assemblies at those places and Exeter. I was often tempted to go by my companions but never could accomplish it, each trip of this kind generally running away with five pounds. I am glad now I acted so prudently (though I lost perhaps the sight of many a fair face that might have enslaved me). And from what I have said above, was it not a danger to which it might only have been a folly to expose myself? I must endeavour now to forget the charms of my own countrywomen and prepare to pay my devotions to the Spanish senoras. Some of our officers who have been there paint them in very attractive colours and sing their favourite ditties.

I anticipate great pleasure from serving with our fine Army in that interesting country. By the time we reach them this year's campaign will have terminated and we may expect to find our troops in cantonments. Once more adieu my dearest Mother, Says your affectate Son, W.T.K.

Berry Head
10th Sept 1812

My dearest Mother,

You are no doubt participating with ourselves in the great anxiety consequent upon our present situation. But the events of a single day are uncertain, so soon are our expectations liable to be frustrated by sudden and unforeseen occurrences. I think this will not be the case with Ensign Taylor or myself, but the other three officers who were destined to accompany us will most probably remain behind in consequence of an extraordinary fracas that happened here last Sunday eveng, the particulars of which I must relate to you.

Our Band had enticed the lasses of Brixham and its neighbourhood to visit the Garrison, and the fineness of the weather had induced many of them to prolong their stay until after dusk. The scene conspired to exhilarate the spirits of all present and frolics ensued, which led to an attempt to intercept their retreat, and there was soon a general assemblage and outcry in the avenue leading to the drawbridge, which had been raised by those most active in the sport. All this was very well (we had before made captives of our fair visitants, and entertain'd them in our Mess room with a dance) and the gay group submitted to their imprisonment with great complacency, some of them returning to the promenade, and kept in tune by the harmony prevailing there, the Band continuing to pour forth strains of melodious music. All at once however the flight of the damsels recommenced owing to an unexpected and secret compliance with the entreaties of a few among them who had succeeded in their supplications for liberty, and the drawbridge obeying the fiat of some amorous but unknown magician descended again. This proved very displeasing to those who desired a continuance of the fun, and Who was it! echoed from every side. It happened that Ensign Parke and Ensign Power (both Hibernians) came like two fiery Sons of Mars in contact at this eventful moment (and never was an occasion more suited to chivalric deeds, one striving to imprison, and the other to liberate the fair supplicants).

Mr Parke hereupon charged Mr Power with having committed this daring offence. (It is supposed they had each their particular Dulcinia in view, whose wishes they desired to consult.) The other boldly denied, or confessed having done so, and then had they been armed their lances would doubtless have been at the rest preparing for mutual attack, but want of weapons at the moment has been their undoing, for not being able to command their rage they flew at each other and commenced to conflict with fisticuffs, in sight unfortunately for them of the private soldiers and townspeople. The senior officers present ordered them to be separated and placed under immediate arrest, and the consequence is that they are going to be tried by a General Court Martial, letters having been written to Plymouth to assemble officers to open the trial, and the two next officers in seniority will be ordered to prepare for foreign service, which will include Ensigns Hill and Colleton. Alexander must be detained as a witness. Mr Taylor and I were

1. An officer of the 28th (North Gloucestershire) Regiment, c. 1811.

2. Arthur Wellesley, 1st Duke of Wellington, 1769-1852. After a painting by Heaphy.

3. Sir Thomas Picton, 1758-1815. Picton was Keep's brigade commander during the Walcheren Expedition in 1809 when he was serving in the 77th Regiment.

4. The interior of the fort at Berry Head showing the old barrack mounds with a capped well at bottom left. Keep was stationed here with the 28th, before leaving for the Peninsula in 1812.

5. British infantry at drill. Private soldiers, wearing their white fatigue jackets, are shown the rudiments of drill by sergeants under the watchful eyes of officers, right.

6. The battle of Vittoria, June 21st 1813. The battle was Keep's first action in the Peninsula. This superb painting by Beadle shows Robinson's brigade attacking the village of Gamara Mayor.

7. British cavalry smash into the French rearguard during the closing stages of the battle of Vittoria.

8. The battlefield of Maya, as seen from the main ridge along which the 92nd Highlanders fought. The French attacked from left to right along the track visible on the left. The rocky height on the right was where Moyle Sherer and his piquet were overrun and taken.

9. Maya. The rocky spur, described by Keep, where he fought and saved one of the 28th's colours on July 25th 1813. The French swarmed up this spur before driving the 28th down the other side into the valley of the Baztan.

10. The battle of the Nivelle, November 10th 1813. Simkin's painting shows the 85th Light Infantry, attacking French redoubts.

11. The western sector of the battlefield of St Pierre, as seen from the main road to the north of the Chateau Larralde. Keep was severely wounded whilst fighting in the trees to the right of this picture. Captain Hartman of the 28th, led the light company out into the field in the distance to skirmish with the French.

12. Wellington and his staff on the Rhune mountain during the battle of the Nivelle, after a painting by Thomas Heaphy. The artist travelled to the Peninsu paint a number of Wellington's officers, many of whom appear in this most detailed painting. Wellington's pose is virtually identical to that in plate numbe in this book, which was also painted by Heaphy.

13. Number 13, Rochester Row, Camden Town, London,
Keep's house from 1841 until his death in 1884. Keep
used to re-enact his old battles in the back garden of
the house with his friend, Henry Alexander,
an old comrade in the 28th.

and commenced to conflict with fisticuffs, in sight unfortunately for them of the private soldiers and townspeople. The senior officers present ordered them to be separated and placed under immediate arrest, and the consequence is that they are going to be tried by a General Court Martial, letters having been written to Plymouth to assemble officers to open the trial, and the two next officers in seniority will be ordered to prepare for foreign service, which will include Ensigns Hill and Colleton. Alexander must be detained as a witness. Mr Taylor and I were entirely out of the fray. I was travelling over the pages of Goldsmith's Comedy of the Good-natured Man, lent to me by Adjutant Gilbert just previously to the event. This occurrence will perhaps occasion further delay in our departure, and we begin to think we shall not go to Portugal until the Spring, particularly as the equinoctial gales have set in.

I saw a letter from Captain Bradby (who is with our 1st Battalion) dated August 12th wherein he says "There is no news stirring here. We have 20 thousand men drawn up in front of Soult's army of 12 thousand, and why we don't attack them wiser heads only can tell. We advance and retreat alternately." He deplores the battle of Salamanca and says Bony's prognostic will be verified that "every British family will be in mourning ere the contest ends." He also says that they have a field officer at Headquarters so sick that he cannot be removed to the rear, and that Col. Abercromby has written for Col. Ross to be sent out, and also for 100 or 150 privates from the 2nd Battalion, and that they have not received a farthing of pay for the last six months. Here again a probability arises of our being detained some time to prepare so large a detachment. It will be very pleasant if Col. Ross should accompany us.

The order is issued recalling officers from the Recruiting Service and we expect several will arrive today, so that we shall have a very strong Mess shortly. No doubt appears to be entertained that Powell and Parke will be dismissed the Regiment, there being no possibility of hushing the matter up, so many having witnessed it.

The rules of the Service are very rigid in these cases, so that no two officers can have the privilege of calling each other names even without being compelled to call each other out. Had they fought with pistols or swords they would have been regarded as Gentlemen and caressed, but fighting with their hands has completely ruined their character, and they must throw up their commissions with disgrace. On this subject I must tell you how I managed lately to get two of my friends out of a scrape of this sort, for you may easily suppose that when we have words with each other (a thing unavoidable among boys who are placed as we are two or three in a room) on recollecting the penalty it is not the most agreeable alternative to be obliged to shoot each other. There is no other however unless you should happen to be quite by yourselves, or compromise your honour in the company of a third person, which indeed most of us have too much pride to do.

I was with two Gents one Evening at supper when they fell into dispute, and passed the limits prescribed in these cases. The consequence was they left each other intending to send a message next morning. They were two high spirited young men, and though they had a great regard for each other, and were previously excellent friends, yet they were not intimate enough to wink at their from his antagonist to breakfast saying he was disposed to forget everything that had passed etc. This gave such surprise and pleasure to his former friend that he called him 'the best fellow in the World' and most forgiving etc, blaming himself entirely for what had occurred, and saying he would certainly come. Having practised this deception with such good effect I returned to the expectant duellist and imposed upon him in the same manner, so that they presently met with open arms instead of loaded ones, and have ever since been ten times more attached than ever. So much so that luckily they don't like to make the smallest allusion to their quarrel; and as I could never undeceive them they go on admirably together, giving each other credit for what is due to me only. But I like them both, and had no wish to see them put their lives in jeopardy upon such ridiculous punctilios, and mere lapsus lingua as it were.

Yet had it been found out I suppose my conduct would have been considered highly dishonourable, and I should have been termed a liar etc and then doubtless I should have quarrelled with any who said I acted improperly in so doing, and have got into a hobble perhaps myself, so that it is only very well as it has turn'd out. I hope we shall not be ordered off before the 24th as I shall then receive another month's pay. I am reluctant to pay off bills too quickly, and hoard the money you have sent me with the rigorous care of a miser. Your letter and Samuel's with its enclosures have added to the regret I feel on account of the demands made at this moment to supply my necessities, for I perceive how delighted you both are to attach the least possible importance to it, forgetting that the very effort of concealment only serves to add an imperishable value to such true love and kindness. Heaven bless you both, and believe me ever yrs most affectionately, W.T.Keep.

Berry Head
20th September 1812

My dear Samuel,

Ten days have glided away since I wrote last in a feverish state of anxiety with conflicting events that thicken around us. Our departure has been countermanded, postponed, interrupted, while fresh discussions have been forming new arrangements made, and in progress, and we are all left in more or less uncertainty and restlessness. Many who looked on with unconcern in the full assurance of eating their Christmas Dinners here are now aroused as by a sudden alarm to reinforce our army abroad; and the letter bag will contain communications least expected, proceeding in all directions with this I send you.

Yet I can say nothing positively about what is doing or the extent of the measures intended. It is to be inferred however that Lord Wellington's designs are dependent upon his means, and the reinforcements he requires are so urgent it seems, that boys enlisted as such are being inspected and drafted for immediate service. It is an animating sight to see how these lads bristle up and stand on tiptoe at the muster, for the spirit that animates them is very warm, and those think themselves most unlucky whose services are rejected.

Among ourselves various feelings prevail according to the circumstances in which each are involved. Our nights are devoted more than ever to prolonged debates upon going on service and equipment for the field, the Mess table soon forsaken, and tea parties formed in our rooms, where maps are consulted to trace the movements of our armies and the point at which our first Battn is to be found. Horse furniture and saddles examined etc and then the more important query discussed of those destined to go. The list being still enlarged with more names as time proceeds. Col. Ross is in expectation of an order to join us, and Col. Paterson although just married is on the alert. How many absent hearts are now set throbbing about their friends here, for the 88th and 11th have received the same order as ourselves and are equally on the qui vive.

Amidst all this confusion you will not wonder at my finding little time to write to you, and am doing so now after an interesting night extended to 2 in the morning — spent with a companion I have become very intimate with, and much attached to, a Mr Taylor who I have named to you before. He has long been very undecided about going with us, and I am truly sorry to add it is now finally settled by his friends at Manchester that he is to leave the army altogether, to follow some other pursuit. This is one of my troubles I could not go to bed without imparting to you, and must now bid you goodnight.

At 10 am: with no perceptible change in the wind, as nautical men would say, I resume the pen, to retrace what I wrote last night and unbosom my feelings to you upon present events. This is a Weathercock World my dear Sam, and we are all the sport of fortune apparently, and subject to perpetual fluctuations of joy and grief. I truly lament the loss of dear Taylor, so gay a spirit with such a feeling heart, are not often found united.

We have cried and laughed through the unheeded hours of the night for weeks together, and become familiar quite with each other's sentiments. He is fond like myself of the drama and poetry (which he reads very finely) and has a philosophic mind that unfits him for a soldier's life. A disappointment in a tender attachment has embittered his existence, and the conviviality of the Mess table been his best relief, where indeed his conversational talents and gaiety have promoted such enjoyment, that his absence there will be much felt. But I have other causes to add to my regret for we know not what extremities fields of battle may produce and at such times with him I should have been sure of a brother and friend.

The Court Martial is to be dispensed with, in consequence of the lenient disposition of Col. Ross as I am informed permitting those officers named in my last to resign their commissions without the disgrace that wd be attached to their names from a public expose of their conduct, and Alexander will consequently be enabled to go with us, and his great desire to do so gratified, for he has been shedding tears of regret at the Col.'s shaking his head and forbidding him to think of it. Dear Taylor and Col. Ross have been very intimate and it is said so reckless in their cups and misanthropic moods as to enrich the sea with banknotes thrown in to it, but as I am certain Taylor is a few months older than myself I cannot believe this. That they might have railed at fortune's spite in good set terms on the sea-beat rocks (for the Col. has experienced vicissitudes) is credible enough, and it is still more so that his departure will be as much lamented by him as myself.

The weather has been as unsettled as everything else here and moonlight nights as well as stormy ones at Berry Head will long be remembered by those who have been in friendly companionship here and who are now about to bid farewell to it for ever! When we leave the Mess table we have no places of amusement such as we might find in a town to repair to, and once having passed the threshold the rocks we are inhabiting, the sea and canopy of heaven are the only objects familiar to us, yet the change is often agreeable from the brilliant light of our banqueting room to the wild nakedness of nature around us, except when clouds and rain obscure the skies, and then we scurry to our wigwams, where the Quartermaster furnishes us with coal and candles and chairs and tables, and with other articles of furniture hired we contrive to make ourselves very snug.

I have agreed with Delmar to transfer to him my camp bedstead, crockeryware boxes etc for which he has paid me £5 (until I can remit him the same or he has no further use for them) for the bedstead I value as having belonged to poor Bowes, and the other things because given to me by my dear Mother.

I had purchased very pretty curtains for the bedstead, but we must oblige each other in this world, where we stand so much in need of each other's assistance, and Delmar is paying 16 shillings a month for furniture hired. I will now refer to your letter last received. I trust my aunt will now be persuaded to come home and join with my mother in some establishment, which I fear her aid will be very necessary to succeed in. Give my kindest regards to Miss Ann Jones. I shall always think of her with affection and gratitude since she has proved such a valuable and dear friend to my dear Mother, and I am delighted to find that Lord and Lady Cavan are as good and kind as ever to her, which is a proof of real friendship that must be most gratifying in a world like this, where a true friend is more precious than a Diadem. I often think of our kind relatives in Windsor forest and hope they are all well.

About myself I can only say that the experience I have had prevents all anticipation of acquiring renown in my present pursuit; the forms of the British service seldom admitting that honour to Subalterns or even Captains, which makes officers of that grade anxious to get their promotion advanced to the rank of Lieut Colonel or Majors at least, and then they might have some chance.

We ought not to complain of being unhappy because we cannot see each other at this moment, when we consider how much such a meeting would add to the distress of an immediate separation. God bless you my dear Samuel, says your affectionate Brother, W.T.Keep.

Berry Head
29th Sept 1812

My dearest Mother,

You kindly assure me that at this eventful crisis you reckon not time by the ordinary standard, but 'regard each day as an age', when you hear not from me, and believe me I have not been unmindful of your anxious solicitude, but only waiting to inform you of our final destination. But I am sorry to tell you I have besides been poorly with an eruptive complaint that has confined me some days to my room, and has partly deprived me of the use of my right arm. However, I must acquaint you that an express has just arrived from Exeter, augmenting the detachment to following strength, viz. 1 field officer, a Captain, 2 Lieuts, 4 Ensigns, and 170 Privates, and that we are beginning to complain of the delay in sending us off, as it is approaching so fast to the decline of the year, and Winter setting in with all her 'rising train of clouds and storms' at this Siberian spot. Last night it blew a hurricane, to the great discomfiture of a large fleet of transports and ships of war that were driven into Torbay.

Guns of distress were firing all night, and this morning a scare presented itself that to us who are accustomed to behold the sea 'puffed up' with winds was truly terrific. The ships ride in sight of our windows, but we generally repair to the head of the rock for a more extensive view. There with glasses we perceived all the devastation of the tempestuous night. Several vessels were blown from their anchorage out to sea, and one had the misfortune to be entirely wrecked, and its disjointed timbers, barrels, spars, etc floating about, bespoke its fate.

We hear that the body of one of the Marines was picked up by a small boat that ventured from the shore to the assistance of the crew. It still continues to blow very hard, and a heavy rain has set in that completes the dismal prospect. The ship that was lost is supposed to have run on a dangerous rock very near this, and the safety of the fleet depending upon their putting out to sea, the Blue Peter (a signal for sailing so called) is now flying at the mast head of the Admiral's ship for them to get under weigh again. Some of them are merchant vessels, and others transports with the Guards on board destined for Lisbon, under convoy of the Marlborough Man of War from Portsmouth. There are also 2 or 3 East India men. We can't yet learn the name of the vessel that went to pieces nor the fate of the unfortunate crew.

September 30th. I have detained this to give you further particulars as we ourselves are likely to be materially interested in what the elements have brought about, for Col. Ross is in expectation of an express ordering us on board (they having put back yesterday and opened a communication with us) though he says that they could not venture to embark us unless the wind moderates, such a heavy sea is running on the coast.

The Honourable General Stewart landed last night with his suite, and dined at our Mess, going off to the ships this morning, which however are still detained in the bay, Rude Boreas in high distraction veering to all points of the compass, so that by land and sea we are all in commotion. In the midst of which I am under the Doctor's hands, a very amiable man named Dakers (who strange to say was our Surgeon in the 77th). He ascribes my scorbutic attack to the effect of too frequent bathing in salt water and takes so kind an interest in my general state of health that he says he shall be glad to give me a sick certificate to remain in England! But I trust I shall not require it as the medicinal chest has afforded me salutary relief in the shape of calomel pills etc, and I am now peeping abroad again. The most mortifying consequence of my complaint was that I could not accept an invitation received to attend a rout at a watering place about 12 miles from this, where all the Belles of Devonshire were assembling to attract the Lotharios from distant parts, as I anticipated much pleasure from it.

The fleet is now under sail and may soon be altogether out of sight, or they may be compelled to beat about only, if the wind is adverse, and return again to port, and perhaps take us on Board. Otherwise we shall see them no more, for with the wind fair they would not wait a minute for us. This changes our destination once more to Plymouth, where we shall certainly now speedily repair to embark. The whole barracks are in disorder, the 88th having by the last express been ordered to send out from their 2nd Battalion a detachment to the same amount as our own. This occasions a complete disorganisation of every thing here, and it is probable the Regiments will be removed after our departure as our own Gents can look for no consolation, but in a change of quarters, to Exeter, and Col. Ross will I suppose effect it, though he is himself now under orders to embark with us for Portugal. You may fancy our situation under all these circumstances. One great pack up prevailing, it reminds me of past scenes at home, so well known to you and I, when everything has arrived at that state of preparation that there is not a chair or table to sit down to. The uncomfortable kind of desolation and agitation we have so often experienced together. Pray write, and without fear of the letter being opened if I am absent, as I have made arrangements in that case. Conceive my dear Mother my anxiety to hear again from you, and believe me, etc. etc. W.T. Keep.

Berry Head
5th October 1812

My dear Brother,

This note will introduce you to a dear friend of mine, Ensign Taylor of the 28th — an unlucky combination of complaints has prevented his accompanying us on service, and he has obtained a sick certificate to return to his friends at Manchester, and on his way home he proposes passing a day or two in the Metropolis, to which at present he is an entire stranger. We cannot as formerly open our doors to welcome our friends, and I have therefore disclosed to him our situation, so that he will not think you deficient in your attentions in that particular.

Pray my dear Samuel escort him to as many places of public amusement as the town at present affords, and make yourself agreeable and affable sans ceremonie, he being a very kind hearted and excellent fellow, and when I say that I mean to imply that he possesses all the valuable qualities of a truly disinterested friend.

You must ask the Colonel to give you leave to be absent from the desk for a day or two. Taylor knows I am but un pauvre militaire, but I am well assured he likes me the better for that, and therefore you have a very reasonable and comfortable plea for being unembarrassed in his company notwithstanding your finances being just now at a very low ebb, as I guess at least from your last evasive reply to my enquiries.

Until time effects a change in our circumstances we must rail on at fortune I fear, that fickle jade who leaves us nothing but our wits to depend upon, except in some instances — our friends. Continue to show every regard to mine, for the more rare the gift the more inestimable.

I am now about to bid perhaps a long adieu to England, and to those whose feeling hearts have beat so long in unison with my own, and whose but yours can better tell the painful import of that most distressing word farewell. Heaven bless you my dear Sam, and believe me ever, Yours most affectionately, W.T.K.

Chapter Four

Voyage to Lisbon

When William Keep and his comrades of the 28th marched from Berry Head to Plymouth in October 1812 they did so with high expectations of what was to follow once they caught up with Wellington's army in Spain. After all, had not the British army taken by storm the fortresses of Ciudad Rodrigo and Badajoz as well as having thrashed the French at Salamanca? All gave great cause for optimism. However, instead of finding himself poised on the Spanish-French border in anticipation of the invasion of France, Keep was to find himself back on the Spanish-Portuguese border after a disastrous October and November, the result of Wellington's one great failure in the Peninsula, the siege of Burgos.

The year of 1812 had begun in spectacular fashion with the snatching from the French of the so-called 'keys to Spain', the fortresses of Ciudad Rodrigo and Badajoz. The first of these towns fell to Wellington's men on January 19th 1812 after a siege of just eleven days, a remarkable achievement given the conditions and the timing of the year, winter, when the campaign season was usually well and truly done with. Indeed, the capture of Ciudad Rodrigo came as a great shock to the French and certainly put paid to the myth of Wellington being a purely defensive-minded general. The offensive did not stop here, however. In February Wellington's army slipped away south to lay siege to the much more formidable fortress of Badajoz, a town which had defied the British army in June 1811 and which, for various reasons too drawn out to enter into here, had long been the object of the men's desire. The army broke ground before the town on March 16th and by April 6th three breaches had been made in two of the town's bastions and in the curtain wall between them. Wellington knew the attack would be a bloody one but even he could not have anticipated the bloodbath which was to follow as he hurled the 4th and Light Divisions at the walls on more than forty occasions, only to see his men smashed and swallowed up in the fiery ditches that lay at the foot of the breaches. Indeed, it was only when the two diversionary attacks by the 3rd and 5th Divisions succeeded that the town fell.

With both fortresses in his hands at last, Wellington could feel confident enough to begin his advance into Spain and on June 13th his army marched from Ciudad Rodrigo. Four days later he entered Salamanca. Then, after weeks of marching and countermarching, he crushed Marmont's army a few miles south of the city at the small village of Los Arapiles. This victory really did nail the French belief that Wellington was not capable of fighting an offensive battle and in fact General Foy, writing of Wellington's victory, said that it raised Wellington's reputation to that of Marlborough. Coming from one of Wellington's adversaries this was tribute indeed. The logical road to take following the victory at Salamanca was north-east towards France but political considerations held sway and instead Wellington marched upon Madrid which he entered on August 12th. After a short stay here he did indeed resume his march north to undertake the siege of Burgos. Here, however, the year of victory was to come shuddering to a halt.

The siege operations in the Peninsula were undoubtedly the most disappointing aspect of the war from the Allied perspective, marked by a lack of proper siege material, trained sappers and miners and a shortage of heavy guns. Nowhere was this more in evidence than at Burgos. In fact, Wellington took with him just three heavy guns to lay siege to the castle which stood high on a hill overlooking the town itself. His veteran storming divisions were absent also, the siege being entrusted to the 1st Division of the army. Only the Brigade of Guards came out of the siege with any credit, but even they failed to make any real impression during the attacks on the castle's defences. Bad weather made for atrocious conditions while the last straw perhaps came when Edward Cocks, one of the brightest prospects in the army and one of Wellington's favourites, was killed repulsing a French sortie. Wellington wept at Cock's funeral and it is almost certain that his heart went out of the siege at this point. The siege of Burgos dragged on until October 22nd when the Allied forces stole away in the night to begin their retreat towards Madrid. The subsequent retreat, in fact, did not end until November 20th when Wellington's army concentrated around Ciudad Rodrigo where it had begun the year eleven months earlier.

Just a few days after the army had reached Ciudad Rodrigo, William Keep came ashore at Lisbon to begin his own personal adventures in the Peninsula. But let us return to early October 1812 and his march from Berry Head to Plymouth.

Plymouth
8th October 1812

My dearest Mother,

I have only time by this post to inform you that we marched from Berry Head on Tuesday morning last for Modbury, and arrived here yesterday, and that we embarked on board the British 'Hero' Transport (I'll send you the number in my next). I have at present the Colonel's leave to be on shore, and I slept last night at an inn, but am going on board in the course of an hour to relieve other officers who are anxious to leave the ship. I have been so pressed and had such various affairs to attend to, that I could not write sooner. The order (as we expected) coming upon us admitted of scarce time to pack our portmanteaus[1]. I was

---

[1] The business of assembling one's campaign kit was an integral part of any officer's preparation for overseas service. Officers carried their campaign kit in a portmanteau or valise and George Gleig, who served with the 85th Regiment, left a detailed description of his preparations prior to departure and of the kit he packed. 'The short space of time which intervened between the arrival of the route, and the eventful day which saw its directions carried into effect, was spent by myself, and by my brother officers, in making the best preparations which circumstances would permit for a campaign.....a selection was made from our respective wardrobes, of such articles of apparel, as, being in a tolerable

delighted to hear from you, and of your intention of removing to the cottage. If you have written since they have not yet come to hand but will be forwarded. Direct to me at the Commercial Inn in future. I say in future, for we may be here some time yet, if the wind and weather continue unfavourable.

I am tolerably well, and am laying in a stock of the best spirits possible to encounter the buffeting of the voyage, for which I thank God I am pretty well prepared. Send me if you can the direction of Mr Brown, my Aunt's acquaintance, in case of anything very unforeseen occurring. I am in the greatest hurry imaginable.

Heaven bless you my dear Mother, yrs most affectly, W.T.K.

On board the 'Hero'
(continuation of 8th October 1812)

My dear Sam,

I have brought my Mother's letter on board to add these few lines to it. We left the old quarters on Tuesday, taking leave of all our friends there, both town's people and military, who were much concerned at parting from us. You would have laughed to see one poor creature — a sort of Mrs Fathom or Moll Hagan, who has been for years in the Regiment, perching upon a rock and giving vent to her lamentations as we filed down the road before her on the way to Brixham, the tears rolling over her weather beaten features, and her fists clenched in a wild paroxysm of grief and heroism, crying out 'fight 28th — fight boys — fight 'em'.

On arriving at Brixham the Colonel gave us permission to proceed in chaises, thinking we shall have been marching enough by and bye, I suppose, leaving the men to the charge of the Adjutant, Gilbert, who is a fine dashing little fellow, and came to Plymouth to see us off.

---

state of preservation, promised to continue for the longest time serviceable; canteens were hastily filled up, and stored with tea, sugar and other luxuries; cloaks were purchased by those who possessed them not before, and put in a state of repair by those who did. Perhaps the reader may be curious to know with what stock of necessaries the generality of British officers were wont, in the stirring times of war, to be contented. I will tell him how much I myself packed up in two small portmanteaus, so formed as to be an equal balance to each other, when slung across the back of a mule; and as my kit was not remarkable, either for its bulk or its scantiness, he will not greatly err, if he esteem it as a sort of medium for those of my comrades. In one of these portmanteaus, then, I deposited a regimental jacket, with all its appendages of wings, lace, &c.; two grey pair of trousers; sundry waistcoats, white, coloured and flannel; a few changes of flannel drawers; half a dozen pairs of worsted stockings, and as many of cotton. In the other were placed six shirts, two or three cravats, a dressing-case competently filled, one undress pelisses, three pairs of boots, two pairs of shoes, with night-caps, pocket-handkerchiefs, &c. &c. in proportion. Thus, whilst I was not encumbered by any useless quantity of apparel, I carried with me quite enough to load a mule, and to ensure myself against the danger of falling short, for at least a couple of years to come.' (Gleig, *The Subaltern*, pp.1-3.)

At Ivybridge, one of the most picturesque spots in Devonshire, there is a grand inn. Here we stopped to refresh, and among the travellers sojourning there was Mr Young of Covent Garden. This was unnoticed except by myself, few if any of my companions being acquainted with London theatricals. Dear Taylor and I took sorrowful leave of each other, and when he pressed my hand he squeezed a note into it, which could not be examined before I had lost sight of him.

I have given him a letter to you, and he will call on you at the office, prepare yourself therefore to receive him and show him all the attentions you can, for you will like him much, and he has been a kind and valuable friend to me.

We have six officers of the 88th embarked with us, and 8 of our own, with between 3 and 4 hundred men of the two Regiments.[1] Col. Ross has a sick certificate and remains at home, and Col. Paterson goes out with us in his stead.

I shall write again before we sail, and remain my dear Sam, your ever affectionate Brother, W. T. Keep.

P.S. Tell my dear Mother to rely upon my being a punctual correspondent, and that I wont forget to address my letters to her little abode in Chelsea, or Rubergall's Cottage, since it must be so called, but I think from the high reputation of its ancient tenant it should still bear the name of Captain Cox's Hall.

On board the British 'Hero'
Plymouth,
10th October 1812

My dearest Mother,

I wrote to you the day before yesterday from the Commercial Inn, acquainting you of our arrival here, and embarkation, since which we have been busy taking in stores, and the weather is clearing, and promises a fair wind to prosecute our voyage, but we are all in a fine quandary for the want of money, and are hoping to be detained in harbour a few days longer.

Just at the moment we were coming to a settlement the paymaster here informed us that without a special authority from the Secretary at War he could neither issue to us the Embarkation Allowance nor month's pay in advance. This is a most unfortunate event as we have no resource but to live upon our rations entirely, without cash on arrival at Lisbon to make our necessary purchases there. Most of the officers astonished at this news have gone on shore, to enquire into it, and Colonel Paterson is so surprised and angry about it that he has sent an Express

---

[1] The 88th (Connaught Rangers) had been in the Peninsula since April 1809 and had established itself as one of the fiercest regiments in Wellington's army. It had fought at Talavera, Busaco, Fuentes de Onoro, had stormed the castle of Badajoz and had been at the forefront of Pakenham's attack which began Wellington's offensive at Salamanca where it captured the Jingling Johnnie of the French 101st Regiment. It was to become one of the most famous regiments of the war.

to Berry Head for our paymaster (Moore) to set off instantly for Plymouth to arrange matters with the paymasters here. In the meanwhile if the wind comes round, in spite of our wants, we must sail. Such is the state of things here at present, and we are quite in arms about it, for it is unprecedented, and we may be said to be all in the same predicament, every one fully depending upon receiving it, and time now through private means not permitting the least chance of making up the deficiency.

We are very fortunate in our ship, which is very large, and we hear an excellent sailor. We have six officers of the 88th with us, making 14 altogether, as follows, Colonel Paterson, Captain Bowles, Lts Burn and Medlycott, Ensns Nelson, Hill, Alexander and myself, and of the 88th Captains Robertson and Walker, Surgeon O'Reilly, Lieutenant Lloyd, and Ensigns Mills and Reynolds.

Leaving my dear friend Taylor behind was a very severe disappointment to me, for he has been a most kind friend on this emergency, giving me the things he had purchased for himself, his saddle, dressing case, etc. I hope Samuel will be attentive to him when he calls at the office, which I conclude he will do either Thursday or Friday next.

Hill, who is to supply his place, is a very generous young man, but as badly off as myself. Not expecting to go on Service he had been expending too much money in other ways at Berry Head. We are doing duty together on board (whilst those with money are on shore) and are living on the rations — salt pork, sea biscuits, rum and flour, and today have fresh meat and wine, but you may imagine how short this allowance is considered to fall, when the extras for the voyage will cost £5 each.

We are looking out for every boat that is likely to bring us news of the arrival of our paymaster, and of the result respecting the £20 each we are in expectation of, flattering ourselves that we shall certainly obtain it. The contents of your last eventful letter I cannot now reply to — the Ryder Street occurrences are too melancholy to bear contemplation. I have exchanged the fur with Lieut Gilbert for an old portmanteau.

God bless you and comfort you my dear Mother, and remember you have a Son who loves you dearly, and will always remain, Yours most affectly, W.T.Keep.

On board the 'Hero'
Falmouth Harbour
14th October 1812

My dear Mother,

We removed from Catwater on the 11th but the next day anchored in Cawsand Bay (an extreme branch of Plymouth Harbour) where we were detained by the unsettled state of the weather until yesterday, which was the means of my receiving a letter from Samuel that otherwise must have remained at the post office. We weighed anchor again from Cawsand at 12 noon, and put to sea with other vessels outward bound, under convoy of the Seaflower Brig, but encountered some heavy gales that obliged us to run in here. This enables me to put another letter on shore, but I have only a few minutes to devote to you, as the Pilot is about to leave the ship, for although the wind continues variable we shall pursue our course.

Our transport promises well, if allowed to proceed (these ships are hired from the merchants by Government at so much per month) and perhaps being paid for thus it is considered advisable to expedite the voyage, but many on board think we shall be obliged to return to port. The wind threatens to be so contrary. We received (after a great deal of trouble) £8.15. on the morning we left Plymouth on account of our embarkation allowance, which was all we could get; but on my departure from Brixham Col. Ross took a very friendly leave of me, shook me kindly by the hand, and lent me nine pounds, with only a 'good bye my poor Boy' and not another word about it. Nevertheless I sent back by our paymaster to the Colonel every farthing of this money and more than I received, leaving myself quite penniless. My other commanding officer, Colonel Paterson, who goes with us, very kindly lent me £3 to pay my share of the stock without my requesting it, which I shall return to him when we arrive at Lisbon, out of the £4 that will be allowed there, to complete our allowance of £12.15., and we shall receive another month's pay there to carry us up the country, so that altogether I shall do tolerably well; but I have been sadly harassed and perplexed to arrange matters and yet I could not have got on without the assistance I have received — having extended the same aid to others, which indeed has taken from me £13 that I cannot at present explain to you the particulars of, but it arose from money I imprudently advanced to the private soldiers during the time I had the payment of a company at Berry Head — Col. Ross intended this as an assistance to me — the allowance being 2s a day, but it has turned out a Frenchman's Benefit; the Quartermaster who took it after me, refusing to let the men remain in his debt, and compelling me to pay it.

We have laid in a plentiful sea stock, costing between £40 and £50 among 14 of us, which is considered a moderate allowance — none of us being very rich, and you may easily suppose I am not at all sorry others are compelled to be economical.

The wind is coming round, and the sails will be unfurled directly, as the capstan is at work heaving up the anchor, and the vessel begins to feel her freedom already. Write to me often when in Spain, for your letters will be the greatest comfort that can be afforded to me.

Heaven bless you my dearest Mother. With kind love to all I leave behind me, I remain yrs ever most affectionately, W.T.K.

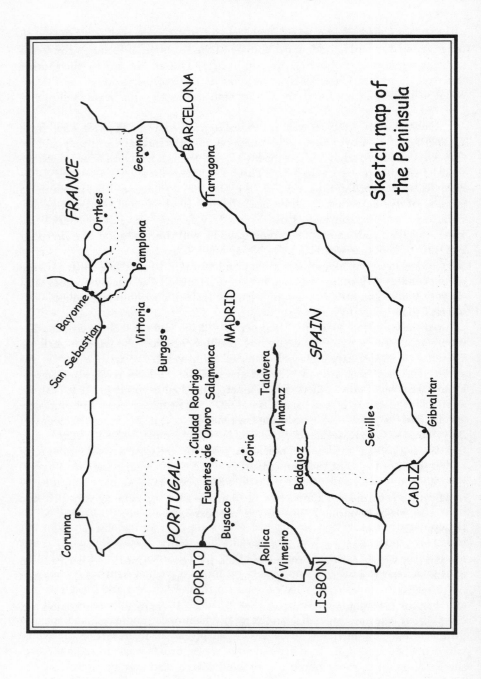

Sketch map of
the Peninsula

My dear Brother,

I hope you have not yet heard that the fleet with which we so recently sailed was entirely dispersed and driven to various ports by a tremendous storm we encountered on the night of the 17th when distant about 100 miles from the Land's End. In that case my dear Sam you will have the satisfaction to learn from me that having parted from the rest of those that sailed in company and after beating about for the last week in what is called the Chops of the Channel, we were forced to put the helm about, and return here, where we are now once more safely at anchor, after very narrowly escaping shipwreck. As this was the first storm I was ever in, I must give you some account of it.

In the first few hours after we sailed we enjoyed sunshine and fine weather, and during this short interval you should have taken a peep at us, when the eyes of all were going before the wind as it were, and to the right about, after taking their last look at old England.

You would then have seen us like a troop of horsemen eager in the face, bounding over the billows, with our gallant Commodore Seaflower leading, vigilant as a hen over her chickens, and the spray occasionally dashing over our decks received with shouts of laughter, and strange outcries from the pigs and poultry that idle time below, when the sun throws its dusty shadows across the cabin, where only a silent pair of card players are to be found or perhaps some pensive passenger, perusing his last billet-doux from a sweetheart. But how brief is human happiness! Two days were merrily passed in posting through the waves in this manner; but on the next, the sky gradually darkening had assumed its gloomiest aspect, and the winds increased so that the crockery began to rattle. On this afternoon the telescopes were employed, but we had lost sight of the Commodore, and the ships were all abroad and dispersed, each providing for their individual safety, according to instructions from his last signal. So threatening was the appearance of the weather that we were soon close reefed and tarpaulin put down over the hatchways. Our mulled wine after dinner on this fearful night was taken in the eastern fashion, that is seated on the floor, from a tea kettle, with the light swinging overhead in an iron lanthorn. Every wave that struck the vessel still disturbing our equilibrium, a sad moment to think of a snug and quiet seat in a coffee house on terra firma. For my part I had no thoughts of sleeping, but my companions being so disposed I braced up my hammock, undressed, and got into it. The wind blew in heavy gusts, more dismally awful from feeling the whole fabric shaking under us, as the ponderous waves broke with dreadful force in succession upon it, every bump of this kind was so distinctly felt that it set the heart in quicker palpitation, and was followed by the immediate crash of things breaking. The light had been extinguished by the wind, that forced an entrance through every crevice above water, but the waves rising like hillocks of snow at the cabin windows gave momentary gleams of illumination equal to moonlight.

The storm still increasing threw the ship so deep in the sea that it was apprehended the stern would be covered, and accordingly the carpenter (a tall, one eyed man) came to make all sure in that quarter by fixing in the Dead Lights (as they are called) or shutters. Being without an assistant for this purpose, I got up and offered my services, and greatly indeed they were needed, for in effecting this object he was obliged to hang his body half out of the casement, so that when the ship pitched he was in the greatest danger of tumbling forward, and I had enough to do to keep good hold of his legs while he was engaged in this perilous business, which when he had completed he departed, not without letting us know, with much indifference 'That it would be well if we found ourselves afloat in the morning' as he had never known it blow harder.

Such an opinion from an old sailor who had been twenty years at sea did not tend to make me, or I believe any of us, feel at all more comfortable as to what would ensue, as the rage of the tempest was increasing and the ship strained and cracked in every timber and rolled most horridly, slipping as it were at one moment with comparative ease down terrific declivities and in the next struck by the mighty billows she came into contact with so that with the shock she seemed stunned and to reel in the water, volumes of which cast up above her, appearing to add to the Wind's distraction and confound its clamours.

As it was not my Watch, I had no business on deck and could not tell what was passing there, but the crew I found were drinking to calm their despair, if they entertained it, as the grog was going round pretty freely. My companions were all silent or asleep around me, but I felt unable to follow their example, the very tumult of the elements quite preventing it. I was wrapped snug enough in my hammock with my boat cloak and blankets over me, three more officers besides myself being similarly suspended, the rest disposed in births above me and below on both sides of the cabin. Thus passed the midnight hour, listening in fearful wonder at the hurly burly above board and around us, about which time the ship laboured most dreadfully, being no sooner relieved from one wave than another assailed her, until for the last time uplifted, and while streaming from her deck in torrents the seas that broke over her, she was totally overwhelmed by a fresh accumulation that brought our fate to a crisis.

The bursting of this wave was like an explosion of gunpowder. Although my hammock was slung close to the rafters I was thrown by the jerk completely out of it, and every thing on one side of the ship breaking loose from its fastenings I fell with the general wreck upon the berths in the opposite quarter, drenched to the skin by the flood gates suddenly opened through the seams and the sky light above us, nor were my companions in a better condition. Col. Paterson rushed from his cabin to bear the perils of the scene with us, and whilst partaking of this foretaste of the salt water in darkness and dismay the ship was on the verge of the fatal gulp, being completely on her beam ends (as the Seamen term it) and another such wave succeeding must have brought with it our destruction and rolled us over. Could we at this period have beheld our helpless vessel, drifting and prostrate in this dreary waste of waters, her situation would no doubt have appeared doubly awful and terrific, lit up as she was in the boiling wrath of the luminous waves bursting over and around her; the overshadowing canopy of deep darkness making her condition more visible from the element she was engulfed in partaking so much of the aspect of fire that a human figure submerged in the transparent fluid would have been seen while sinking.

Providentially we did not present so frightful an exhibition, but nothing surprised me more than this strange appearance of the sea, changed from ordinary water into rolling mountains of sparkling foam. While the ship was in this forlorn state we were all huddled together, and what had been the floor turned into a side of the cabin; this position gave horrible evidence of danger in it, so much so that when it suddenly took place a general cry issued from those on board, not only abaft the binnacle (that is in our cabin) but in the ship's waist, where 400 men and several women were closely battened down, and it is curious and deplorable to think how they must have been tumbled together, half drowned and stifled. In falling I struck my ribs against a table, and was bruised sadly, but I heard the outcry in the same moment of these unfortunates, and now the time had arrived in which it would have been good policy to have given 5 or 15 years pay, for one yard of good substantial ground, covered with brown furze or anything, as Shakespeare says.

Could you have held a light to us, it must have been frightfully comic to have seen so many blue faces. Perhaps I suffered as much as any during this dread moment of suspense, until the ship righted. Unused to such dangers they appeared very terrifying to an imagination as soon disturbed as my own; and yet there was a grandeur about it exciting a sort of stern heroism to brave the worst that might happen.

I could but hope that life would be extinct before the gulp opened and the cataracts followed us, if it was our fate to go down, but my fear was that it would be otherwise and if we sunk rapidly in soundings we might feel the last dreadful concussion on reaching the ground, particularly as you and I had so often successfully practised holding our breath in a basin of water a sufficient length of time. But providence mercifully did not forget nor forsake us in this hour of need. The vessel however was not relieved from this state without further apprehensions attending it, for she fell over into a chasm on her other side, which shook her dreadfully, but meeting a friendly wave to break her fall in that direction she maintained her upright position and happily in this manner continued supported during the night.

When day broke the great stress upon her timbers and the damage she was found to have sustained rendered it necessary to give up the intention altogether of proceeding, her bulwarks, binnacle, wheel etc having all been carried completely away in the height of our danger, so instead of steering for the rendezvous at Ferrol the helm was put about for England, and now the scene was quite of a novel character, going right before the wind in such a gale as was blowing, the ship seeming to leap straight from billow to billow as she proceeded with amazing rapidity under a storm stay sail upon her bare poles. She was now altogether relieved from the rolling and accidents before liable to from beating up against the wind, but it was almost as frightful to see her bound over the deep troughs of the sea at the rate she was now going at, with the rain blown into a thick mist ahead, involving us in partial obscurity.[1]

On once more approaching our native shores, we found her guardians on the alert, for whilst scudding thus the Frodroyant frigate shot past our leequarter like a meteor, coming so close to us that it was almost superfluous to hoist our Union Jack except to be the more speedily secure against the showers of iron balls she was prepared to put into us had we proved to be an enemy. Passing suddenly so very near that we could see every face on board of her, with her beautiful blue silk standard flying (another denoting her name at the mizzen) and totally disappearing again as instantaneously, made a fine phantasmagoria of it. And now Sam our voyage is nearly concluded, and you may conceive you have been sailing with us, luckily exempt from the perils we have experienced in it; for as evening advanced we had the superlative pleasure of beholding the Lizard Lights at the Land's End. A thousand times as welcome a sight as those at Hyde Park Corner after a wearisome journey. Sailing on, we dropped our anchor in Falmouth Harbour off St Mawe's Castle, and slept that night comparatively speaking in smooth water. Thus ended our first attempt to cross the Atlantic, and it is to be hoped the next will be more prosperous.

For two days the surf ran so high that a boat couldn't approach the shore, but today I have been sent there at a venture as the men are said to be sadly in want of clean linen and we are all very glad to have at hand what the sailors call a clean Jaycee. I descended into an eight oared boat with the women and piles of baskets for this purpose and we pulled off and dashed through the water very swiftly until we came to a point of the coast it was necessary to pass round to get to the appointed landing place. But here the wind and current ran so strong against us that with half an hour's hard pulling we couldn't get the boats length forward, shipping besides the spray by hogsheads. I wished the baskets at the devil with their contents, the danger was so great in persevering, especially when the seaman at the helm begged to know from me (being in command) if I would risk it, and the lives of all depending upon my decision. I was mightily perplexed what to do. However while in consultation with the most experienced, the wind in some measure abated and we determined to push for it, in which after great hazard we at last succeeded. I was rejoiced enough to put my foot on land again, and soon came

---

[1] This most graphic account of the storm illustrates just how much British ships were at the mercy of the weather. Indeed, the memoirs of Wellington's men are rife with accounts of tempestuous journeys to Portugal and Spain across the notorious Bay of Biscay. Captain John Cooke, of the 43rd Light Infantry, gives a similarly vivid account of a storm in his wonderful *Memoirs of the Late War*, pp.63-65. Others, like Jonathan Leach, of the 95th, experienced a fine, trouble free passage. 'we.... opened another heavy and destructive fire on such unfortunate gulls and sea-birds as ventured within reach. We pursued our course with favourable winds and heavenly weather...' (Leach, *Rough Sketches of the Life of an Old Soldier*, p.68.). Robert Eadie, in his *Recollections*, records a hair-raising episode on his voyage to Portugal in 1809 when a large cask of cannon shot, 'that was lashed to the mast between decks, by the rolling of the ship became loose, and before we were aware of the danger, the balls were pitching over the deck in all directions. Such a scene of confusion as this occasioned, I almost never witnessed.' (Eadie, *Recollections*, p.65).

to the inn from which I am writing this. Put ashore in this part of old England reminds me of having been fictitiously here about this time 2 years when acting in John Bull at Richmond. My host being an Irishman makes the resemblance more exact, and what completes it is that the waiter here would make an excellent Dan. I may easily suppose myself to be Peregrine, just escaped shipwreck, although my adventures are not quite so marvellous, not having gone far enough to drink sloe juice with a simple Gentoo as he did.

Outlandish as this place is I find it under present circumstances a blissful retreat, since it affords me an opportunity to be thankful to God for our preservation and to send you this assurance of our safety.

So adieu for the present my dear Sam, and believe me to be, Yrs most affectly, W.T. Keep.

I hope this will prove a great relief to my dear Mother's mind, in case the wind should have alarmed her lately by shaking the chimney tops. Give my kindest love to her, and to all who enquire after me best compliments.

Falmouth
26th October 1812

My dearest Mother,

Being on shore in a very cheerful room at a pretty inn, in this remote but pleasant place, I cannot enjoy my present quiet without thinking of you, and taking up the pen to communicate my situation and feelings to you after our recent providential escape, described in my letter to Samuel, which I trust you have duly received. The contrast this place now presents to what we have just experienced brings the two extremes of safety and danger so conspicuously before my eyes that it is only with devout thankfulness I behold the change, and endeavour to describe it to you.

Put ashore here again from the turbulent ocean, Falmouth appears paradise. It is a town in itself with many claims to commendation, being on a fine hill in a most picturesque nook of our native shores, called the Land's End, but were it a desert we should hail with supreme joy our return to it, after such perils as we have escaped.

To be tossed about in a ship in a storm occasions such derangements in bodily feelings that persons never having been to sea can form no idea of. Everything on first landing appears in movement with the whirligig impressions left upon the brain, and you must be some time on shore to be convinced you can stand steadily on your legs, after the long disuse of them. With me, a feverish dryness of the skin, the want of an opportunity of washing oneself, as well as the giddiness, makes the transition to a house most desirable, and a wash hand basin in a snug bedroom is the first thing sought after by us fresh water mariners. After which, to occupy with the breakfast table spread, a window, with objects beneath it, such as are now presented to me, compensates indeed greatly for all we have endured. As everything in sight is rendered a hundred times more agreeable than usual — bells ringing, waiters coming, landlord bawling etc, within doors; And without, country people passing in market carts, chaises running with dust flying, boys playing and dogs basking in the sunshine on dry ground, are all great adjuncts under present circumstances to the enjoyment of our sojourn and I trust I shall never forget this blessing bestowed upon us.

In time of our despair our young and gallant Colonel, getting up for a moment from the table, I could not resist the desire I had to know what he had been perusing in the book before him, and I found it was a Chapter in the Bible, the first verse of which was very appropriate to our situation that selected for such an occasion and read to us would have been very edifying to us all; but our profession inculcates different doctrines, and dangers once escaped are only laughed at and forgotten. It may be necessary perhaps to treat them thus lightly in a pursuit like ours, so replete with dangers of all kinds, which we are expected to encounter with the utmost resolution, and think little of; but some among us are found to be more irresolute than the rest, and the last night on board, when below at supper, a disturbance occasioned us to run upon deck. Two men had just made a bold effort to desert, and had cut the slings of a small boat and were rowing to shore. At first it was suggested to fire at them; this the Colonel did not permit, but another boat was immediately prepared to pursue them. The night was calm with splendid moonlight, and the chase commenced across the wide expanse of water to the wildest part of the opposite coast. A rowing match on the Thames never offered better occasion for the odds to be taken between the pursuers' and deserters' success.

All eyes were intent upon the result, the fugitives being first afloat, and urged by terror to use their most vigorous exertions, kept well ahead, but the six-oared boat followed swiftly and was gaining upon them. An unclouded sky with the moon at the full enabled us to watch their progress, but after long rowing both boats became blended in a line, that we could not judge the distance between them. It appeared however that time and distance were in favour of the deserters for we saw them land. On the return of the boats we heard the pursuers were within a dozen yards of them, when they sprang on shore, but that short space was sufficient to ensure their escape from the wild state of the country and thick woods abounding there.

Another circumstance has given us more surprise — a Lieutenant of ours named Medlycott has taken French leave of us, and gone from hence not intending to return. A subscription was obtained for him at Berry Head among the officers of two Guineas each to pay his extravagant debts at Plymouth, where he had been long recruiting, and to enable him to come onboard with us, which makes the matter worse, as it proves his ingratitude to his contributors: Surgeon Johnson, Colleton and I, with 2 or 3 others were exempt from this subscription (being too poor).

Col. Paterson is so incensed at this conduct that he has written a statement of it to the Adjutant General, and he will of course be dismissed the Service, and we shall see him no more, which is considered no loss.

The news lately received gives good hopes of Bonaparte's being fully employed with more powerful enemies than ourselves, at least with larger armies to meet him in the field,[1] but our reinforcements will no doubt be very desirable in the Peninsula, to carry out the measures pursuing there, and are we find more numerous than at first supposed. We are very desirous to effect a quick passage, and to be favoured with propitious winds to waft us speedily to the shores of the Tagus, whose fabled golden sands us raw recruits are eager to behold.

God bless you my dear Mother, and believe me always to be, bearing you in mind, in the midst of whatever joys or vicissitudes may befall us, Yours most affectly, W.T.Keep.

On board the 'Hero'
Falmouth Harbour
4th November 1812

My dear Brother,

I wrote you on the 22nd from St Mawes with a full description of the Storm, and our preservation and arrival in this port, and on the 26th to my Mother from Falmouth. Since our return here, shipwrights and workmen of all sorts have been night and day employed in repairing the damages received, and refitting us for sea, so that the ship has been like a carpenter's shop encumbered with shavings, and mice and men have been running about in full activity preparing for another voyage. I am very unhappy in not having heard from you. Why have you not written, as you must be aware of my anxiety to receive a few lines. Every night the boat goes off for the letters, but only returns with disappointment for me. This is very mortifying, and you ought to consider it will be some time ere a letter can reach me, when we are once gone. We have been on board 4 weeks, and shall be heartily glad you may be sure to get out of this transport. Every day affords us fresh reason to congratulate ourselves on our late escape. A fine vessel No. 199, with a detachment of the 11th has gone to the bottom, and all on board perished. Another transport met with a similar fate having on board 40 horses and a troop of artillery drivers, and other ships are still absent and unaccounted for.

We have spent a fortnight here very pleasantly. Every morning early, when not on duty, the Colonel has given us permission to rove about the surrounding country, and our transport has moved to the opposite side of the harbour, which has enabled us to go frequently to Falmouth, and to visit Pendennis Castle, etc but Adieu to these diversions.

The wind has just come round, and we are likely to have our anchor up immediately. The Commodore has deferred sailing till tomorrow, and the boat has

---

[1] Napoleon was by now, of course, embarked upon his ill-fated invasion of Russia which was to end disastrously in the retreat from Moscow. He had crossed the River Niemen on June 24th 1812 but by December the same year re-crossed the same river having seen the destruction of his Grande Armée in between.

once more gone on shore for the letters. It has just returned, and there is no letter for me from you! What can be the reason of it? Pray write immediately directing to me at Lisbon, and it may arrive by the Packet as soon as the Fleet.

Our stock being expended, I wrote to our Paymaster to send me 5ú; he has not yet answered my letter, and I have left directions at Falmouth that it may be forwarded on to you.

5th November. We are now under weigh, with a fine breeze at N.W. and happy shall we be when we come in sight of the Spanish coast. This will be put into the Post Office at St Mawes by the Pilot. I have nothing more to say, only that my prayers are always with you, and with tenderest recollections to all at home, I remain my dear Sam, Your affectionate Brother, W.T. Keep.

> Rua di Monti Olivate (or Mount of Olives)
> Lisbon
> 26th November 1812

My dearest Mother,

At length I have the delightful task of relieving your anxiety, and of resuming the pen on this side of the water, having crossed that vast ocean that separates Old England from the country of our Allies, after a passage of fourteen days in most tempestuous weather, during the early part of which we were tossed about by contrary winds that threatened a second return to our native shores, and the fleet was again dispersed in a gale, that was sufficient to remind us of the horrors of the storm of the 17th October. Fortunately it blew from the north west, and we scudded away at an amazing rate through torrents of foam, at night presenting the appearance of liquid fire, which with darkness over head, the melancholy cry of the sailors working the ship, and raging winds that you would every moment expect to split the sails to pieces, forms a sight as extraordinary and sublime, as any the mind can contemplate. Twenty four hours afterwards we discovered land ahead, having made more way in that short time than we had done during the preceding days of the voyage. It proved to be the summits of the lofty mountains of Galicia on the northern coast of Spain, and the wind continuing favourable, on the morning of the 19th we had at last the satisfaction of casting anchor in the Tagus, in sight of the wind mills and opposite hills, or blue mountains as I should call them. My bed is made up of the finest muslins with rich damask curtains, the pillows such as you would admire very much, edged with lace, with rosettes of crimson ribbons. The approach to these apartments is quite different from ours, the ground floor being perhaps once a hall, and since apparently converted into a stable — no inmates to be seen, one old servant merely guarding the doors of admissions. I regret very much that I can't speak or understand their language, for it gives rise to continual mortifications and perplexities.[1] However I hope I shall

---

[1] Keep was not alone when it came to trying to understand the Portuguese language. The more diligent officers availed themselves of a copy of William Guthrie's *Historical*

"pick up something daily" and become an interpreter myself one of these days. We are in orders to march to join the army by the end of this week, allowing us these few days to prepare ourselves and provide animals for conveyance of baggage etc.[1] I have only been enabled to purchase the half of a donkey with an Ensign Nelson, for which we paid 33 dollars, this kind of cattle is in such high request here just now. To tell you the truth, I was more choice in my pannier than about the animal to carry it. These are basket trunks slung across the donkey's back in equilibrium (as you may have seen the bags of brick dust conveyed about London). They make them here of various kinds with great ingenuity. I chose one of leather, with a padlock, and it will contain all that is needful. Thus one donkey serves for two of us, each having a trunk apiece. I hope never the less to purchase a mule to carry a pair of gay panniers for my own use by and bye (the great point of ambition among us) £15 or 20 will be necessary to do this. Some Gents are rich enough to have another to ride, which is permitted, if you can afford it, but few of us can achieve this. I don't regret it much because if I have the fatigue of marching I am relieved from the solicitude of shoeing, feeding, stabling etc the said nag (a very nagging business it is too I believe). You will perhaps hear before this reaches you of the retrograde movement of our army, and of its abandoning its late possessions.

Very melancholy rumours of disastrous retreat greeted us on our arrival here, but by the latest Courier we understand the Headquarters are at Ciudad Rodrigo, which is approaching the frontiers, and seems to indicate that we shall rest quietly in cantonments until the spring in this country.[2] What a dispiriting service is the

---

and Commercial Grammar, published in 1770, which provided Wellington's officers with a useful guide to the language. Mordente's *Spanish Grammar* was one of the more well-known books on the Spanish language. The problems faced by Wellington's men are dealt with in Brett-James' *Life in Wellington's Army*, pp.135-144.

[1] One of the first tasks facing an officer upon arrival in Portugal was to procure a mule to transport his baggage. A market was held every Thursday near the Rocio, an area in northern Lisbon, where horses, ponies and mules were sold. The 33 dollars paid by Keep compares very favourably with the price paid by John Rous for his two mules. One cost him 130 dollars with another, for his servant, costing 140 dollars. (Fletcher, *A Guards Officer in the Peninsula*, p.31.) Moyle Sherer was another visitor to the market. 'In an open space near the gardens of Salitre, a fair or market for the sale of horses is often held. The contrast between this scene and a horse-fair in England is great indeed; the small size, long tails, and flowing manes of the Portuguese horses; their paces, either a slow prancing amble, or a high short gallop; and the clumsiness and singularity of their horse furniture and saddlery, strike an Englishman at first very forcibly.' (Sherer, *Recollections of the Peninsula*, pp.10-11.)

[2] Keep wrote this letter barely a week after Wellington's army had concentrated around Ciudad Rodrigo after the disastrous retreat from Burgos. The siege operations at Burgos were handicapped from the start by a lack of heavy guns. Indeed, Wellington rather naively assumed that he would be able to take the place with just the three heavy guns at his disposal. On this occasion, however, the Gods were to conspire against him and things went from bad to worse almost from the start of the operation. The weather was bad, the French garrison tenacious and brave and when one of the brightest lights in the Allied army, Charles Cocks, was killed during a sortie on October 8th, Wellington's heart appeared to go out of the business. Indeed, it is said that Wellington shed tears at Cocks' funeral. 'I consider his loss as one of the greatest importance to this army and to

British for a great General to serve or command in, having only such a handful of troops, thus Lord Wellington's successes are neutralised at pleasure, by the French Marshals, for a little ink and paper sent to Paris soon brings a reinforcement of 50 thousand men to their armies.[1]

I have just received a letter from England with the well known seal of office, and the contents are extremely pleasing as it assures me of your all being well, which is the principal source of happiness. I have no time to say more than that I am in better health now, than I have been for these two or three years, and think the air of this country will agree with me very finely.

With most affectionate regards, believe me to remain. Yours most affectionately, W. Thornton Keep.

His Majesty's service,' wrote Wellington to Lord Bathurst. (*Despatches*, 11th October 1812, IX, p.483.). The army abandoned the siege on October 22nd and so began the retreat to Ciudad Rodrigo which was likened to that of Sir John Moore's army to Corunna in 1808-09. Indeed, some who experienced and survived both episodes considered the 1812 retreat as by far the worst. The weather was appalling, the Commissariat broke down and hundreds of stragglers were lost to the pursuing French army. After the successes of the first seven months of the year it came as a bitter pill. Indeed, John Mills, of the Coldstream Guards, considered the retreat so bad that there was little prospect of a satisfactory outcome to the war. 'Our want of success at Burgos and the subsequent retreat will cause a great deal of dissatisfaction in England. I think it has turned the tide of affairs here and Spain I think is lost. If ever a man ruined himself the Marquis [Wellington] has done it; for the last two months he has acted like a madman. The reputation he has acquired will not bear him out, such is the opinion here.' (Fletcher, *For King and Country*, p.253.)

[1] On the contrary, the French had seen a large number of troops withdrawn for service in Russia. On December 13th 1811, Napoleon ordered all of the light and heavy cavalry of the Imperial Guard, the chasseurs, grenadiers a cheval, dragoons and Polish lancers, to be brought back to France along with the Guard's horse artillery and the gendarmes d'elite, in readiness for the war against Russia which at the time seemed inevitable. Eventually, some 27,000 veteran French troops were taken from the Peninsula. (See Oman, *A History of the Peninsular War*, V. pp.83-84.)

Chapter Five
The Vittoria Campaign

Villiam Thornton Keep set off for the front at a time when Wellington's army was well on the road to recovery after the traumas of the retreat from Burgos, that most unhappy episode which soured what had otherwise been a year of splendid triumph. The army had concentrated around Ciudad Rodrigo in mid-November 1812 after what some considered a retreat far worse than that experienced by Sir John Moore's army in the terrible winter of 1808-09.[1] One could have excused the army if it had simply gone into cantonments for the winter to reflect ruefully on what had been a momentous year. Far from it, however, for Wellington and his men quickly took stock of the situation and were soon on the road to recovery. However, this was not before Wellington issued his infamous Memorandum of November 28th 1812, in which he gave his officers and NCOs a real lashing for failing to control their men on the retreat from Burgos[2]. This gave rise to much complaining within the Allied camp from many officers who felt they had been unfairly blamed. The atmosphere soon changed, however, and with the onset of winter both officers and men turned their minds to matters domestic, as there was to be little activity at least until spring arrived.

---

[1] Sergeant David Robertson, of the 92nd Highlanders, was one such soldier who had experienced both the retreat to Corunna and the retreat from Burgos. Of the latter he wrote, '...such confusion I never saw. The four divisions came on the road all at one time, pushing forward, so that the best part of it fell to the strongest. All the waggons and ammunition that could be dispensed with were destroyed. The rain now began to fall in torrents, so that the roads were rendered nearly impassable. At the same time the French dragoons were close on our rear, and all that fell out of the ranks were taken prisoners. The retreat to Corunna never presented any thing to equal this, for all was uproar and confusion.' (Robertson, *Journal*, p.89.) Robertson's sentiments were echoed by William Gomm who, writing home on November 22nd 1812, wrote, 'During the last few days it revived many recollections of the dreadful race to Corunna. In some respects the hardships were greater, for on that occasion the troops were generally under cover, such as it was, during the night; but here the only resting place, after a day spent as I have just described, was a bleak, swampy plain, with more temptation in it to watch than sleep, and to look out with impatience for the break of the following morning. (Gomm, *Letters and Journals*, p.290.)

[2] This was Wellington's infamous Memorandum of November 28th 1812, addressed to Officers Commanding Divisions and Brigades. (See *Despatches*, 28th November 1812, IX, 582-585). The Memorandum infuriated Wellington's officers who thought it totally unjust. John Mills, of the Coldstream Guards, wrote, 'And now, after a most severe campaign, successful as far as the courage of soldiers could make it, the army, naked, without hay, and reduced by sickness, is told that they have conducted themselves so ill, that they have brought all the evils upon themselves. Is this fair? What encouragement has a man to do his duty?' (See Fletcher (Ed), *For King and Country: The Letters and Diaries of John Mills, Coldstream Guards, 1811-1814.* p.264.)

Wellington himself was far from idle. Indeed, he may have been temporarily at peace with the French but the fight with Horse Guards and the Duke of York was waged by him with some good measure of success. Reinforcements were despatched from Britain to bolster his depleted army, including fresh regiments of that much maligned branch of the army, the cavalry. Indeed, it was not until the Vittoria campaign that the Allies were able to put anywhere near the same number of cavalry fielded by the enemy.[1] One of Wellington's more significant victories over the Duke of York was his retention of the so-called Provisional Battalions. These battalions were made up of depleted line battalions whose numbers had so been reduced that Wellington was moved to merge them together to form one strong battalion. Tradition and practice dictated that when a battalion had been drastically reduced in numbers, either through enemy action or sickness, it returned home to recruit. This often meant the loss to Wellington of a few hundred good veteran soldiers who had become acclimatised to the Iberian climate, unlike their replacements, fresh from England's shores, many of whom quickly fell victim to the rigours of campaign life beneath Spanish and Portuguese skies at a time when Wellington could ill afford to lose them, hence his fight to retain them as Provisional Battalions.[2] Take, for example, the 1st Foot Guards, not present in the Peninsula since the Corunna campaign in 1808. The 1st Battalion 1st Foot Guards arrived in Spain in October 1812 to find themselves in the midst of the retreat from Burgos. Going into winter quarters at Viseu the battalion was quickly

---

[1] When Wellington, still Arthur Wellesley at the time, fought the battle of Vimeiro on August 21st 1808, his cavalry numbered just 240 men of the 20th Light Dragoons, a ridiculously low number. At Fuentes de Onoro, May 3rd-5th 1811, his cavalry was still only 1,854 strong whilst at Salamanca the number had grown to 3,543, still fairly low in ratio to the rest of the Allied army. By the time of the battle of Vittoria, however, Wellington's cavalry numbered some 8,317 and for the first time matched the numerical strength of their French counterparts.

[2] Wellington fought hard to retain his veterans in the Peninsula even when their battalions had been so reduced that under normal circumstances they should have returned home to recruit. On December 6th 1812, Wellington wrote to the Duke of York, informing of his decision to merge certain under-strength battalions into a single battalion. For example, four companies of the 53rd and four of the 2nd Queen's, were formed into a single battalion, as were a similar number of companies of the 24th and the 58th. The same instruction was given to four companies of the 30th Regiment and four of the 44th. 'My reason for adopting this arrangement is,' he wrote, 'that I have for the service in this country the whole number of men of which these provisional battalions will be composed, all of whom are seasoned to the service and climate. Experience has shown that they could not be replaced by three times their numbers brought from England, or any other part of the world.' (Despatches, 6th December 1812, IX, p.609). He followed this up on December 26th 1812, referring to his cavalry in much the same vein. 'Experience has shown us in the Peninsula that a soldier who has got through one campaign is of more service than two, or even three, newly arrived from England; and this applies to the cavalry equally with every other description of troops.' (Despatches, 26th December 1812, X, p.5.) Although the composite parts of some Provisional Battalions were later sent home some remained in service until the end of the war. For example, the 2/31st and 2/66th, following heavy losses at Albuera, were formed into the 1st Provisional Battalion and fought as such until the end of the war in 1814. (See Oman, Wellington's Army, 1809-1814, pp.187-189 for more on Provisional Battalions.)

hit by an outbreak of low fever. Brigaded with the 3rd Battalion of the same regiment the brigade lost 800 men dead from sickness in the first three months of 1813. The two battalions suffered so much that they were sent far to the rear, to Oporto in fact, to recuperate and did not take any part in the Vittoria campaign, eventually marching from Oporto on June 24th.[1]

The battle of Salamanca had established once and for all Wellington's reputation throughout the halls of Europe as a military commander of the highest order. Indeed, it was a crushing victory. But it was to be his victory at Vittoria, on June 21st 1813, that broke the back of French resistance in the Peninsula. From then onwards there was no stopping the Allied army which rolled on like a juggernaut, stopping only briefly now and then to glance over its shoulder, checking that the political winds were blowing in its favour. Vittoria was to be Keep's first action in the Peninsula, and what a battle he saw. His own regiment, the 28th, played its own vital part, opening the battle as part of Hill's 2nd Division which attacked the French left flank. After the opening stages Keep was left with a grandstand view of the proceedings from his vantage point on the heights of Puebla as Wellington's army rolled over the French and drove them back beyond Vittoria and, eventually, back beyond the Pyrenees and into France. Indeed, it was only the vast wealth of treasure found amongst the abandoned enemy waggons that saved the French army from total destruction, as thousands of astonished and wide-eyed Allied soldiers stopped to plunder them, filling their pockets with a lifetime's worth of gold, silver and jewellery.

Our chapter begins, however, with Keep's sometimes disturbing account of his journey from Lisbon to Coria, graphically described, and an account which illustrates the extent to which British soldiers often got out of hand, officers seemingly helpless as their charges ran amok amidst nameless Portuguese hovels. It also illustrates the confusion and perils encountered by officers with drafts, fresh from England who, with little or no sense of direction and with no good maps, made hard work of the march to the front. Our story resumes with Keep's account of his march to join the 1st Battalion of the 28th Regiment of Foot, then in billets at a village called the Casa de Gomez.

---

[1] A return of the 1st and 3rd Battalions of the 1st Foot Guards for 25th November 1812 showed a total of 700 sick out of 2,541 present. The 3rd Battalion had been on active service at Cadiz for some months but the 1st Battalion only landed at Corunna on September 30th 1812. The two were afterwards brigaded together to form the 1st Brigade of the 1st Division. It is possible that the outbreak of low fever started within the ranks of the 1st Battalion before spreading to the 3rd Battalion. The main body of Wellington's army marched east to begin the Vittoria campaign in May 1813 but the 1st Brigade of Guards remained behind, having been averaging four or five deaths per day since December 1812. The brigade eventually marched on June 24th 1813 by which time it had buried some 800 out of 2,500 men. (Hamilton, *The Origin and History of the First or Grenadier Guards*, II. pp.447-450.)

Casas de Gomez
9th January 1813

My dear Mother,

The Casas de Gomez — or houses of the Don, so called, on the borders of Spain — is the name of the village, where we have found our 1st Battalion quartered, after a month's march through Portugal. Here we have arrived, to join our brave comrades, whose weather-beaten features and time-worn habiliments plainly indicate them to be soldiers long inured to rough service in the field. Heartily they congratulated us, and with pleasure most truly expressed, on joining their ranks to partake in their toils, now that our own are over in the tedious and dreary marches we have made.[1]

I must lead you from Lisbon briefly through the vast extent of country we have passed, toiling through the day to find obscure and remote villages on our line of march, to rest in at night. This route has been so often followed by our troops that depots for a supply of provisions have been formed generally at every third day's halt, otherwise we should not have been able to proceed for never was a more beautiful land left in so destitute a state. It has conformed to its fate, and

---

[1] The journey by a new draft to the front to join the main army was often accompanied by a sense of excitement at the prospect of seeing old comrades once again. It could also, on the other hand, be a tough and strenuous ordeal. Cooke, of the 43rd, left a wonderful description of his journey to the front in July 1811. 'Every eye was on the stretch, and in the distance we descried a cloud of dust rolling towards us, the bright sparkling rays of the sun-beams playing on the soldiers' breastplates, when suddenly the leading regiment of the light division burst forth; their bronzed countenances and light knapsacks, and their order of march, all united to inspire a conviction that their early discipline had not only been maintained amidst privations, battles and camps, but had become matured by experience. They had traversed mountains, and forded rivers; the grim and icy hand of death had grasped many in the unhealthy marshes of the Alentejo, and with sure effect had scattered balls amidst their ranks without distinction; yet the remainder of these veterans were still bent onwards, to gather fresh laurels in the rugged and uncertain paths of fortune. Seven regiments of light infantry and riflemen defiled before us with their thread-bare jackets, their brawny necks loosened from their stocks, their wide and patched trousers of various colours, and brown barrelled arms slung over their shoulders, or carelessly held in their hands, whilst a joyous buzz ran through the cross-belted ranks, as their soldier-like faces glanced towards us to greet many of their old comrades now about to join in their arduous toils after a long separation.' (Cooke, *Memoirs of the Late War*, pp.76-77.) For others, however, it was not such a happy story. Rees Gronow, the famous raconteur of the 1st Foot Guards, recalled in his *Reminiscences*, a story of Sir Thomas Styles, a young, aristocratic Guards officer, who travelled to Lisbon in 1813 only to find that his battalion was somewhere in the Pyrenees. Styles found the long journey from Lisbon all too much to bear and when he joined his battalion he was exhausted, adding that, 'the fleas and vermin on the march had nearly driven him mad and that when the peasant girls observed him scratching himself, they would laugh, and shaking their petticoats over pails full of water, tell him how much more they were to be pitied than he.' Styles was soon confined to bed in a state of great distress, suffering from what the surgeon called 'brain fever' and during the night he took out his razor and cut his own throat from ear to ear. (Raymond, Ed. *The Reminiscences and Recollections of Captain Gronow*, pp.331-332.)

become indeed a fit arena for warfare and strife. The invaders of the territories of these unhappy people have driven them away, so that very few are to be met with transacting the ordinary pursuits of civilised life. The roads are infested with bandits, who find no difficulty to escape justice, and thus utterly prevent all travelling on them by the peaceably disposed.[1] We met none whatever, but such as were under military escort, and this of course is enough to give a dreary aspect to the prettiest spots on earth. The vicinity of Lisbon presented for our admiration that fine addition to the beauties of nature such climates enjoy — something more pleasing than easy to express, especially agreeable to me, who am such a lover of the enlivening sun beams, that I never think I can have too much of them. The abodes of the wealthy in this neighbourhood show very clearly what taste they would display in the decoration of their premises under different circumstances to the present, which does not permit the public eye to penetrate their recesses, so that high walls enclose them too frequently. Nevertheless luxuriant vegetation creeps over them in a thousand forms, exhaling a delightful perfume, and concealing their deformity. These country seats I believe are called Quintas, and we passed many most inviting ones on our way to Santarem. The next town we arrived at was Punhete, worthy of observation. Here there is a very fine river scenery, with a picturesque bridge of boats meriting the skill of an artist to convey an idea to you of its beauties, so singular and uncommon. At first I had the pleasure of being billeted for the night in the habitations of people in good circumstances; many families I thus for a few hours became acquainted with, and was not only charmed with the owners of the house, but often with the house itself, the situation, furniture or accommodations.

Everywhere I found they thought it necessary to surrender the best bed chamber; the roosting place is often very curious in its fittings up, and generally with the image of our Saviour (according to Roman Catholic custom) to be seen somewhere in the apartment, or attached to the head of the bed, the decorations often showing the respect in which it is held; and I have reposed beneath the trappings better calculated for the altar, such as fine rich red counterpanes with golden embroidery etc.

Setting out each day to a new scene on the day's march, we sometimes met with streams to ford or mountains to ascend by zig-zag roads, plains of immeasurable extent before us, or thick forests to seek a promiscuous path in, and as we progressed a great contrast was frequent between the places we arrived at. Now and then a miserable village on the top of a hill in the most forlorn and primitive state, carrying the mind back to centuries past, and possessing nothing suitable to our wishes, perhaps only a very large oaken trunk to stretch one's weary limbs upon, and no fire to dry our clothes, but such as brought clouds of smoke from green wood to smother us, or else to make the eyes overflow and

---

[1] These bandits often operated under the guise of guerrillas, acting in the cause of Spain. Much revisionist work has been done recently, particularly by Charles Esdaile, to show that many of the so-called guerrillas, far from acting in alliance with Wellington, simply took the opportunity to rob with impunity the people of Spanish villages. See Esdaile, 'Heroes or Villains? The Spanish Guerrillas in the Peninsular War,' *History Today*, XXXVIII, April 1988.

smart most cruelly. Nothing can equal the melancholy impressions induced by these human abodes, arriving at them perhaps amidst torrents from the clouds at night fall.

Grey stones, not at all indebted to the labours of the masons, but in the rudest state, composing the few houses, and the low walls enclosing them. Having arrived at the wildest part of the country in our approach to Spain, and halted at a town there, the Commandant informed us that owing to the heavy rains lately the route was uncertain, but that we had the choice of two to pursue, that by the usual road, much the shortest, to the next station, yet he could not promise that we could pass in safety, the floods having risen so. Our Captain in command, who gave us very unnecessary trouble at times from his ridiculous punctilios in observing the General Orders (such for instance as obliging us when off each day's march to trouble the men by an examination of their packs, often when tired and falling asleep, their heads were reclining upon them), this officer in fear for, if not in compassion to a lame animal conveying his baggage, deciding upon the most unpromising course. The men's packs, lest they should have disposed of any of their wardrobe for liquor on the march, are thus required to be looked into, but as the desolate roads we passed over offered no such opportunity it was very often an unnecessary annoyance to all parties, particularly the suspicion of it to good soldiers who had no intention of the kind, and he was very unpopular with them, for this and other similar causes.[1]

When at the distance of some miles from this town the Captain remembered he had left a valuable watch, for which he gave 40 guineas, at his billet, we were halted for a long time whilst a man was sent back for it. This was only the commencement of our troubles. At the next halt we were to be supplied with provisions, now nearly or quite consumed, and the men were therefore extremely anxious to push on. The day was far advanced when we arrived in a wood, and at the side of it a very wide expanse of waters opposed our progress. Here was the difficulty we had been apprised of, and our commander was exceedingly perplexed, yet most anxious to proceed, and called us all into consultation upon it (that is

---

[1] There are several General Orders instructing officers to inspect the packs of their men, although the practice was usually for the purpose of discovering plunder rather than to ensure that the men had not sold any of their equipment for the purpose of buying liquor. For example, on 3rd October 1810, a General Order was issued stating that, 'General officers commanding the divisions are requested to direct that there may be an inspection of the soldiers' packs, both British and Portuguese, this day after the march, and every thing, not strictly regimental necessaries, is to be taken from them and burnt, and those who have these articles are to be punished, as they have certainly procured them by plunder.' *General Orders*, 3rd October 1810. Similar General Orders were invariably issued following the successful storming of a town. After his men had taken Badajoz in April 1812, Wellington issued the following General Order. 'The Commander of the Forces observes that there are several carts on the march loaded with private baggage, and other articles, which ought not to be so carried; to which subject he calls the attention of General Officers commanding brigades and divisions. He likewise observes that the carts are very much overloaded, in consequence of which several are broken; he begs that the knapsacks of the soldiers may be inspected, and all articles not necessary for a soldier may be destroyed.' *General Orders*, 15th April 1812.

Lieut. Burns, Ensigns Alexander, Hill, Nelson and myself). Both Nelson and I had been much under his censure in the early part of our journey for letting the men help themselves to oranges growing unprotected on the road. He even went so far as to make a complaint against us to the Commanding Officer of a town we had passed through some time before, who deemed the affair too frivolous even to reprimand us. Yet Nelson shed tears of vexation at our misfortune, though I cared little about it, the poor soldiers being often so distressed with thirst.

As it was expedient to give the men something to eat as soon as possible, and they were by no means disposed to retrace their steps to go by the other road, even if we could find it out, attempts were made to ford this vast sheet of water, quite as broad as the Thames at Westminster Bridge, and running with remarkable impetuosity. Yet we hoped to find it sufficiently shallow to effect it; for this purpose two grenadier sergeants were ordered with their pikes to sound the depths. We were all assembled in great suspense during this experiment. One sergeant had got into the centre of the stream, but at great risk of his life, and a long time was spent in watching his progress. At length he succeeded, and got across, but another, less fortunate, turned his pale face to us as he was sinking fast. At this perilous moment Mr Hill (who I have told you was once in the Navy and is an excellent swimmer) dashed into the tide to his rescue; and it was a truly pleasant sight to see so bold an effort made to save the poor sergeant, which as Hill is a powerful young man, was soon effected.

It was evidently out of the question to let the men venture, so that we halted here for the night, as nothing better could be done and it was getting dark. In a little time we discovered a forsaken building, fallen long before to ruin, that had been once a hunting lodge as we conceived. Here Hill and I decided upon passing the night together; the only habitable part remaining of this ruin consisted of one room only with a very large window, low to the ground, but long deprived of all the woodwork, and none left to the floor, and as we had no inclination to lay upon the dirty ground we were soon busy in collecting wild lavender by moonlight in a gap of the wood in front of this building, where it grew in profusion. Having spread our boat cloaks upon it, we were going to sleep when suddenly our Captain came to us requesting shelter as the men were disposed to be outrageous, and all control over them was lost. We placed him directly between us, and nestled quietly down, but one or two suspicious looking fellows we observed to come to the window and to be prowling about apparently with no good intentions.

We however fell to sleep, and did not awake until the morning, when we were once more on foot with a strong desire to get forward as fast as possible. For this purpose we set out, but having no guides the men fell into terrible disorder and we had the greatest difficulty to keep them together. After marching all this day in various directions, as chance directed us, towards evening we found no signs of roads or human habitations, but were threatened to be again benighted in an open forest. Here dreadful to say we met with a most frightful and startling apparition, such as was perhaps never before seen under such circumstances, and almost incredible. It was the corpse of a lusty full grown woman, seated as if in life, perfectly upright, with her back against a tree. Such was the fearful situation we were in, with the men from the cravings of hunger and exhaustion in a state of total insubordination, hurrying about in all directions to extricate themselves from the mazes we were involved in, that no one paused a moment scarcely to look at her. I observed no blood whatever about her garments (for she was completely dressed) and her face was as composed and unchanged in colour, as if she had been seated at a cottage door, but she was probably not left long unmolested for when darkness came on we heard wolves howling most distinctly and only through using extraordinary exertions could we hope for relief. Mr Alexander was most active in this dilemma to render assistance, and we got clear at last of the trees, and had the surprise and pleasure to espy a peasant or shepherd as we supposed him to be, on the top of a neighbouring hill.

Some of our most nimble-footed light Infantry were sent in pursuit of him, but the peasants not liking to be pressed for guides, always shun us where they can as to them it is no small punishment to be forced to walk miles from their beaten tracks. Night was now coming on, but we had not to wait the issue of this, as some of our men had found a village called Ladoeiro at a short distance from us. This was a cluster of poor and miserable houses encompassed with woods and yelping wolves, but what was worse when we arrived our ravenous soldiers were beating the doors open with the butt ends of their muskets, and crying for 'Bread' or 'Pan blanco' in most vociferous terms. This was a dreadful night of horrors of one kind or other, as the men were dispersed, seeking food, and no longer amenable to any direction than their own will. It is only to be hoped that they did not disgrace their country by any more desperate acts than satisfying their hunger. Yet these are occasions that soldiers too often gladly avail themselves of, when it can be done with impunity, and the smallest error of those in command placing them in such difficulties is sure to be resented in this manner (as it has been ever proved with all armies in retreat). When morning broke, the well disposed mustered again, and most of them we were glad to see did so. With proper directions we proceeded on our march to Zibreira, but a dreadful tragedy had been acted here just before our arrival, and the first sight we witnessed was heart rending, of a distracted mother with a beautiful babe, appealing to every one around her at the brutality of some barbarous individual who in a scuffle with the parents had thrust his bayonet into its temple. This called for immediate steps to be taken against the offender; but whilst this was doing, much to our amazement a sort of joy seemed to possess the people assembled. We soon learnt the cause, which was that a Portuguese Regiment on the march was coming there, and within a few miles of the town. This intelligence had quite a magic effect upon our refractory men, who fell into their ranks immediately, and the word was scarcely given before we were all off in double quick time on the road to our right destination.

These untoward events are not known or discussed here, and are of too frequent occurrence to excite surprise, but our Captain has been ordered to Lord Wellington's Headquarters at Freneida, to give an explanation of them, and no doubt his Lordship will command a strict enquiry to be made, and Courts Martial will ensue, but as we junior officers were only passive spectators, we shall probably hear no more of it.[1]

When the supplies were again issued, we started for the frontiers and passed the little stream that divides the two countries. There we halted to read the General Orders issued to all British troops on entering Spain.[2] The men were drawn up at a memorable spot in front of a stone detached from the earth beneath, and as large as a moderate sized hay stack. Such are not infrequently met with, and form an interesting subject for scientific enquiry, as the wonder is how they came in such places, no such stone being found above or below, or near them. From thence we proceeded to the first Spanish town called Zarza la Major, or mayor as it is pronounced. A very striking change is immediately observable here, greatly in favour of the Spanish nation, and here we spent our Christmas day. Through the lower compartments of a large and lofty house in the principal street, with iron balconies from the top, to each window, we were led (Hill, Nelson and I) into a spacious kitchen (occupying that portion of the house we should call a parlour) but bearing even as a kitchen not the smallest resemblance to ours, with the deal dressers, shelves, and tea kettles etc. It resembled a hall hung in black for a dead body to lay in state in; here, seated upon three legged stools, before a flaming fire burning on a hearth, with no recesses of chimney at the sides (but the smoke caught by its projecting at about 6 feet from the ground) were to be seen the male personages of a family consisting of four young men of nearly the same ages, who rose with a peculiar stateliness upon our entrance. They were all fine fellows, fit for Grenadiers; the graceful nobleness of their carriage was very remarkable. It impressed us at once with a proof of the proverbial pride of the Spaniards. A

---

[1] A report of this unfortunate incident did in fact reach Wellington himself. On January 26th 1813, he wrote to Sir Charles Stuart, 'I likewise enclose the proceedings of a Court of Inquiry on an affray in the town of Zibreira between the inhabitants and a detachment of the 28th Regiment, in consequence of which a child lost its life.' Wellington went to ask what the Portuguese government wished to do with a lieutenant, corporal and private of the regiment who had been arrested. (*Despatches*, Wellington to Sir Charles Stuart, 26th January 1813, X, p.37.) In fact, an investigation by the Assistant Adjutant General of the 2nd Division showed that the child had not been killed, as was first thought, and that by May 1813 it was enjoying perfect health. The three offenders were subsequently released 'by desire' of Sir Rowland Hill. (*Despatches*, Wellington to Sir Charles Stuart, 2nd May 1813. X, 341.)

[2] There were dozens of General Orders issued by Wellington to his men stressing the importance of good conduct and discipline when on in Spain and Portugal. Unfortunately, there is an even greater number of General Orders rebuking the men for breaking them and for ill-discipline on the march. This, of course, was detrimental to the war effort in the Peninsula as it aggravated an already irritated population, tired of seeing their homes, harvest and livestock requisitioned by Wellington's army. The Iberian people could at least take some comfort from the fact that the Allies paid for their goods (sometimes) unlike the French who bought their provisions at bayonet point. Good behaviour by the troops was of paramount importance when the Allies entered France as the last thing Wellington needed was a resistance movement similar to that waged by the people of the two Iberian nations against the French. Fortunately, discipline was largely maintained and Wellington's men were generally welcomed by the French people of southern France who, hitherto, had been somewhat anxious at the prospect of the Allied invasion of their country.

domestic came and led us forward, and by a door he opened in approaching we saw a light in a remote chamber, prepared for us. We followed him observing hams overhead suspended from the rafters, and cased in brown paper, and a great many frying pans hooked to the walls (these I must tell you are the chief utensils of cookery in this country). But I must cut short my descriptions to bring you to our next march when we arrived here.

Passing over a cheerful succession of hills crowned with olives (which are very like cherry trees) we came to a rivulet where a working party in the well known uniform of the 28th were busy laying a small platform or bridge under the charge of a fine soldier looking young Lieut. (named Gordon) of our 1st Battalion Light Infantry.

Now that winter has come, we wonder at the few signs of it observable, but more striking still is the isolation of our military associates from the rest of the army, none of whom were to be seen on joining them, our 28th friends being the only sojourners at this very quiet somewhat dingy and retired village. Ourselves and villagers being shut up together closely for the season presents a winter piece of peculiar interest. Not that we expect frost or snow to incommode us, although the mountain tops are covered with it, and rise in gloomy magnificence in the distance to be seen from our parade ground. This battalion now, with the addition of recruits we have brought to it, makes a strong muster of more than a thousand bayonets, and in the disciplined state they appear in the 28th must make a fine component of our army.[1] As each Company moves out from their quarters to the parade where the Band are playing, we seem indeed to be taking our places in an actual battlefield.

Colonel Abercromby who commands it is a fine handsome young man, not more than 30, very sprightly and extremely animated with that kind of esprit that shows him to be devoted to the service. He has been 4 years in the Peninsula already, and is not inclined to return home, although he must soon resign his command to Colonel Belson[2], who is on his way from England to join us. We have the most funny little bedrooms in the world for repose in this village, with small oil papered windows, not larger than a boy's slate to give light to them, excellent but coarse bedding, perfectly clean, and such as we might expect to find in the rural districts of our own country; under the table is placed a pan of hot coals, in what is called a brazilio, a capital contrivance to keep the feet warm, but we have seldom occasion for it, the temperature is so mild.

Pray give me as long letters as I am disposed to write to deserve them, and believe me my dear Mother to be, Yours etc. etc., W.T.K.

---

[1] The 1/28th was indeed one of the army's strongest battalions and at Vittoria was 818-strong. Given that the average strength of a battalion was 550 this figure shows just how strong the battalion was. It would need to be, too, for during the next few months the battalion would see heavy fighting and suffer many casualties.

[2] 40 year-old Charles Belson joined the 28th Regiment on November 23rd 1804. He was to serve with the 28th for the remainder of the Peninsular War and commanded the regiment during the Waterloo campaign in 1815. He was promoted to major-general in 1819 and died in 1830.

Coria,
General Hill's Head Quarters
11th February 1813

My dearest Mother,

We marched to this town from the Casas de Don Gomez on the 28th last month, a few days previous to which I had the delight of receiving your letter of the 16th December with the joyful tidings of your all continuing well, with the promise of a happy Christmas etc, which set my mind at rest with regard to you, and afforded me a real treat, and being accompanied by Samuel's view of the cottage, made it complete. Let me be situated how I may, the knowledge of there being a spot where happiness reigns around my dearest ties will reconcile me to my fate. The little circle in which you preside is my only point of attraction in this great world, and my father and yourself are the only persons I am bound to please in my actions through life, and while you continue so I shall do my best to buffet on, to deserve the smiles of fortune, but not to be daunted by her frowns. My last letter has informed you of every occurrence up to the time we joined the Regiment. No reason is assigned for our removal to this town, where we are likely to remain until the general remove takes place at the opening of this year's campaign. We have letters and papers up to the 26th January by which you have heard I perceive of Lord Wellington's visit to Cadiz and from thence to Lisbon. It would seem that the Cortes have refused to enter into the measures his Lordship went to propose.[1] What they were we know not, except that they were said to relate to the Spanish Army, of which however at last they have conferred upon him the title of Generalisimo! The expectation of a peace has been very prevalent in the minds of the army in this country lately, however the return of Bonaparte

---

[1] Wellington had left his headquarters at Freneida on December 12th 1812, reaching Cadiz eleven days later. He went there as a consequence of his being appointed Generalissimo of the Spanish armies by the Cortes at Cadiz some two months earlier. Once at Cadiz, Wellington set before the Cortes his schemes for the reorganisation of the Spanish armies but with mixed results. As usual, Wellington found dealing with the Spaniards a tiresome business but when he arrived in Lisbon to deal with the Portuguese Council of Regency he wrote to Earl Bathurst, saying, 'I left Cadiz.... having arranged everything tolerably well and nearly as I wished.' (*Despatches*, Wellington to Bathurst, 18th January 1813, X, p.31). His frustrations when dealing with his allies were revealed in another letter to Earl Bathurst, written upon his return to his headquarters at the bleak, windy village of Freneida. 'I am astonished at the patience of my brother [Henry Wellesley, British ambassador to Spain], and that he has been able to do anything with such people.' (*Despatches*, Wellington to Bathurst, 27th January 1813, X, p.55). The story of the relationship between the British army, whether it be commanded by Wellington or Moore, and its Spanish allies makes for sorry reading from 1808 right up until the close of the war in 1814. (See Oman, *History of the Peninsular War*, VI. pp.194-213, for a full account of Wellington's business in Cadiz and Lisbon.)

to Paris etc has done away with that opinion, and war seems threatening to rage some time longer.

Lord W. is certainly determined to make a vigorous push this spring, and it is to be hoped this year's campaign will decide the contest. We shall certainly advance beyond the Ebro, and most probably without impediment or opposition (Burgos having been abandoned.)[1] Our first stand will probably be at Saragossa or Valencia, both cities with strong defences, the last on this side of the Pyrenees. This is Col. Abercromby's opinion and I am sorry to say he has been forced to solicit another command, and must leave us, Colonel Belson being daily expected to join us, who is the senior Lt Col. Col. A. does everything with such an Esprit de Corps that it is the highest gratification to serve under him. He is very young and bids fair to rival his gallant uncle, the unfortunate Sir Ralph who was killed in Egypt.[2]

At our last quarters in a village so secluded, there was much to interest us, that has left impressions not soon to be effaced, the chief features of which were derived from our Commanding Officer who kept us continually employed, requiring all our movements in the field to be done in double quick time, that the General when he came to review us had enough to do in riding about after us into different positions continually exclaiming "That will do, Colonel, that will do!" who never failed to reply "O pray General let me put them through another manoeuvre," and there was a good deal of fun in all this to us young soldiers. Col. Patterson has returned from the command he was sent upon, and his presence with the Battalion affords us much satisfaction, as I am indebted to him for numerous kindnesses and feel assured he would serve me in any particular. I believe I told you he left England at a very short notice and at a time when Mrs P. was in a most interesting situation. This lady I might have described as the Hebe of Devonshire, whether I did so or not I don't remember, but she is certainly a most charming woman and he must feel his separation from her very acutely, at this period particularly. He is besides only the junior field officer with this Battalion, there being in addition to Cols A and B, a Col. Nixon senior to him here, but both he and Col. Patterson are merely Majors in the Regiment but Colonels by brevet from having commanded in action.

I had the pleasure for the first time of seeing Sir Rowland Hill last Sunday during Divine Service. He is very plain in his attire, a red waistcoat appearing between the folds of an undress blue coat, and you might suppose him to be a

---

[1] The castle at Burgos, which had caused Wellington so much pain in September and October 1812, was blown up by the departing French troops on June 13th 1813, and so the Allies were spared any chance of a repeat of the disastrous episode of the previous year.

[2] Sir Ralph Abercromby commanded the British expeditionary force to Egypt in 1801. Born in 1735, he had seen active service in Germany during the Seven Years War, in Ireland and in the Low Countries. The Egyptian campaign of 1801 remains his most famous contribution to British military history, a campaign which saw him command a host of generals who were later to win fame in the Peninsula, including Moore, Baird, Beresford, Fletcher, McGrigor, George Murray, Hill, Colborne, Lumley, Kempt, Colville, Houston, Edward Paget and Dalhousie. Sadly, Abercromby was mortally wounded during the battle of Alexandria. The best recent account of the Egyptian campaign is Macksey's *British Victory in Egypt*, London, 1995.

farmer, of a very thoughtful and grave deportment, but a man you would feel to like very much.[1]

And now my military news is ended, let me endeavour to entertain you with another subject and to surprise you, at the same time, for I must inform you that we have become Theatrical Amateurs to relieve the tedium of our present situation. And Sir Rowland's Aides (Lord Chas Fitzroy, Captains Egerton, and Churchill of the Guards) have got up a theatre to relieve the General's mind from the pressure of more weighty matters. For this purpose a fine old palace of the Duke of Alava's has been fitted up for our performances, and I have had the pleasure to join the Company, being requested to take the part of Mrs Malaprop in the Rivals, vacant by the absence of Colonel Payne, who was to have acted it, and for which there was a great difficulty to find a substitute. This part, which I did not much like, I resigned, not thinking I could do justice to it, and gave the pedantic old lady into the keeping of a young volunteer (a pleasant young Gent named Radford, who has lately joined us in that capacity) who it happens has a penchant for the Drama and that character.

With regard to financial concerns I have not received a penny since I left Lisbon, nor are we likely to have an issue of pay till March at the soonest. This would be a bad business for poor Pil Garlick, but that fortune and friends have not quite deserted me, and our wants are much more moderate here than at home. Hill and I have been living together in accordance with our circumstances at the village we have just left, where as few things were obtainable even with money, we contrived to preserve appearances with our new associates and got on very comfortably. Our allowances from Government are very liberal and don't oblige us to go to many extra expenses, though provisions are very dear here — eighteen pence for a small white loaf and 3 shillings a pound of salt butter, with other articles in proportion.

With respect to my equipment, I have been very badly off for shirts, so much so as to request the Quartermaster to let me have half a dozen coarse white linen ones such as he serves the private soldiers with, but many other officers are as badly off in this particular and they are quite good enough for campaigning. The packet you prepared for me contained indeed a very valuable collection of things. Most of them will be serviceable for Samuel or Alfred, and it would not be worth while reserving them for me as it is uncertain when I shall return, and I should never be able to get them further than Lisbon if you was to send them out. I am happy to hear my Aunt intends returning in a twelve month, as her presence in

---

[1] Rowland Hill (1772-1842) was undoubtedly the most respected of all Wellington's senior officers. He showed great compassion towards his men which earned him the nickname 'Daddy' Hill and, as Keep says, was more akin to an English farmer or country gentleman than a soldier. Certainly, he was as different to Craufurd and Picton as chalk is to cheese and is claimed to have been heard to swear on only two occasions, at Talavera and St Pierre. He enjoyed great success at the head of an independent command in the Peninsula, notably at Arroyo dos Molinos and Almaraz and later succeeded Wellington as Commander-in-Chief at Horse Guards between 1825 and 1839. The Rev. E. Sidney's *The Life of Lord Hill* (London, 1845) remains the best biography.

England will be a great comfort to you. I am delighted too to hear you are so well, and the little girls growing apace.

I enjoy thank God very good health here. It seems the very climate suited to my constitution. Our soldiers look remarkably well, quite healthy, although they have so recently come off hard service, though not on the retreat from Salamanca, which was almost as bad a one as that under Sir John Moore. We may perhaps leave this very soon, of which a great idea prevails at present. The 28th is in the 3rd Brigade of the 2nd Division.[1] Samuel had better notice this in his directions.

I hope to see Madrid in our advance from which at present we are distant about 100 miles. Tell Sam I hope he will think of me very often, and under the same cover that he puts your letters give me all the news he can collect, with many thanks for his drawing of the cottage. Our army occupies at present the frontier towns and villages from Lamego on the Douro to a considerable distance beyond our position in the south, so that with a map of the Peninsula you will see the line we're upon, the French being distributed in cantonments like ourselves, at a respectful distance in our front, but of course in possession of the capital. Though I have not seen places of high renown like Seville, Toledo or Granada, and its Alhambra etc, what I have beheld has excited a great desire to see more, and Coria has attractions different from any in England, with a climate more genial and warm, and landscapes superior to Richmond; but there the comparison ends, for there are no grand hotels, carriages and four, with postilions in jockey caps and silk waistcoats and gay company moving about in all directions with brilliant shops etc. But there is a place of resort to which we go about half the size of St James's Square called the Plaza and where the Town Hall is now converted into a Guard house, and here when on duty, seated on a bench in front of it, it is amusing to see our companions promenading, pacing to and fro in busy talk, about events occurring, General Officers and others looking so soldier like, though in dishabille, and brought together so promiscuously. The officers' room in this temporary Guard house contains a fine painting upon a religious subject, that connoisseurs would highly appreciate, but though the French are so apt to covet such things we look upon them with indifference. Pray write to me often for your letters and news from you is so dear to me, that I am always wishing for them long before they arrive.

I have no room to say more my dearest mother, and must conclude therefore with more affectate regards to my Father and Grandmother, and all at home with an assurance of my continued love and affection, I remain, Yrs ever, W. T. Keep.

---

[1] In February 1813 the 2nd Division was as follows: Cadogan's Brigade (1/50th, 1/71st, 1/92nd, 1 coy 5/60th), Byng's Brigade (1/3rd, 1/57th, 1st Provisonal Battalion [2/31st and 2/66th], 1 coy 5/60th), O'Callaghan's Brigade (1/28th, 2/34th, 1/39th, 1 coy 5/60th), and Ashworth's Portuguese (6th and 18th Line, and the 6th Cacadores). O'Callaghan assumed command of the 3rd Brigade only at the end of January 1813 following the death of Wilson, the previous incumbent. (See Oman's *Wellington's Army*, pp.343-373 for Divisional and Brigade organisation in the Peninsula, 1809-14.)

Coria
Spanish Estremadura
27th March 1813

My dear Sam,

I imagine you are becoming impatient to get a few lines from me in acknowledgement of your long and entertaining letter, received just as I had joined our brave friends after our tedious march, with the neat little drawing it contained, so precious an object for me to look at, when I think of home, and peruse its contents. I do not trust my letters where they are liable to be lost, and have too often a desire to refer to them, to leave them behind me, so that I have enclosed them in the parchment of my commission (sometimes not an unnecessary thing to produce quickly in case of being taken prisoner). Within this, in a breast pocket of my red jacket I deposit them, where they be snug enough and next my heart. By my letter to my Mother you will have read of occurrences in our march through Portugal, a varied scene of tempest and sunshine, gleams of brightness succeeding often a deluge of rain, yet when descending in mighty torrents, soon disappearing again through chasms in the mounts in their progress to the main. A climate so sultry as this in the hot season, disposes of these overflowing waters in a very short time, leaving not that sparkling and refreshing brilliancy in the dew deposited upon our rose leaves at home, but something very characteristic of a different land, with its olives and oranges and other unusual productions that spread a very perceptible perfume around that is extremely agreeable; nor can the eye wander far without being assured the scene indeed is changed, deserted roads and dilapidated houses, embankments and fortifications with all the munitions of war being visible at every turn. We passed no towns of great repute whose history I am acquainted with, Abrantes and Castello Branco the largest, and Niza and Vilha Velha the most noted on this route, the first for the sportsman's recreations and the latter for its inaccessible position and miserable recompense for the Traveller's toils; thus I must close my account of Portugal, but this more interesting country you may expect me to be very desirous to recommend to your notice.

Not alone in my first arrival among strangers here, we soon fell into their ranks and became a part of themselves. Joining them at the obscure little village they were quartered in, we found them mixed up with the interesting and rural folks around them, and they gladly made room for us and gave us proofs of brotherly attention. An interchange of invitations to a social glass in cosy places brought us acquainted with soldiers we were prepared to look up to with great respect. In these snug and pleasant abodes we scarcely noticed how time flew, enlivened by their presence, and when I laid down at night shut up with these Spanish villagers I could but admire the vicissitudes of life, and wished you was again my Bed fellow to talk them over and participate in them. Still a lingering care will assail the mind with a desire to know when we shall meet again. This world is nothing more than a succession of such anxieties and separations. From this pleasant obscurity an order came to march here, where we have had fresh introductions to more fine fellows of our noble army. But let me contemplate the dear little cottage where you now reside. How different are the places we are both occupying. Chelsea Common and the high walks by the riverside, I love to think of, how you are there and of the pensioners and their old abode. I fancy I see them seated in their large hall at dinner, as we used to do when boys, and little did I dream then of becoming so intimate with their pursuits. At the time Captain Cox occupied your cottage it must have been a desolate place though so near London, and he was a bold man to live so completely alone there. The inscription plate over the door marking such an ancient date accords with the tale of highwaymen by whom he was beset, but here how many places appear a hundred times more alarming surrounded by thick woods, and infested with wolves and bandits. I hope you will be amused in gardening and every day better pleased with it; how I shall like to seek it out on my return!

We gave a grand dinner lately, and invited Sir Rowland and his Staff in commemoration of the Battle of Alexandria in Egypt on the 21st March, where the 28th fought very gallantly when attacked by the French on two sides, with the front and rear ranks back to back, and repulsed them (for which service we have the peculiar honour to wear a plate on the hind part of our caps) and I think Lord Cavan's motto would be appropriate to us "Ut quocunque paratus" — "Prepared on every side".[1]

I spoke a speech from Shakespeare on the occasion, and we had some excellent songs, one in particular sung by Major Lluellyn of the 28th — "Sound, sound for War" — which made the walls of our Banquet Chamber echo again. We did not fail to drink the health of our gallant General, and he returned a speech very complimentary to us. We have a great number of officers present with the Regiments here, and many pay us a visit from other Divisions, so that Coria, like ancient Troy, is full of gallant spirits, and such a number of fine fellows as are now assembled with her army England may be justly proud of. Amongst the Spaniards most renowned is a Duke del Infantado — this old warrior is the most remarkable personage here, he being besides the most funny and diminutive of men. He is a great favourite with the 28th and was feasted to his heart's delight and placed upon the table itself. Altogether our festival did us credit.

I am happy dear Sam to tell you that I continue in excellent health and fancy myself to be better looking than I ever was, in that cold climate I was born in. No faces are to be seen here unsunburnt. How do the ladies do then you will ask. Of course you have heard of Mantillas, and with these they continue to preserve their complexions. You know that some of the pale Beaux of our native Isle might in fairness vie with their enslavers, but here it is by no means probable, and you will truly think the girls of this country are consequently more captivating by the contrast, and the Gents in their eyes proportionately more attractive. At least I

---

[1] The 28th was awarded the privilege of wearing their regimental badge on the back of their caps following a celebrated incident during the battle of Alexandria on March 21st 1801 when the regiment faced about to repulse French cavalry. (See Macksey's *British Victory in Egypt*, pp.127-128.) The 44th (East Essex) Regiment performed a similar feat at Quatre Bras on June 16th 1815 during the Waterloo campaign but received no such accolade.

suppose so, and am therefore of opinion I should do more terrible execution in a ballroom now than ever I could hope to do before. My Mother, when you read this to her, will decidedly conclude I have become terribly conceited; but my Grandmother when she hears it will say, "Never mind that, so long as the Boy's better in health and quite well", and then I sigh to think how I can repay them both for all their tender care of me.

I have had a grey great coat made with a few marks of my vanity attached to it, and have set the tailors to work at a forage cap. Our noble Commander I must tell you cares little how we equip ourselves, and leaves it entirely to our convenience and option. Among the vagaries this license admits of, I ordered the said article to be made of cloth similar to the coat but in the form of the Westminster scholar's caps — but after it was finished I was not so proud of it, as I expected to be, and thought it too grotesque and pedantic.[1]

Delmar has just arrived from England, and has brought a forage cap with him, the gift of Robert Taylor, that he wore at Berry Head, and for that I have gladly exchanged my new and extraordinary one. It is of light grey, with a black tassel and broad band of velvet. With this, and said coat, sash round my waist, black belt and sword, grey trousers, shoes and black gaiters, you may figure my equipment, which is the same as worn by one half the officers here. On parade occasions the regulation cap only is worn, but universally covered up with oil skin concealing its ornaments. We all therefore look equipped for bad weather, even in the very finest. We were very glad to see Delmar again, and my pleasure is increased to behold him with the cap he is now wearing of my invention, which is really not so inappropriate as he looks so very young, and is indeed a student of military tactics.

I was quite delighted to hear such good news from the Western Indies. Our dear Aunt seems to be enjoying herself there at the Governor's Balls, and is quite among the military. Her letters therefore must be frequently on the same topics with my own, as she is so intimate with the officers' ladies, Colonels and Captains

---

[1] The study of military uniform in the Peninsula is a subject in its own right which has generated scores of books. Passages such as this by Keep only serve to draw attention to the fact that so much non-regulation clothing was adapted and worn by Wellington's men that one suspects that, given the aid of a time machine, we would have great difficulty recognising the British troops in the Peninsula. Indeed, judging from the accounts left to us by Wellington's men, their appearance was a far cry from that set down in the official Dress Regulations of 1802. William Grattan, of the 88th, summed up the situation with his famous quote that, 'Provided we brought our men into the field well appointed, with their sixty rounds of ammunition each, he [Wellington] never looked to see whether trousers were black, blue or grey; and as to ourselves, we might be rigged out in any colour of the rainbow if we fancied it. The consequence was that scarcely two officers were dressed alike!' (Grattan, *Adventures with the Connaught Rangers*, p.50.) These sentiments were echoed by Robert Mercer, of the 3rd Foot Guards, who wrote, 'Every person here dresses as he likes. These fancy dresses occasion much surprise and horror to the martinets who arrive from London.' (Quoted in Fletcher, *Gentlemen's Sons*, p.34). Good studies of military dress in the Peninsula include Windrow and Embleton's *Military Dress of the Peninsular War*, Philip Haythornthwaite's *Uniforms of the Peninsular War*, Fletcher's *Napoleon's Wars; Wellington's Army*, and the various Osprey 'Men-at-Arms' titles by Don and Bryan Fosten. There is also a fine chapter on military dress in Brett-James' *Life in Wellington's Army*, p.78-86.

of the gallant 96th Regiment. Whenever you write give my kindest love to her, and detail as many of my adventures as you think will amuse her.

I was likewise much pleased to find you entertain such a favourable opinion of dear Taylor and like him so much. He is indeed a very superior and uncommon young man, and we have had a sad loss in him.

How entertained he would have been with what is going on here, and our convivial parties and theatricals, of which more in my next, and with love to my dear Mother, and all who may be around you when reading this, I remain, My dear Sam, Yr affectate Brother, W.T. Keep.

Coria
2nd April 1813

My dear Mother,

The time has now arrived at which we shall soon set off, upon the momentous issue of this long continued struggle, for the independence of Spain, and freedom of the world. We are only waiting now I believe until the battering train comes up, and pontoon bridges, and it is said their equipment is complete, and they are on the march from Lisbon to join us. Yet I don't know how it is in England, but doubts have been entertained here, whether hostilities would be renewed in this country and that our army was awaiting the orders of its Parliamentary leaders, ready however to continue the war with undiminished ardour or to attend to the voice of peace, and retire contented with the laurels it has reaped.

For my own part I have neither participated in the hopes or fears engendered by this uncertain state of things, but ad interim contrived to pass my time in a very agreeable way, always finding some object or other to engage my attention in this new scene.

Last night but one I had the pleasure of supping at Sir Rowland Hill's, and I mingle occasionally in most of the gay circles of this place. I finished my last letter to you with a short account of the theatrical mania that has raged here, and thus you may conceive the channel through which I arrived at this honour. How often I wish you could behold the ever varying scene, to be sure I've been buffeted about lately but like a true soldier I reconcile myself with a good will to the rough as well as flowery paths before me. As my father may desire some military information from me, I shall first communicate all I am acquainted with. Hitherto Sir Rowland Hill has had a separate command of 15 or 16 British Regiments with a few corps of Spaniards and Portuguese, and was employed last year to keep Soult in check, while the northern army as it is called, consisting of six other Divisions under Lord Wellington, marched against Burgos in Castile.[1] His Lordship was not able to

---

[1] Rowland Hill enjoyed great success with his independent command in 1811 and 1812. His force between September and October 1811 consisted of what was virtually the 2nd Division, of which the 1/28th, along with the 1/34th and 1/39th, being Wilson's

make a lodgement there for his troops (the French having received reinforcements) and he was in full retreat when we landed at Lisbon, which he continued, until the army arrived where it is at present when General Hill's army was again united to it, so that with our whole force thus assembled we may be said to encompass Portugal in our rear, which is entirely cleared of the foe.

The British force is divided into 7 Divisions, which are again divided into Brigades, each Brigade being composed of 3 or 4 Regiments. Ours is the 3rd Brigade of the 2nd Division, and is commanded by the Honourable General O'Callaghan, comprising 1st Battalion 28th, 2nd Battalion 34th and 1st Battalion 39th Regiments, so that whenever either of these last corps are mentioned you may be sure we are not far off.

The present position of the army is different to what we expected. It cannot be said to be in the field, but has been leisurely recruiting its resources for the Campaign ensuing, with more than ordinary preparation. The reinforcements from England, and supplies of all kinds (except money) are very considerable so that our numbers have rapidly increased and we do not fall far short of 50 thousand British troops, besides the numerous forces of Spain and Portugal united to us. This indicates vigorous measures, and when once in movement God knows when we shall again be in quarters.

We see nothing whatever of our enemies, and should not know they were in the country, a sort of truce prevailing so that we only mount a Subaltern's Guard here for ordinary purposes. The French I hear are not to be seen within 7 leagues

---

Brigade, formed part. The other brigades were Byng's (1/3rd, 1/57th, 2/31st and 2/66th) and Howard's (1/50th, 1/71st and 1/92nd). There were also seven battalions of Portuguese troops (Ashworth's Brigade and Hamilton's Division) as well as 3 brigades of cavalry (Long's, Le Marchant's and a Portuguese brigade), a troop of Royal Horse Artillery, two companies of Royal Artillery and two companies of Portuguese artillery. (Oman, *History of the Peninsular War*, IV, 649.) His greatest exploit during this period was the surprise of Girard's force at Arroyo dos Molinos, on October 28th 1811, during which he took 1,300 prisoners including General Bron, the Prince of Aremberg, the colonel of the 27th Chasseurs and thirty other officers at a cost of just 71 casualties to himself. Hill's second famous victory came on May 19th 1812 when he attacked and destroyed the French bridgehead and forts over the Tagus at Almaraz. Other senior officers exercised independent command in the Peninsula, such as Graham and Craufurd, but none was as consistent and successful as the reliable Hill. Graham's greatest achievement came at Barrosa, on March 5th 1811, a battle which saw the first capture in battle in the Peninsula of a prized French 'eagle', but there were few other shining lights during his independent operations. Robert 'Black Bob' Craufurd exercised by far the most celebrated independent command in the Peninsula at the head of his famous Light Division but, in spite of his undoubted genius and his exploits at Fuentes de Onoro and Busaco, not to mention his operations on the Coa and Agueda rivers in the spring and summer of 1810, there were too many uneasy moments, such as the debacles at Barquilla and the fight at the Coa river bridge, for him to be considered the most successful independent commander. Craufurd often drove Wellington to his wits' end but, fortunately, the Commander-in-Chief knew his merits and recognised him as the finest commander of his light troops. Indeed, had any other officer been in command of the Light Division during the events of July 1810 they would almost certainly have been removed, and when Craufurd was mortally wounded at the storming of Ciudad Rodrigo in January 1812, Wellington said his death was a great blow.

of us, but we shall soon pay them a visit now, as all things are very nearly in readiness. Most of the officers are provided not only with baggage animals but others to ride (an order has just been issued permitting it) but I am very well content to trust to my own legs, and don't mind the fatigue at all of doing so, as we shall have nothing but our swords to carry. I am billeted with Alexander and we are now the best friends in the Regiment and have done ourselves some credit by the gentlemanlike course we pursued to wipe away the stain of our silly squabble. I must tell you that he is more than kind to me, and has such a generous consideration for an empty purse that he makes use of his own as freely as if I was a relation of his, and is ever ready to supply my wants. He is rich, the eldest son of a Major who served in the East Indies, and was the friend and adherent of the Nabob of Arcot.

A few mornings ago, when seated at breakfast with our window open which looks upon walls and gardens beneath, I was much surprised to perceive on the balcony of an adjoining house, in conversation with Col. Paterson, Gifford (Marquis of Tweedale) an old schoolfellow of mine at Dr Burney's. His person and exploits there I fully remembered, but had no expectation of being as quickly recognised by him, as I was then known by the nick name of Billington (in some imitations I had attempted as heard from you of that celebrated Singer). Gifford and I must indeed be the oldest companions here, living besides so constantly under one roof. But time makes wonderful alterations, and now I don't suppose he would know me. As I informed you would be the case, Colonel Abercromby has left us, and Col. Belson is in command. He was received very cordially by the officers previously acquainted with him. He left this Battalion after Sir John Moores's campaign when he signalised his name by the admirable style in which he conducted the 28th through the retreat, since which he has been moving in the walks of fashion in the purlieus of St James's, and is said to be a favourite with the prince. It is more to the honour of Col. Belson that he is very humane to the soldiers, and the first parade he visited they showed their regard for him, they cheering their old friend 'Charley' as they familiarly call him. I have received every attention and politeness from them both, and must consider myself very fortunate in this respect, having always met with pleasant Commanding Officers hitherto in my military career.

Our time is very little engrossed by military occupations as we have no raw recruits here, but fine experienced soldiers who have done with the drill. We have therefore only the usual parades at morning and evening and two field days in the week. We call a field day the junction of the Brigade for exercise, our own Regiment and 39th being stationed at Coria, and the 34th at a small village a league distant. Coria is a town resembling Richmond in its situation, being little larger than that or Hampstead. It is seated on a hill overlooking an extensive plain, through which a small river called the Alagon winds its course, or more properly speaking, it overlooks a narrow but level track of land enclosed on opposite sides by a chain of hills running parallel with each other. Part of the town is built as most towns are in this country in the mountainous districts, on the edge of a steep declivity requiring a parapet wall to protect the descent. On this eminence stands an old Gothic cathedral with a fine walk enclosed like that in front of Somerset

House in the Strand, though here the river is at a greater distance in the plain beneath.

At this beautiful spot, I often pass an hour very agreeably on the seats fixed to the walls for the accommodation of the Holy Brotherhood. These old Friars are very good friends to the military, and many of them well informed men, with whom some of our learned Gents converse in Latin. The Interior of this cathedral is fitted up as all the monasteries and churches are in Spain and Portugal, with great attention to display, and the rites of the Romish church as they perform them appear very imposing, but are too theatrical, having all the decorations and ceremonies we are accustomed to see on the stage only — the monks chanting requiems, youths bearing in procession to the altars burning censers etc. The devotees come to perform their solitary devotions at all hours, passing in silence and abstraction over the nicely matted floors to kneel before their favourite Saints formed in wax, and enclosed in glass cases.

The Priesthood seem to have trained the people to abstain from all diversions, and accordingly make the church service as attractive as possible, and it appears to be their only business in this world to say their prayers and leave it again. A road, as I said before, runs along the plain to the station of the 34th where we are joined by that Regiment on field days. This little review takes place on the loveliest spot in nature — overgrown with broom and wild lavender without any spectators to witness it, the Spanish people possessing little curiosity of that kind. Sir Rowland generally pays us a visit to hear Divine Service on Sunday mornings. He dresses very plainly but his Staff Officers rival each other in the costliness of their attire, with cocked hats and waving plumes etc. As soon as the clergyman has closed the service, we perform some evolutions before the General whose presence is sufficient to animate the troops, and then return to Coria, where we arrive about one or two o'clock, with excellent appetites for a luncheon, or dinner (which generally consists of cold boiled mutton, English pickles, fine Spanish white bread, and a good quantum of vino Porto). The mutton here is such as you never taste in England, and delicious, owing I suppose to the aromatic herbage the sheep are fed upon, and so small that you can with ease put a shoulder in the coat pocket (a whole sheep not weighing more than 13 pounds when prepared for the table). This is the way in which my Sunday mornings are spent. On these occasions I frequently recall to mind past scenes at home at the same hours, where we have been used to meet en famille in so many various places, under such odd circumstances. A remarkable contrast to the scene I am engaged in here, and thus, falling into reflection on the diversity of things around me compared to the past, wonder how the pages of the future will be filled up and what turn fortune will take next.

I believe there is something peculiar in the climate of Spain which forcibly operates against remaining indoors for I seldom return to my quarters from the time of morning parade except to dine until I go to bed at night. Nor is it surprising for we enjoy the most uninterrupted fine weather here. I don't think it has rained more than once or twice for the last six weeks. I assure you, one's morning ramble here would afford you infinite delight. The novelty is so striking of every thing you meet. The air itself impregnated with odours from the soil, clothed with myrtles and various scented shrubs, so new and strange, and the silence and tranquillity in the immediate vicinity of the villages adds to the charm, and serves to convince you at the first glance that you are in a foreign land, and in Spain, so fittingly called the land of romance. It is indeed a fine field, if well cultivated. It only wants English customs to make it a paradise, or rather I should say English industry, as by substituting the former it would certainly lose much of the picturesque, which in my eyes constitutes its chief attraction. The country rarely affords a vehicle of any kind for the rich or the great, in any town between this and Lisbon, and it therefore has the appearance of being inhabited solely by the peasantry. You never by any chance see a carriage or chaise on the road with dashing belles or beaux as in England, so that little care is taken of the roads which are intolerable, the communication from one place to another consequently difficult. The soil is generally sandy, with few stones for repairs of suitable magnitude, yet strange to say some are frequently met with so immensely large, that the road is formed round them (as I have before alluded to). They appear quite separated from the earth beneath them, and to have stood in the spots they are found in, from the first formation of the world. You can't expect to meet a jolly Woking coachman smacking his whip to the tune of six inside, and eight out, instead of which you may now and then fall in with a party of merry muleteers, bestriding their lazy footed animals, and winding down the road amidst magnificent mountain scenery, singing as they go, with little jingling bells attached to the mules' collars to aid the concert, some laden with sacks of flour, or skins of wine, with great wrapping cloaks around them, and muskets slung at their backs to protect them from the Ladrones or robbers, a race of men (they may be almost termed who live in the wildest retreats, and perpetrate the most desperate acts on the unguarded traveller). My last letter from you is dated March the 11th, in which I find nothing particular to reply to, except with congratulations that you all continue well and have found such a pleasant refuge at the cottage from the ill treatment of the world. What a different fate might ours have been, had that Chancery suit been settled. Such a breach of trust in a trustee was a most scandalous robbery, but it is equally so in the lawyers, not to bring that horrid man, Bolt, to account at once. I trust my dear Mother, nothing will prevent your remaining at the cottage, as it appears to please you so much.

I have received not a farthing of pay yet. The army is so much in arrears in this country (at which all the officers are constantly complaining).[1] Mr Dewes, the

---

[1] Arrears of pay was a constant irritation to Wellington's men, not to mention the Commander-in-Chief himself who realised that the men's morale and discipline depended largely upon regular pay. At the beginning of the Vittoria campaign the army had been in arrears for some time, although this was nothing new. The previous year Wellington had written to the Earl of Liverppol, complaining of the lack of money to pay the army and of the impossibility of carrying on the campaign without funds. 'I beg leave to point out to your Lordship how impossible it is to expect that this or any other army can carry on operations in Spain so ill supplied, as this is, with money. We can get nothing from the country without payment in ready money, and every day's march increases our distance from our magazines and the difficulty of communicating with them. The troops are 4 months in arrears of pay; the Staff of the army 6 months; and the muleteers nearly 12 months; and we are in debt for every article of supply, of every description.' (*Despatches*,

paymaster of this Battalion, advanced me however four guineas within this last month, and that he thought doing me a great favour, which he could not extend to others. Of the £13 I advanced the privates at Berry Head, I have received £2.17 found to have been due to me from the officer I took the payment of, and advanced to them by him in the same way. The rest of the £13 I shall most probably never get, as the poor fellows must be put under long stoppages for it, so that I have very greatly distressed both you and myself by this present, as I may call it, of ten pounds to them. For they it is that are now in our debt. What odd things occur in this life: but what can be more scandalous than that breach of faith in the trustees.

I left you in my last on the eve of going to the theatre. You will laugh to think we should be thus employed, but be truly astonished could you see what excellence our dramatic labours have arrived at. Captain Egerton, Aide de Camp to Sir Rowland, is the Manager. A very clever gentlemanlike man, and excellent actor in Dowton's style, or Farren's (the latter of whom he much resembles). The performers have an advantage that encourages them to attempt it, in the selection of characters suited to their inclinations. Under this proviso I was induced to make one of the corps dramatique and to enact a character offered to Captain Hartman of the 28th, but which he felt a reluctance to undertake, as it was the part of an old man in the Honey Moon, Signor Balthazar, the father (or Padre as they say here) to the shrew, and I think I may venture to say — although you have seen it so well acted at Drury — you would have been highly pleased with my exertions. At least I am sure you would have been much gratified with the plaudits I received, particularly from Sir Rowland and the English ladies of his party, who laughed heartily, and broke their fans in my behalf, in that part especially where Balthazar compels Lampedo to swallow his own physic (to be sure the scene speaks for itself, and the author has a just claim to a share in it). The rest belongs to the apothecary and myself.

Wellington to Lord Liverpool, 30th June 1812, IX. pp.263-264.) One wonders how seriously Liverpool considered these complaints given that Wellington was to achieve one of his greatest victories, Salamanca, just three weeks later. The problem of arrears amongst the muleteers was a serious one, for at the beginning of the Vittoria campaign a large number of them deserted from Hill's division owing to no pay. The army depended enormously on these men and Wellington could ill-afford such desertions on the eve of such a great campaign. (See *Despatches*, Wellington to Earl Bathurst, 30th March 1813, X. pp.245-246.) The problem of arrears of pay had been recognised by Wellington at an early stage of the war and he drew the attention of the Earl of Liverpool to the consequences of such a situation on March 20th 1810. 'The constitution, and the whole system of the discipline, efficiency and equipment of the British army, depend upon regular payments. All the soldiers' necessaries, and much of their provisions, and the provisions, equipments, and comforts of the officers, are purchased and paid for out of their pay; and if these articles cannot be paid for, the soldiers will take them without payment, notwithstanding all the exertions of the officers to prevent them.......... and fresh opportunities will be afforded for the disorders and outrages to which I have more than once drawn your Lordship's attention, at the moment at which everything may depend upon the efficiency, discipline, and good order of the troops, and upon the good will of the inhabitants of the people.' (*Despatches*, Wellington to Liverpool, 20th March 1810. V, p.562).

Captain D'Arcy of the 39th played Lampedo, and acted it admirably, as well as Mathews could have done it, so complete was our success that a second representation was ordered by the General a few nights since. It was my first attempt in the comic line and I should like nothing half so much as to continue in it — if the French would permit us. We have a superb theatre, in the palace of a traitor (whose estates I hear have been confiscated) the walls of the house before the curtain lined with fine tapestry, representing the adventures of Telemachus and Ulysses, with the figures as large as life. The audience part rising from the orchestra and forming an elevated pit with two stage boxes, one fitted up in great style for the General, the other in imitation, painted very cleverly, as if containing spectators, and to complete the effect our Bands furnish musicians for the orchestra, and the scenery wouldn't disgrace a Greenwood and Assistants, in short the whole got up with a surprising combination of talent, and at great expense, paid by admission of one dollar each to the performance.[1]

This has been one cause of the great influx of visitors here from other parts of the army — our fame having spread. But we have two or three rivals in the field, other Divisions having their own houses of theatrical entertainment, but whether upon so grand a scale or not I can't tell, as I have not had the pleasure of visiting them. We had to prepare our dresses according to our own ideas, sending in the tradesmen's bills to the Treasury, and I think I dressed the old Don in good taste as he appeared on the London Boards. Adjutant Day of the 34th played Elliston's famous character, and really acted it very well, Captain Sherer,[2] Bannister's, of Rolando, and that with the others were extremely well sustained.

After the play, we partook of refreshment in our Green Room, the most singular and to me agreeable scene in the piece, the window commanding a beautiful view by moonlight of the silver tide of the Alagon, and all the romantic features of the real place. When I had partaken of libations from the punch bowl a five minutes' reverie and survey of this splendid night piece was worth all the rest. The balmy breathing air of this lovely landscape so delightful, I could have lingered over the enchantment for hours. I thought how you and Samuel would have enjoyed all this, and seeing me in my Spanish dress with a grey wig in silent contemplation here (ignorant of the occasion) how your wonder would have been raised. Such a thought was an evening's diversion in itself!

---

[1] Wellington's men were very adept at organising 'theatrical entertainment', particularly during the winter months when the campaigning season had died down. The Light Division was noted for its theatre and on October 30th 1811 produced its own version of Edward Young's *The Revenge*, a performance attended by Wellington himself. Hill's 2nd Division proved more than capable of presenting its own plays whilst at Coria. 'We likewise got up an excellent theatre,' wrote Cadell, of the 28th, 'and were as happy as possible, Sir Rowland doing every in his power to add to our amusements.' (Cadell, *Campaigns of the 28th Regiment*, p.147.)

[2] Captain Moyle Sherer served with the 34th Regiment in the Peninsula. He later wrote what has become one of the most entertaining of Peninsula memoirs, *Recollections of the Peninsula*, published in 1823. As we shall see, Sherer was taken prisoner during the fight at Maya on July 25th 1813.

The Farce was the Mayor of Garratt,[1] excellently acted, Egerton playing the Mayor, and comically delineating the humours of the Volunteer force. As soon as the whole was concluded, we went to Sir Rowland's to supper, the General having invited all the dramatis persona, desiring us to come in the dresses we wore on the stage. We accordingly left the house, passing the streets of Coria in this whimsical attire. Four or five Gentlemen in petticoats, one being an officer of the 28th who impersonated the Duchess and two more as Zamora and Violante, besides other ladies appertaining to the farce. We sat down to an elegant supper on our arrival, where I met some Spanish Grandees and other personages of no small consideration.

Could you have seen us here at this brilliant entertainment, your surprise would have been on the increase, and it must have proved a night of wonders to you, not to be solved, a fairy dream. You might indeed have then exclaimed

"This World as far as I can understand
Is all enchanted fairyland."

Among other persons assembled at this odd masquerade was the Marquis of Tweedale, the Duke del Infantado, Lord Chas Fitzroy (the two last rather than be left out, having acted Waiter and Servant in the performance) and young Brunton (Brother to the famous actress, and Countess of Craven). He is a Captain in a Portuguese Regiment, and a very facetious, merry young fellow, and many other remarkable persons were present could I find room to describe them, but as my limits are exhausted I must prepare again to bid you adieu.

Trusting this very long and rambling letter will amuse you and excuse my long silence. As all the world is merely a stage, and the men and women players, I must fancy I am only acting a temporary part in this grand drama, though the scenes I have next to describe I can promise will be quite new and not devoid of interest that I am now preparing to encounter, so God bless you my dear Mother, Says yr affectate Son, Wm Thornton Keep.

---

[1] *The Mayor of Garratt* was written in 1764 by Samuel Foote and was based upon actual events in Wandsworth in the latter part of the 18th century. The play, a farce, was evidently very popular at the time because it was also performed by the Connaught Rangers (Grattan, *Adventures with the Connaught Rangers*, p.286-287.). It is quite possible that Garratt's House, a building held by the British on their right flank during the battle of the Nive, in December 1813, was so named because on the left flank of the British line there was a house owned by the Mayor of Biarritz, which was called by Wellington's men the Mayor's House. I have yet to come across any reason why Garratt's House was so named. Was it named after the very popular Foote play? William Thornton Keep later acted at the Theatre Royal, Richmond.

Coria
23rd April 1813

My dear Sam,

As a short postscript to my letter to our dear Mother cannot fail to be acceptable, I resume the narrative of events here, where I often wish you could spend a few hours with me. I am billeted with my very kind friend Alexander, in the first floor of a house, close to an antique gateway leading by a gradual descent to the suburbs of Coria, with a fine view on emerging from it in front of an extensive plain, shut in by mountains in perspective, with a narrow river shining like silver and gently winding through it, enlivened by constant sunshine and imparting warmth without any heat that is oppressive.

Here the Spanish girls are often to be seen so prettily attired that you would think them fit to appear in a melodrama. Fancy one of them about 14, in a short yellow petticoat descending no lower than the knees, with legs bare, and brown as a berry, and nicely proportioned, with a bodice laced above a slender waist, and on the head a coloured cotton cloth rolled in a band, and supporting a large water Jar (such as convey the grapes to us in London) other lasses kneeling at the river side in little wooden boxes and employed in washing. Our days pass only too rapidly at this delightful place in the presence of so many fine fellows of the different Regiments who impart such life to it — particularly when brought together at our playhouse as aspirants to theatrical honours or the festive board. At our grand banquet in celebration of our victory in Egypt, we mustered strong. Songs and recitations going merrily on, a Captain D'Arcy of the 39th singing from a well corked face on the back of his hand (at the top of a bottle) so well contrived that the tips of it seemed in motion, and where a Captain Hartman of the 28th was invited to recite "Alexanders Feast" by Captain Churchill (Sir Rowland's Aide de Camp) who made an appropriate introduction to it in the following quotation from Hamlet — "For Hartman and his tragedy, Stooping to your clemency, We beg your hearing patiently" which I hope you will do, as I proceed to tell you something more of our theatrical entertainments, in which our rehearsals made such a droll contrast to our military duties, and produced great merriment in the Green Room. Egerton, our Manager, being full of fun and anecdotes of actors, imitating one who came on the stage exclaiming, "To arms, brave comrades! To arms!" extending his own in ridicule of him. I often think what a famous trip it would be for some of our countrymen to spend a few weeks here, where they would find a new set of performers, very clever in all departments of the drama, and it is really surprising how complete a company might be formed from the ranks of our military heroes, with nothing wanted but ladies, and those supplied by the other sex, as in Shakespeare's days. I have no time to say more, and remain, Dear Sam, Your affectate Brother, W.T. Keep.

Toro (Province of Leon)
3rd June 1813

My dear Mother,

On the 5th of May we marched from Coria. Our joyful days of revelry there being suddenly closed by the stern mandates of war. All our trappings in the hurry of the order to move were directly prepared. Horses saddled, baggage animals laden, and we bade adieu to scenes we can never expect to revisit.[1]

I have witnessed frequent removals from different places, but none equal in interest to this, where so many friendly and jovial companions met for the first and last time to participate in the amusements I have described to you.

I have now to conduct you through perpetual transitions in the distribution of so many troops led forward as we trust to victory. Sad as our departure was from Coria, we had none of the usual sources of regret on this occasion, as we were only like travellers proceeding together to the same destination, and all united besides in one pursuit.

Uninterrupted fine weather, and all the necessary appurtenances to our comfort following us on each day's march, it was a very agreeable and by no means toilsome task; even to those on foot, and to such as were relieved from all fatigue by riding it was a journey of pleasure, though certainly a very long and rapid one, for we moved constantly forward with little respite, meeting with few obstacles to our progress from the French.

After leaving Coria, and that part of Spain we were best acquainted with, we found a chain of mountains on our path. This was the Sierra de Gata,[2] through which a rugged and very narrow road makes this a desirable post of resistance,[3] and

---

[1] Wellington himself knew he would never again see Portugal, once the advance into Spain began, and it must have been a very poignant moment when, turning round in his saddle and waving his hat, he said 'Farewell Portugal, for I shall never see you again.' (Longford, *Years of the Sword*, p.307.) And he was right, for he would never again set foot in the country in which he had spent so long, forging his army and earning his reputation as one of, if not the, finest soldiers Britain has ever produced.

[2] The Sierra de Gata is a particularly bleak range of mountains to the south of Ciudad Rodrigo. Any troops marching between the towns of Badajoz and Ciudad Rodrigo, and the majority of troops marching to Ciudad Rodrigo from Lisbon, would have had to cross the mountains. The main road during the Peninsular War ran across the mountains and, indeed, still does today, where some spectacular and rugged scenery can be viewed. The Sierra was the subject of a poem by an officer, 'J.A.', which appeared in *The Royal Military Chronicle* entitled, 'The Subaltern's Complaint, on Piquet at Pena Perda, a Very Lofty Mountain, One of the Passes of the Serra de Gata, In Spain.' The 22-verse poem began;

'Bleak was the wind, and dreary was the night,
  When posted at the pass of Gato's Height,
A luckless sub, with cold hunger pressed,
  Look'd on the Moon, and thus his grief expressed.'

(*The Royal Military Chronicle*, March 1812. pp.341-343.)

[3] Keep's views upon the Sierra de Gata were echoed by Moyle Sherer. 'The passage of the rude and lofty Sierra de Gata, and the descent from the top of the pass to the town,

immediate measures were taken to secure it, and we ascended the highest points of it and were soon in a much colder climate than we had left, with snow around us. From this freezing position however, after a short stay, we again descended to the sultry plains. Our Commissaries attended us, and provided what was needful for our sustenance on the road, one pound of beef a day to each officer soldier, and another of biscuits or bread, with a small quantum of rum or wine. Our servants accompanied the baggage, and at the end of each day's march brought into the appointed ground the long train of animals with our cooking apparatus, and other essentials.

Along the dusty and well beaten high roads which we most frequently followed, the thirsty soldiers hailed with delight the sight of a village or town, where we found the people at their doors with jugs in readiness to answer their impatient outcries for agua, or water, and the pleasure these good women took in thus offering relief to the soldiers was an agreeable sight, joy beaming on their countenances upon the "Ingleses" or Buenos Amigos — our very good friends, as they called us. A hurried draught only could be taken, as we did not halt in the towns, but on the road for a quarter of an hour, generally at the end of every 3rd or 4th mile.

Arab looking men in light linen garments, with sandals on their feet, then made their appearance among us, having small barrels with long tin tubes slung to their backs, crying "Lemonade" to those who had a tintun, or halfpenny, ready to buy it. Discipline was easily preserved for the conduct of the soldiers was exceedingly praiseworthy. Burdened as they were with the heavy loads they had to carry, some of these poor fellows were often deplorably jaded, but cheerful and uncomplaining.

The passage of so large an army over such an extent of country left some melancholy traces behind it of dire disasters to man and horse; the dead bodies of both being occasionally met with, where misfortunes had happened, or deeds of rapine by the native robbers committed on stray travellers (particularly officers' servants with baggage) and this even in the paths of so numerous a body of men. But these mischances were effaced by the delightful scenes of lively interest to us young soldiers, who were such strangers to the country. I messed with Alexander, Hill and Delmar, or others as chance permitted, and you could not have been more amused than to have been our hostess to make our tea on each day's halt. The officers of the Quartermaster General's department usually rode forward to select the ground for each Regiment to encamp for the night, with a running stream near and fuel to supply our wants.

The neighing of the long cavalcade of animals as they approached our encamping ground was a welcome sound in the beautiful woods and luxuriant green shady spots chosen to build our huts in, or pitch our tents for the night.

---

abound with subjects for the pen of Salvador Rosa. A rugged and dangerous road winds amid the thickest brushwood, and around the boldest rocks; below it, on one side, are precipices the most frightful, while, above, on the other, huge masses of mountain-stone terrifically impend, and seem to threaten the traveller with instant destruction.' (Sherer, *Recollections of the Peninsula*, p.222.)

These quite in the gypsy style — fine Bohea (16s) was first poured into the tea kettle, and made to boil there and then into our horn cups — as tea was the refreshment invariably in request among us all. Parties so numerous thus dispersed in preparation for it would have amused you much. Every opening glade with the green sward having its occupants, and like a fete champetre or vauxhall, each part of the company having their own box — though not quite such close neighbours — yet sometimes a Gent's tent and attendants only separated by intervening trees or a bush. Before the intensity of the sun's rays could well be felt, we were again on the move, and thus continued for nineteen days until we arrived at Salamanca.

The scene of conflict was pointed out to us here by our friends, where our General and Marmont had long contested for the disputed Arapiles — a parallel chain of hills — where the French Marshal lost an arm, and was vanquished by the superior skill and tactics of our Chief, who I must tell you we first beheld here — as he halted his staff in compliment to the arrival of the 2nd Division, and received us on the march.[1]

The bustle this threw us into precluded much observation on our part as we moved before him in slow time, and were employed with our swords to salute — with eyes front — and a very large group of officers all mounted and in various costumes were closely assembled all round him. The victories won were not forgotten, whilst on the road to fresh achievements, for on the 16th of May, the anniversary of the Battle of Albuera, at the end of a short day's march, a vacant space amidst a grove of pines was selected to make a rural banquet, and an oblong square marked out for a table, with trenches cut by our pioneers to admit our legs, so that our knees came to a level with it, whilst others were employed preparing broom to spread upon it and raise it for the reception of our plates and dishes. Here under the greenwood tree, like foresters of old, we made the woods ring with our jovial glee.[2]

---

[1] The battle of Salamanca, fought on July 22nd 1812, was one of Wellington's greatest and most decisive victories. After a protracted period of manoeuvring by both armies they finally got to grips with each other on the rolling plains and low range of hills around the tiny village of Los Arapiles. Two of Marmont's leading divisions, those of Maucune and Thomieres, in attempting to cut across Wellington's route back to Ciudad Rodrigo, became separated by some distance, prompting Wellington to launch his divisions against them. The result was a crushing defeat for the French as one after another of Marmont's divisions crumbled. Only Clausel's division offered any initial resistance, at one time threatening to bring the battle to a drawn result after throwing back Cole's 4th Division. However, Clinton's 6th Division stepped forward to plug the gap and continue the inexorable advance of the Allied army to victory. The day, won by Wellington at a cost of 5,214 casualties against some 14,000 French losses, nailed the lie that Wellington was a cautious, defensive-minded general, something which came as a shock to Marmont and his generals who were stunned by Wellington's lightning move against them.

[2] Charles Cadell, one of Keep's comrades in the 28th, left another fine account of this dinner. 'On the 16th, being the second anniversary of the battle of Albuera, the regiment gave a dinner to Sir Rowland Hill, and the staff of the 2nd Division. Being encamped, we had no tables or chairs, but the deficiency was ingeniously supplied by Lieutenant Irwin. A nice piece of turf being selected, he marked out the length and breadth of a mess table, for 100 covers. The sward was carefully lifted, and a trench dug

Col. Abercromby presided, and many other officers were present who had been engaged in that hard day's battle. A Dragoon unluckily deprived us of the company of our gallant Colonel in the midst of the feast by arriving post haste with urgent orders from the Commander in Chief, which required his immediate presence elsewhere, but our festivities continued until the shades of night obscured the sun's pale beam and threatened to leave us in darkness.

When we first set out, the French Army under Marshal Jourdan and Joseph Bonaparte immediately broke up from their quarters and continued their retreat without offering to impede our movements, except by occasionally putting their rear guard into hostile array to cover their stragglers etc, until we reached this place, and crossed the Tormes (which is a very pretty clear and shallow river, running close to the Walls of Salamanca).

The different columns of our army were here arrested as they arrived by a demonstration of a large body of cavalry, that indicated a resolution on the part of our enemies to come to action. Our Regiment halted on the roadside in a field of Indian corn, and uncased their cartridges and loaded for the first time, expecting to be forthwith engaged. The usual hurry and ferment previous to a battle was here displayed, the dust rising in clouds at the hoofs of cavalry passing to the front — artillerymen with ammunition carts, Staff Officers riding forward whose minds seemed occupied with the importance of orders they had to communicate, and light cavalry changing position with perspiration dripping from their brows, from the rapidity of their movements under a burning sun etc. Yet we had little means of knowing what was going on until the silence was broken by the first discharge of fire arms from the carbines of our cavalry very close in advance of us. These were soon lost in the distance, and our attention was presently directed to a range of what in England would be called Downs, where the French Cuirassiers[1] were manoeuvring with some of our heavy Dragoons conspicuous in their red cloaks (the morning having been rainy), some of whom on both sides were hurled from their horses, and the animals running wildly about with their bridles flying loose.

---

round large enough to accommodate the party; the sods and mould were then carefully placed in the centre, and levelled; this centrepiece was excavated sufficiently to give room for our legs underneath; when the mass was raised to a proper height, the sward was carefully laid on, so that we had a beautiful green table, novel and ingenious. The dinner was cooked in every way the old soldier could invent — roast and boiled — soup and bouille; camp kettles were reversed for ovens to bake pies, and every guest brought his knife, fork, and plate. The wine of the country being excellent, we all enjoyed ourselves much; so much so, that some of us bivouacked under the table for the night. (Cadell, *Campaigns of the 28th Regiment*, pp.148-149.)

[1] The incident to which Keep refers almost certainly took place on May 26th 1813, when Wellington's cavalry, the brigades of Alten and Fane, caught up with the French rearguard under Villatte outside Salamanca. The Allied cavalry drove off Villatte's cavalry and tried, rather half-heartedly, to get in among the French infantry but without success. Fane's battery of Royal Horse Artillery was brought up and sent a few round shots into them to hurry them on their way, leaving the Allies in possession of around 200 prisoners. The French cavalry regiment was the 12th Dragoons, of Digeon's division. There is no mention anywhere of Cuirassiers being involved. (See Oman, *History of the Peninsular War*, VI. pp.316-318 for an account of the fight.)

Our cavalry, which since the commencement of the Peninsular War had been greatly undervalued by the very high repute the French Dragoons had attained, as well as by the novel weapons they were so dextrous in the management of as Lancers, made us very glad to see such a manifest superiority as our men now exhibited in the contest, that was so plainly to be seen, from the hills being so close to us where it took place; and from whence the French galloped off, and continued the retreat.[1] Thus we were left in quiet possession of a pleasant spot, where we encamped, adjoining this famous city. The desire to visit it was so universal that a General Order was directly issued forbidding all who had not especial permission to enter it.

I was sadly disappointed at this, but as Hill and I were lamenting the restriction, a very good natured and gentlemanlike officer of the 28th — a Captain Wilson — most politely offered us a pass he had obtained for two, which enabled us immediately to repair thither. We entered this Spanish seat of learning through an antique porch passing the walls of colleges and convents and brilliantly lighted palaces for the rejoicings, and were presently in the Plaza or great square amidst a blaze of illumination from very large houses with gittiron balconies, and all the fun that was going on; and where we heard that Lord Wellington attended by all the great personages of the place had been enthusiastically received, and sumptuously entertained. Here we passed a few merry hours delighted with all we saw in this joyous scene.

The next morning we resumed the march over roads now beginning to exhibit proofs of obstinate strife, where bridges had been blown up, and immediate engineering skill required to facilitate our advance; the roads encumbered with dead horses and mules, killed or knocked upon the march, and vultures feeding on their remains. These voracious birds were not so easily frightened from their prey, as horses were apt to be frightened on approaching them. Col. Paterson, commanding the Light Companies, was urged to dismount to put them to flight, and actually had a very fierce sword in hand encounter with them — so much ill fortune attended it — that his sabre was broken at the hilt in contending with them. They are hideous looking creatures, always on the wing in search of the offal of cattle slain, or anything else they can fall upon. A few day's more march brought us to Toro; a large town on the road side commanding a very extensive view of the surrounding country with Moorish forts and towers — just forsaken

---

[1] The British cavalry enjoyed an unfavourable reputation in the Peninsula, due mainly to some very high profile misadventures, such as Vimeiro, Talavera, Barquilla and Maguilla. The charge of the Union Brigade at Waterloo was an unfortunate echo of these antics. However, there were many fine achievements, such as Usagre, Sahagun, Benavente and Salamanca. Wellington considered his cavalry as unreliable and wherever possible kept them on a fairly tight rein. Indeed, it was not until the Vittoria campaign, when Allied cavalry numbered around 8,000, that he felt able to use them with any degree of confidence. Ironically, the terrain was such that effective cavalry operations were impossible and it would not be until February 1814, when the army was well clear of the Pyrenees and across the Adour, that Wellington's cavalry became involved in offensive operations in any great depth once again.

by the French — and here again we take breath, until the next order is given for pursuit.

Awaiting the first opportunity to commit this into safe hands to be conveyed across the seas to you, I remain, My dear Mother, Yr affectionate Son, William Thornton Keep.

Camp near Vittoria
Morning 22nd June 1813

My dearest Mother,

I have only a few minutes to write a few lines to you, to assure you of my safety, after our engagement of yesterday with the enemy on the heights at this place. We have been marching on many successive days without halt since my last — generally from sun rise to sun set — and I am at this instant in momentary expectation of the bugle sounding and of being under arms again in the pursuit, but shall avail myself of the first quiet moment to give you an ample account of our successes and proceedings — in the meanwhile Lord Wellington's dispatches must content you, remaining confident of my well doing after this glorious victory.

I am now amongst my companions who have been lucky enough to escape uninjured, with a pannier for my writing desk, whilst they too are busy in gratifying their friends at home with the glad tidings of the results; I am sorry to say, we have many other fine fellows who did not get through the glory of the day with equal good fortune having eighteen officers (one half) wounded — some severely, and one or two I fear dangerously. Poor Col. Paterson had his thigh broken, that must make his recovery very uncertain. Our loss altogether in the 28th is about 200, during a close engagement of six hours, and more than any other Regiment in the Division.[1] It was a great triumph, and a day that may well be numbered in the brilliant annals of old England, being as complete a defeat of her foes as ever happened through the bravery of her troops — than which there is no better soldiers in the world.[2] We were opposed to the left wing of the French

---

[1] Keep was very accurate in his estimation of the casualties in the 28th. The battalion suffered 12 men killed and 17 officers and 171 men wounded, 200 in all. Altogether the 2nd Division suffered 1,110 casualties. Total Allied casualties numbered 840 officers and men killed and 4,040 wounded. (Oman, *History of the Peninsular War*, VI. p.758.)

[2] The battle of Vittoria, fought on June 21st 1813, effectively broke French resistance in the Peninsula and from then on there was little doubt as to the outcome of the war. Wellington's army numbered some 80,000 troops against Joseph Bonaparte's 66,000. The battle began at 8.30am when Hill's division, Keep and the 28th included, drove the French from their positions on the heights of Puebla, their left flank. There followed a series of co-ordinated attacks along the entire Allied front which gradually drove the French back but only after some severe fighting. Indeed, it was not until about 5pm, when Cole's 4th Division was thrust into a gap between D'Erlon and Gazan, that the battle was effectively won. The French retreat along the great road to Bayonne was cut when Thomas Graham's force, pouring down from the heights to the north, took the

army which was constantly reinforced from other parts of their line, and the strongest, as we had rough ground to get over and obstinate contention. In this formidable position the French were not easily to be displaced but it was unnecessary as their right wing was turned by the 5th Division under Sir Thomas Graham, so that they abandoned all at once, the ground in front of us, at about 3 o'clock in the afternoon, when we heard their bugles sounding retreat, in the precipitancy of which we have taken the whole of their baggage, they having left all they possessed behind them. It is a fine chance for some of our poor fellows, many of them obtaining 50 or 60 guineas (or Louis D'ors) each as waggons loaded with money fell into their hands. The spoils of the day pretty well compensate for its toils to some of these heroes, and they are certainly deserving of it, for there is no describing what they endure in these campaigns.[1]

---

village of Gamara Mayor, forcing the French to retreat via the road to Pamplona. This took them through the area of the French baggage park which partly accounted for the panic which set in and for the vast amount of treasure abandoned by them in their efforts to escape the clutches of the pursuing Allied troops. The victory was the decisive point in the war which cost the French 8,000 casualties, 415 caissons, 151 of their 153 guns and 100 waggons.

[1] The haul of plunder taken by Wellington's men after the battle of Vittoria was immense and is probably the greatest ever in military history. Some five million francs had arrived in Vittoria a few days before the battle and which Wellington knew lay somewhere out in the chaos following the French rout. His efforts to secure the money failed, however, as several red-jacketed scoundrels beat him to it and the Commander-in-Chief had to make do with just 250,000 francs. John Spencer Cooper, of the 7th Fusiliers, estimated the amount to be even greater. 'In the course of the night the money waggons taken from the enemy were plundered of perhaps nearly seventeen million francs. One of my company got his pockets filled with doubloons and dollars.' (Cooper, *Rough Notes*, p.87.) Moyle Sherer wrote, 'For two or three days, I was employed with strong fatigue parties, collecting the guns and caissons scattered on the roads, and among the fields to the north of the town. We dragged into the park 174 cannon; of these, ninety were field pieces, all foul mouthed from recent use. The ground, for nearly a square league, was covered with the wreck of carriages, cars, chests, and baggage; and, here and there, whole fields were literally white with thickly scattered papers. In their search for money and valuables, the soldiers had ransacked everything; they had torn out the lining of the carriages, and cut open the padding; they had broken all the correspondence chests of the various military and civil offices, and had strewn out papers, returns, and official documents, that had been, for years, perhaps, accumulating. You saw the finest military books and maps trod under foot, and utterly spoiled by the rain, that had fallen the day after the battle.' (Sherer, *Recollections of the Peninsula*, pp.243-244.) Wellington reserved his own condemnation of his men's conduct for a Despatch to Earl Bathurst. 'We started with the army in the highest order, and up to the day of the battle nothing could get on better; but that event has, as usual, totally annihilated all order and discipline. The soldiers of the army have got among them about a million sterling in money, with the exception of 100,000 dollars, which were got for the military chest. The night of the battle, instead of being passed in getting rest and food to prepare them for the pursuit of the following day, was passed by the soldiers in looking for plunder. The consequence was, that they were incapable of marching in pursuit of the enemy, and were totally knocked up.' (*Despatches*, Wellington to Earl Bathurst, 29th June 1813. X. p.473.) Wellington repeated his exasperation at his men's behaviour three days later, again in a Despatch to Bathurst. It was the Despatch in which Wellington made perhaps his most famous, or infamous, remark about his men, the famous 'scum of the earth' remark. 'It is

I received a letter from you to my great delight, on the march from Toro with an account of Taylor's visit. Pray write often to me, and believe me to remain, Your most affectate Son, W. Thornton Keep.

In a few moments I find we shall be again on the move. Heaven bless you, till I have next an opportunity of writing. Affectionate regards to all at home.

Vittoria
8th August 1813

My dear Mother,

Once more in the agreeable possession of time and opportunity, I sit down to describe my pleasures and pains to you and to all those most dear to me at home.

Fancy me in Covent Garden in one of those houses there with piazzas beneath — which will give you an idea of the principal square in this neat and modern looking town, which is now destined to be perpetuated in the annals of fame to the renown of the British Army. A succession of bustling scenes and moving accidents by flood and field have engaged my attention since I wrote the few lines after the victory we obtained here on the 21st June. The triumph over our enemies has left some very grievous vestiges of the perils of the day. Soldiers are now crowding the vacant space before my windows, with disabled limbs in bandages, or are moving about on crutches to take the air. But when I arrived here a few days ago this square was in a tumult of preparation for a Bull fight to rejoice the natives with what one would suppose they were little inclined to be diverted with, after the more interesting and absorbing events that had occurred so recently within view of the town. As I have much to tell you yet about this famous field I must take you back to Toro, to continue my narrative. Here we made but a short halt, again descended into the plains, and passed so near Valladolid that we saw the nuns' handkerchiefs visibly waving from the high walls and windows of their convents to joyfully hail our arrival; and we then followed the French to that place of fierce contention in the previous year — the castle and fortifications of Burgos. On coming there the intentions of our enemies were not apparent, and a part of our force (with the 28th) were concentrated round it.

Our comfort and security during the night is confided to the vigilance of such of our comrades as are in turn appointed to this duty — which is called being on picquet. On this momentous occasion I was thus employed, and as the greatest uncertainty prevailed as to what the French intended to do, when I arrived at the

---

quite impossible for me or any other man to command a British army under the present system. We have in the service the scum of the earth as common soldiers...... It is really a disgrace to have any thing to say to such men as some of our soldiers are.' (*Despatches*, Wellington to Earl Bathurst, 2nd July 1813, X. pp.495-496.) It was to be another eighteen years before he rather belatedly added the postscript to this, when, in 1831, he remarked to Earl Stanhope, 'It is only wonderful that we should be able to make so much out of them afterwards.' (Stanhope, *Notes of Conversations*, p.14.)

outposts I found more importance attached to it than I had ever known before. The Brigade Major with great care pointed out the limits of our position, and moreover informed us (there being another officer detached from the lines with men under his orders for this purpose) that one of us must take the post of advanced sentinel with a Corporal in attendance.

We then (a young Baron of the German Legion, but an Ensign like myself) awaited his further directions, and alighting from his horse the Brigade Major plucked two stalks of grass from the ground and placing them in his hand told us that which ever drew the longest was to undertake this duty, and it fell to my lot. (Not a very desirable one as we should certainly have been the first sacrificed had the French advanced.) Being thus the advanced sentinel I took my post, and as night came on seated myself on a stone upon an open heath, my sword in the ground, and chin upon the hilt with the Corporal ready loaded at my back, and my eyes intent as the lynx to watch the first move of our foes, a very short distance in front.

It was a quiet starlit night, with a light wind blowing in mournful gusts, and remembering the trust reposed in me I did not relax in watchfulness but was wide awake. The hours rolled slowly on in this dreary spot, but with the first indications of dawn a terrible explosion took place. The earth shook, and a ball of smoke arose from the town and settled over it like a cloud. We started forward, and our companions coming round us in a moment we soon found what the French were at, and that the works were blown up.[1] It spread immediately like wild fire through the camp, and the picquets were withdrawn and we continued the pursuit.

On our advance we came into the neighbourhood of magnificent mountain scenery amidst the great fountains of the River Ebro, which takes its rise here. Cascades and waterfalls (descending from towering rocks overgrown with myrtles and blooming shrubs) making with their clattering sweet music; and the only sounds heard to disturb the repose of nature, on this beautiful road. Here we could have prolonged our stay with great satisfaction, but no time was allowed, except just enough to excite an admiration and regret to leave such places behind us, and again we entered the plains on our march to the north after the French.

Another week elapsed in following their steps, and then we approached Vittoria. But I must tell you that previously, on emerging from the fine mountainous scenery of the Ebro, we had the gratification of seeing most of our army on the march, concentrating towards each other on their advance to this point, and appearing in the long perspective like glittering scarlet threads, requiring the aid of telescopes to discern their numbers. One or two Divisions had already

---

[1] The abortive siege of Burgos in September and October 1812 was the low point of Wellington's campaign in the Peninsula. The siege was undertaken with just three heavy guns, in filthy weather and without the veterans of Ciudad Rodrigo and Badajoz, the siege being entrusted largely to the 1st Division of the army. On this occasion, however, there was to be no need for any siege operations, for as Wellington's army advanced the French garrison, worried lest they be cut off by an outflanking manouevre, took the decision to abandon the castle and blow up the works before retreating.

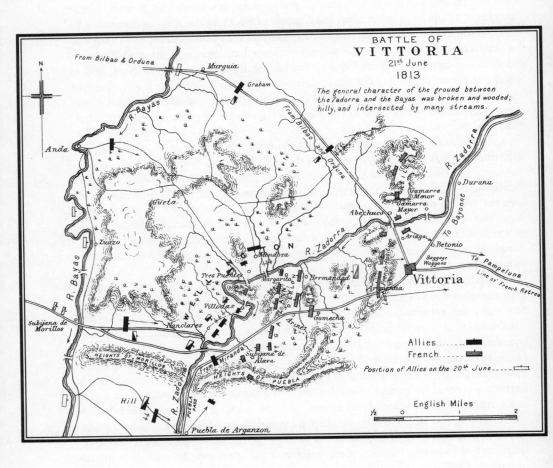

BATTLE OF
VITTORIA
21st June
1813

The general character of the ground between
the Zadorra and the Bayas was broken and wooded;
hilly, and intersected by many streams.

From Bilbao & Orduna

Murguia

Graham

N

R. Bayas

Anda

Gueta

Zuazo

R. Bayas

Subijana de
Morillos

HEIGHTS OF MORILLOS

Hill

Puebla de Arganzon

Nanclares

Villodas

Tres Puentes

Margarita

Subijana de
Alava

HEIGHTS OF PUEBLA

From Miranda

R. Zadorra

Puebla

Mendoza

Hermandad

Gomecha

Arinez

From Bilbao and Orduna

R. Zadorra

Gamarra
Menor
Gamarra
Mayor

Abechuco

Durana

R. Zadorra

To Bayonne

Ariaga

Betonio

Baggage
Waggons

Armentia

Vittoria

To Pampeluna

Line or French Retreat

Allies.........
French.......

Position of Allies on the 20th June.......

English Miles
½   0   1   2

come in contact with the French army and shots had been exchanged, but on the 20th Lord Wellington commanded a general halt and reconnoitred the position they had taken up. At nine o'clock on the morning of the 21st the services of the 2nd Division were required to commence this memorable battle. We had crossed the Zadorra (a dark current of little width in that part with a small bridge) in quick march to support a Spanish Division, under General Morillo, on the heights above. They had commenced a brisk firing but not within view of us. Climbing over banks to a village on an eminence called Subijana de Alava we came within cannon shot of the French. One approach was so open to the range of their guns that we were saluted with a peal of artillery that did immediate execution upon a soldier of the 28th and cut his head completely from his shoulders leaving his body prostrate on the ground before us, unsoiled with blood. Lieut. Bridgland, our Adjutant, stopped a moment to look at him, and informed by a sergeant of his name observed that the worst man in the Regiment had been the first struck; the same shot took effect upon the shoulder of an officer of the 39th and his mild and amiable countenance was turned to us without exhibiting any symptoms of suffering, though the wound was too severe a one to hope he could long survive. As it was advisable not to remain longer than we could help thus exposed, Colonel Belson who commanded us led the Regiment for present shelter behind the village church, which was on the slope of the hill, and encompassed with beautiful cornfields with the grain then nearly ready for the sickle, and divided, as I had never before seen in this country, with hedges. From this post, as we were required, each Company moved to the front, and occupied the narrow lanes and banks within musket shot of the French.

Captain Meacham, with that to which Lieut. Moore and I belonged, took in turn our places on the line of action, but from the field in our front few shots were fired, and the Frenchmen kept themselves well concealed from us. It is a saying that 'every bullet has its billet' and we had not been there five minutes before one whistled past my ear and penetrated the cap of the sergeant by the side of me. Luckily the height of it permitted its passage without going through his head; such escapes we continued to experience during this long and oft suspended action. Yet I found nothing more remarkable than the rapid flight of time. The day was the finest that ever shone from the Heavens. Towards one and two o'clock the fire so slackened that we supposed the action was over, but no change took place in our position, nor did the 28th advance until suddenly at last, when the enemy had fled, from the battle being won, on the French line being turned, by the left wing of our army. Then immediately we scampered over hedges and fields to a road, where the French had been stationed, and where the 14th Light Dragoons under Col. Hervey (a very gallant officer who had in a former battle lost his left arm) had been ordered up to follow them. The high pinnacles upon which our Division was placed during the battle gave us a decided advantage in the view it commanded of the whole field as we now moved forward and the splendid sight of it became fully displayed to us. Yet it was very tantalising, for had the treasures of a hundred palaces been turned out upon the plains, it could not have exceeded the multitude of things to be seen in all directions scattered about, and in the midst of them the whole of our cavalry force at full gallop, and all the infantry Regiments that had been engaged advancing together in line.[1]

We were now mere spectators of the scene, the grandeur of which was lost in the contemplation of the spoils. Sir Rowland as he galloped off after surveying it cried out "Never mind 28th, you shall have your share of it yet," but the 6th Division which had just arrived after a long day's march, and hadn't fired a shot, came into the field quite at the nick of time for the good things. We moved only a few miles further that night in the pursuit; in the morning Alexander came to seek his quarters in the camp upon a fine horse laden with all manner of things picked up. He had been struck in the hip, but the ball fortunately intercepted by his sash, the wound was less serious than might have been expected, and he came to join us once again.

Some of our drummers made a rich harvest, and one little fellow entered the camp (who was only big enough to play upon the triangle) mounted on a French General's charger with holsters and bags of valuable commodities. The spirit that prevailed in this battle between the French and English was of the most chivalric kind, and admitted of mutual good feelings when it was over.

The Frenchmen we found wounded were carefully removed into the high roads where they might be soonest found by our Surgeons. After a brief suspension of exertion we followed Jordan's routed Army and arrived in a few days within sight of Pamplona. Defiling down the sides of a mountain, this fortified city presented a most formidable appearance, in the centre of a plain; and here we expected many broken heads, but Lord Wellington escaped this necessity by the French not having left supplies in it, and he determined to blockade it (that is, encompass them with troops to starve them out). And for this purpose employed a part of the Spanish Army, and we pursued our route to the Pyrenees, the French whilst retiring before us, showing the bitterness of their wrath against the Spaniards after their late defeat — houses being left in ashes, and their blackened walls indicating the utter ruin of villages and places they passed through. Without much further resistance we had now the satisfaction to drive them into their own territories, and took up a position at Roncesvalles, a pass of these mountains where we halted.

You will be glad my dear Mother to do the same after this long description, and as I intend to enclose a letter with this to my Father, giving an account of our subsequent battles, I will change the theme.

You would be much pleased to take a peep from the window (for I have one only, with glass doors) of my apartment here, on the second floor. The gay company assembled at the Bull fight in this square would have amused you more than the diversion itself, which is very cruel to the animals, infuriated to resist a few Cavaliers, dressed up like Rope Dancers at Astley's theatre, and armed at all

---

[1] The image of long lines of advancing British infantry is one of the more enduring of the Peninsular War and was probably the greatest tactical difference between the two armies. Indeed, the British line continually triumphed over the French column from the early days of the war, at Vimeiro, and was still doing so some eight years later at Waterloo. The best recent study of tactics can be found in Brent Nosworthy's *Battle Tactics of Napoleon and his Enemies*, London, 1995.

points to attack them. Palisades enclosed the whole space, with a fine band of musicians in light blue uniform placed at one end. The Spanish ladies give an interest to these amusements by their presence — and my attention was drawn to the applause they bestowed — and their pretty faces half veiled by their mantillas upon the balconies around. I sighed to think I could not participate in their mirth at the drolleries of a set of clowns, similar to those in the circle at Astley's. I am endeavouring to acquire some knowledge of the language as a preparatory step to their good graces. I live extremely well here — their bread is very peculiar and good, of as fine a grain as our pound cakes, in flat loaves of about the size of a circular frying pan. Their chocolate is exquisite, and their mode of dressing rice worthy of our imitation, having the finest spices and making use of a profusion of ground cinnamon.

I have an excellent serving man named Robert, who has a sister a lady's maid in Grosvenor Square, and he is very careful, and attentive to all my wants. And I never was in better health. This is encouraging news to go to sleep upon, and I hope you will have pleasant dreams about me. Pray think of me often, and when at leisure indulge me with a letter from you. And believe me, Dear Mother to be Yours most affectately, W.T. Keep.

Chapter Six
Over the Pyrenees

Wellington's victory over the French at Vittoria effectively broke the back of the French army in the Peninsula and there would be little doubt as to the eventual outcome of the war now. Indeed, such was the decisive nature of the battle that Napoleon sought to suppress its news from reaching the ears of the Austrians and Prussians who were dithering and playing a waiting game at the Congress of Prague following the armistice of Plaswitz. However, steps were taken to inform the Allied powers of Wellington's victory and sure enough, on July 12th, news reached them which, of course, had the desired effect. Upon the expiry of the armistice, Austria immediately declared war once again which allowed the waiting Wellington to resume his march towards France.

The battle of Vittoria was a crushing blow to the French campaign in the Peninsula. Indeed, Napoleon was moved to appoint a new commander to try and restore the shattered morale of his soldiers. The new man was Marshal Nicholas Soult, Duke of Dalmatia, the man who had harried and hustled Sir John Moore's army out of Spain some three and a half years earlier. The task set before Soult was perhaps the most daunting to be set before any of Wellington's adversaries in the Peninsula. For not only was he ordered to pull the threads of Joseph's defeated army together again but he was, in effect, entrusted with the defence of the sacred soil of France. Soult was to remain in command until the end of the war in April 1814, during which time he proved himself a worthy but largely ineffective adversary to Wellington. Soult was a master of logistics and a superb planner. His main drawback was, however, that he was often unable to carry out the ingenious plans which he himself had devised.

Soult's first task in Spain was to restore the morale of the French army which had been shattered on June 21st at Vittoria. Soult was no great commander on the battlefield but he was a fine organiser of troops and Wellington's march into France was far from easy. Perhaps it was the prospect of entertaining British troops on French soil that drove Soult's men to greater efforts but whatever the reason, Soult managed to get his troops into some sort of fighting force before squaring up to Wellington's victorious legions which were advancing relentlessly into the passes of the Pyrenees. It was here, from these lofty peaks, that Wellington's men, after almost five years of hard fighting, finally gazed out across the green, rolling landscape of southern France. Amongst them was William Thornton Keep and it was in the Pyrenees, at Maya, that he found himself in one of the hottest little actions of the war during which he was to save one of the Colours of the 28th Regiment. He resumes his story two weeks afterwards.

Vittoria
10th August 1813

My dear Father,

It was with much pleasure I put pen to paper to describe to my Mother my lucky escapes with a whole skin, after our late engagement with the enemy here — a day of arduous toil to our Regiment which was employed for several hours in skirmishing, a kind of service for which we were not so well adapted as Riflemen would have been, our bright red jackets being too palpable a mark for the French in their dark clothing.[1] The consequence was that we suffered severely but our Division maintained its position against the continued reinforcements supplied to the enemy to resist us, and thus drew off upon ourselves their best troops from other parts of their line, where our brave companions succeeded in turning their flank and secured the victory. We then pursued the French to the Pyrenees, passing Pamplona, and arrived on the beautiful wooded heights of Roncesvalles, from whence after a few days we proceeded to the pass of Maya in the valley of Bastan, another road leading to France through these intricate defiles, where we enjoyed some respite from our more active duties and took possession of its green pastures. The soldiers' joys after fatiguing service are at best but of short duration, and Bonaparte sent his ablest General Soult[2], to command the French army, one Division of which under the Count D'Erlon[3], was on the other side of this mountain pass at which we were stationed. Sir Rowland and the Count had

---

[1] The riflemen of the 95th Rifles and the 5/60th wore green uniforms which were well suited to their role as skirmishers, as were the brown uniforms of the Portuguese cacadores who frequently operated alongside their more famous comrades of the 95th. These regiments were armed with the magnificent Baker rifle, slower to load than the ordinary India pattern musket but far more accurate. The role of skirmishing was not confined to these regiments, however. Each British line battalion had at least one light infantry company which was used in a similar role. Quite often several companies of light infantry were banded together to form a light battalion, although this did not happen too often in the Peninsula. The role of the British light infantry is examined in Gates' *The British Light Infantry Arm*, London, 1987.

[2] Marshal Nicholas Jean de Dieu Soult (1769-1851) was an able strategist but a relatively poor commander of troops in the field. He had a distinguished career and had risen from the rank of private in 1785 to become a marshal of France in 1804. He drove Moore out of Spain in 1809 but was in turn driven from Portugal by Wellesley in May 1809 at Oporto. Prior to his appointment in 1813 as Commander of the Army of Spain he had served in Andalucia and had seen action around Cadiz, and Seville as commander of the French Army of the South from 1810 to 1812. His greatest battle during this period was the bloodbath at Albuera on May 16th 1811. He later served as Napoleon's chief of staff at Waterloo.

[3] General Jean-Baptiste Drouet, Count D'Erlon (1765-1844) had seen much action during the Napoleonic Wars including the battles of Austerlitz and Friedland. He was sent to the Peninsula in 1810 as commander of the French IX Corps and subsequently fought in many of the war's major battles. He later fought at Waterloo where he commanded Napoleon's 1st Corps.

occasion to be in frequent communication[1]. Our trespasses and other causes being the subject of them, for now that we had come within the immediate vicinity of France, many constant depredations were unavoidable.

The peasantry here are called Bascoes, and are a race of very supple limbed men, who traverse these wilds with habitual activity, and give great life to the country hereabouts. Though our camp was chiefly in the valley, the tents of some other regiments were perched upon verdant spots half up the mountain.[2] For three or four weeks the intercourse kept up between all assembled in this position made us forgetful of any interruption occurring to disturb our tranquillity. The rest of the army were distributed at long distances from us upon other parts of these mounts and the cross paths from one to another were of difficult attainment. Thus shut up by ourselves, no better enjoyment could have been desired — if it had continued uninterrupted.

The country people, to whom at first we were such great strangers, seemed to assume their holiday apparel when better acquainted with us, with the happiest blooming faces. They are said to be descendants from the Welsh, and their language is quite unintelligible, not only to us but to most of the Spaniards, whom they do not at all resemble, their complexions being unremarkably fair and features thoroughly English. Our little marketing transactions brought us much together, and all our men being well behaved, and officers disposed to be most friendly, proposed them evidently greatly in our favour. With these cheerful people, and our own cheerful pursuits, and the constant life and bustle in these pleasant valleys, enlivened with our bands, and echoing with our bugles, and our enjoyments in camp, we could scarcely believe we were at the foot of the rugged Pyrenees. At intervals however we ascended the steep paths, and climbed the cloud-capped acclivities to enjoy a peep at France, and discern with our telescopes our distant enemies. Here we sometimes came upon our advanced picquets, and seemed to breathe another air, with the silent and deserted French valleys immediately beneath us. The Highlanders[3] of our Division were on watch here, and observed no changes or movement in the enemy, but at the end of the third week an alarm was one morning given. Three large minute guns were fired (according to preconcerted arrangement) and we toiled in haste to the top, expecting an attack from the enemy, but when we arrived it proved a false alarm.

---

[1] Communication between opposing commanders was nothing unusual in the Peninsula. Indeed, Wellington himself frequently found himself corresponding with French commanders, usually relating to matters concerning the exchange of prisoners of war. Much of this goes back to the spirit of 'live and let live' which existed between the British and French. There was a time and a place for killing each other but neither side saw any profit to be gained from the killing of the odd sentry or piquet. This is not to say that it did not happen but the relationship between British and French was much warmer than that which existed between French and Spanish, for example, the latter having an absolute hatred of the French after enduring years of occupation.

[2] Tents were not issued to Wellington's infantry until March 1st 1813. They were issued at the rate of 3 per company and were carried on the mule which had previously carried the large camp kettle. This was replaced by the much lighter tin camp kettle also on March 1st 1813. (See Ward's *Wellington's Headquarters*, pp.200-201.)

[3] The Scottish battalion in the 2nd Division was the 1/92nd.

Exactly that very day week however, on Sunday the 25th July, at about eleven o'clock, when we had formed a square for Divine Service, the guns from above in three heavy admonitory peals apprised us once more of their real approach.[1]

You must remember that we were left quite to ourselves, with no hope of immediate aid, at the force of the French, be what it might. Every man therefore was put into the ranks that we could muster, and yet our whole strength amounted to only two Brigades. With all the speed we could use we ascended again these steep hills upon hills to the summit, where we found the 92nd Highlanders had struck their tents, and were seated on the mountain brow, until their services were wanted in front. A brisk firing had commenced, and was becoming more sharp and continued, and we advanced with increased alacrity, leaving the 92nd where they were, and took up, under the command of Col. Belson, a position well secured on one side from approach. It was a level piece of ground extending like a promontory, and covered with short grass, without any trees or bushes, but having here and there pinnacles of rock rising to the height of 12 or 14 feet.[2]

The peculiarity of it was, that it did not admit of our line being formed except at a right angle from the true front, so that only as the French advanced on a platform on the other side, the ravine dividing us, could we come into action with them. There was no means of changing this position, awkward as it was, and we had therefore no alternative but to keep our eyes right (as men in the houses on one side of a narrow street might be supposed to do, expecting an enemy to enter at the end of it).

Though the firing from small arms was increased, and approaching very close, we were left for about a quarter of an hour without a single object in sight. The depths of the ravines of these mountains is often very great, though as frequently very narrow; this was so, and a somewhat wider platform, but level like our own, was opposite us, and at the extremity of it a small hill, which shut out every thing beyond it from our view. For the few minutes therefore of that quarter of an hour, we remained in anxious expectation of what might occur, but quite alone, and within a stone's throw of that little hill I have mentioned, to which all eyes were now directed.

Our consternation you may imagine, when we perceived heads suddenly rising above it from the other side — and the 34th Regiment retreating most rapidly. At this juncture the 92nd was advancing on the platform to which the 34th descended. They ran for shelter to the Highlanders who could only form in

---

[1] Four Portuguese guns, under Major Cunha, had been positioned to the west of the main road which runs over the Col de Maya with orders to fire in the event of a French advance. The alarm was duly given at about 11.30am, just when Cameron's Brigade, the 92nd, 50th and 71st, was preparing for Divine Service. These four guns were later lost when the French overran the pass. Two were rolled down into a ravine and were later recovered. They were the only guns 'lost' by Wellington in the entire war.

[2] This 'level piece of ground', as Keep calls it, is easily discernible today. It lies to the east of the track which runs through the Col de la Zurrela and forms the southern end of the ravine which lies to the south of the Aratesque hill, on which Sherer's piquet was positioned. The rocks lie towards the end of the spur while the ledge from which some of the 28th opened fire is just forward of the rocks. Keep would have had a superb grandstand view of the fighting as the French came on from right to left in front of him.

separate wings from want of room. As soon as the French appeared following them, our fire opened, though at first in a very slanting direction and with difficulty, friends and foes were so mingled. The 92nd, a very fine strong Regiment, who would no doubt have come to the charge had the ground permitted, and for a time would certainly have repulsed the Frenchmen — who now found they had only two Regiments to oppose them and knew they had a dozen at least coming forward in their rear. In this confined space in which we were all enclosed a woeful tragedy directly ensued. Poor Lieut. Day of the 34th (our Duke in the Honey Moon) was killed while rallying his men in sight of us, but the volleys of the 92nd strewed the smooth green turf of that little hill with the French that fell before them. To fire with greater precision some of our men had descended to a ledge running along the edge of the ravine. Here I stood at the station of the company I belonged to, and with Col. Belson and the Honble Major Mullins by the side of me in a state of inactivity, and merely looking on. Captain Meacham was wounded, having been firing from the ledge (very few officers make use of the musket) and having actively retreated between our legs to the rear. At this moment Mr Bridgland's voice called for me to the Colours, and I proceeded directly there and found that poor Delmar had been shot through the heart.

In the confusion of the moment a mistake had been made, and Mr Hill, being junior to me, should have been called. This the Adjutant discovered, and I returned to my company. But I had not been long there when a second call was made for me, and I found that Hill had been struck in the breast similar to Delmar, and carried away. (Luckily in the hurry of his movements, Hill had thrust his handkerchief in the bosom of his coat, and this repulsed the ball and saved his life.)[1] I now took the fatal Colour, and entered into conversation with Ensign Tatlow, bearing the other.

The description he gave me of what had happened to our friends was whilst the action was going on, for these battles are slowly performed. I had leisure even to think of Delmar's watch, and requested Alexander to enquire for it, that it might be preserved for his family at home. The loud greetings that saluted my ears between our busy combatants now attracted my attention, and my eyes were turned to the fierce contention going on (which nothing impeded, for the smoke rolled away immediately over head). Many shouts were sent across this narrow ravine in mutual support of each other, such as 'Well done, 28th, Bravo 92nd' etc. The French were checked in their progress at the foot of the hill, and several Highlanders were unfolding their blankets to convey away wounded comrades

---

[1] This incident is also mentioned by Cadell. 'Early in the action, a fine young man, Delmar, of the 28th, while carrying the colours, was shot through the heart by a French sharpshooter. Ensign Hill, seeing the colours fall, instantly ran and took them up, exclaiming at the same time that, "the colours of the 'slashers' should never want a person to display them to the enemy." He had scarcely spoke, when the same Frenchman, having reloaded, hit him in the same place as poor Delmar. Fortunately for Hill, he had a handkerchief in his breast, which saved him; the ball passed through his coat, waistcoat, thirteen folds of the handkerchief, and his shirt, giving him a severe contusion in the breast; he suffered from spitting blood for a long time afterwards.' (Cadell, *Narrative*, p.165.)

without any hurry being shown[1]. But as the numbers of the enemy increased, they made another effort to advance. A very gallant French officer was leading them, but he was struck to the ground where he was still waving his cocked hat. I became very much interested in the result and my attention so absorbed in it that I did not observe what was passing behind me.

The enemy had been busy surrounding us, and the Regiment had been forced instantly to flight and had left me there. A young French conscript levelled his piece at me within 20 paces, with a smiling countenance, intimating that I must surrender. A violent zeal seized me to preserve the Colours, not caring for my life, and I turned immediately and pitched myself headlong down the ravine, grasping most tightly the staff. Through bushes and briars I rolled, and scrambled, hearing shots after me. The exertion was such as under other circumstances would have been impossible. Rough stones rattled down with me, and it was some time before I put my feet to the ground, and then I set off again in the right direction. After a rapid race I was relieved from my anxiety by the shouts of a Sergeant of the 28th who waved his arm to guide my steps, and I had at last the satisfaction to join the Regiment then in close column, and preparing to move off.

Col. Belson and the officers were highly rejoiced to see the Colours again, which they feared were lost, and I fell into the ranks to bear them away on our retreat. So far Marshal Soult's object in the relief of Pamplona was achieved. He had with overwhelming numbers forced the pass of Maya, but the fortress he was proceeding to was still a long distance in front. To increase his difficulties probably we chose the most mountainous road to retreat by.[2]

---

[1] The 92nd fought like demons on the heather-topped ridge at Maya which must have reminded them of their Scottish homeland. Just 400 of them held up the French advance before they were pushed back by sheer weight of numbers. George Bell, serving with the 34th Foot, in an oft-quoted passage wrote, 'The 92nd were in line pitching into the French like blazes, and tossing them over. They stood there like a stone wall overmatched by twenty to one, until half their blue bonnets lay beside those brave northern warriors. When they retired, their dead bodies lay as a barrier to the advancing foe. O! but they did fight well that day. I can see the line now of the killed and wounded stretched upon the heather, as the living retired, closing to the centre.' (Bell, *Soldier's Glory*, p.83.)

[2] The battle had been a particularly fierce one, fought over a bare ridge not more than fifty yards wide. A more spectacular battlefield can hardly be imagined, with the beautiful valley of the Baztan to the south and the low, undulating hills of southern France to the north with the Atlantic in the distance. D'Erlon had attacked in two columns, one by the Aratesque hill, on which was positioned Sherer's piquet, and the other by the main road which ran over the Col of Maya. The 92nd and 50th bore the brunt of the fighting until Pringle's brigade, the 28th, 34th and 39th, got up from the valley of the Baztan below. These troops were exhausted by their efforts to reach the ridge, however, and after initial resistance were pushed back into the valley. D'Erlon's troops finally managed to drive Cameron's brigade from the pass but only after some severe fighting. The resistance did, however, allow Barnes' brigade of the 7th Division to get across from Echellar and it arrived in time to fall upon the left flank of Maransin's division just as it was about to push down the main road towards Elizondo. The pass remained in French hands with losses to the British of 1,484, the French losing around 2,000. The historian of the Pyrenees campaign later wrote, 'And so the long summer day wore itself out. Night fell and the bivouac fires of both sides shone out on that Pyrenean

Night was approaching when we set out, and by the time we reached the first town on the route it was quite dark. The news of our disaster and the threatened arrival of the French added to the number of fugitives, many of all ranks, and some natives, being forced to pack up and accompany us. For you have no conception how many followers are indispensable to an army in the field.

No rest or refreshment had passed our lips since 11 in the morning and we now set out to march all night. Long trains of bullock cars and mules coming with supplies intercepted us as we moved on as rapidly as we could, but still at a slow pace. Ascending the vast Sierra of Mountains that extend to Pamplona we found ourselves at every point on the road blocked up by a crowd of obstacles to our progress. General Sir William Stewart had been most active during the contest to resist the French at other points with our 2nd Brigade and what other troops he could collect, but all in vain, and many of these came on our line of march to join in the retreat. Our men began to fall into disorder, being unable to preserve their ranks. Cattle were slaughtered in the road, and they helped themselves to great pieces hastily cut off and stuck bleeding at their bayonet's points. It was the darkest of nights, but pine branches flaming in the hands of a few afforded some assistance when jumbled together thus, and these were often the bearers of litters with wounded officers mixed with men bearing bundles, or children on their shoulders, accompanied by the soldier's wives in great distress (I must tell you that Col. Belson had given them all the drummers spoils at Vittoria and some of them were consequently rich in the estimation of their own property). The French it is probable were desirous enough to get back all they could. At all events they were close at our heels, so that we were forced to move as quickly as possible. About midnight poor Tatlow dropped with fatigue at the side of the road, and I was not much better able to proceed.

Thick clouds charged with heavy rain now began to pour down upon us, and when on the highest parts of the mountains we met a train of cars coming with barrels of rum and wine. These could only add to our calamities, for the men soon found it out, and some officers there ordered them all to be hurled down the dark and deep declivities, where notwithstanding some desperate men followed them and were lost in the abyss beneath, and where I dare say they got immediately drunk and remained. You may judge how completely we were exhausted, from our tongues being so glued to our mouths that not a word could be spoken, and a silent shake of the hand given as the only tokens of farewell to such as fell behind and had to await the tender mercies of the French Dragoons who very unceremoniously on these occasions cut and slash the poor unfortunates who come in their way, and it is not unusual for dispirited men to commit suicide, and blow their own brains out rather than fall in their hands.

---

ridge which, to those who know its history, must ever be sacred ground. For there on that day hundreds of brave and gallant men of both nations had fought their last fight and take their long rest beneath its grassy slopes.' (Beatson, *With Wellington in the Pyrenees*, p.123.) Beatson's is by far the best account of the Pyrenees campaign. Good eye-witness accounts of the fight at Maya can be found in Bell's *Soldier's Glory*, pp.82-84, Sherer's *Recollections*, pp.256-260, Patterson's *Adventures*, pp.324-335, Cadell's *Narrative*, pp.162-167 and Robertson's *Journal*, pp.107-111.

About this time, the most welcome sound that could salute our ears was given to halt. I resigned my charge to my Colour Sergeant and staggered forward to a bank by the side of a tree, where I directly rested my legs, and was left in the dark. Dreadfully fatigued, but not drowsy, my attention was soon attracted to a scene very remarkable.

A small kind of amphitheatre was here formed by the hand of nature, round which others less tired it seemed than myself were striving to get a light, the puffing and blowing that followed the flashes from their musket pans set many competitors at work, and long and anxious were the moments expended to obtain the desired flame. But when it was effected a majestic tree was selected, to the dry bark of which it was instantly applied. I sat motionless to observe the progress of this fire, until like a red hot sentry box it sent forth a great heat. I was wet through with perspiration from my previous exertions as well as the rain, and my limbs were now so still I could not easily move. I crawled therefore on my hands and knees to a large circle of men in front of it to dry my clothes. The ground around this bright furnace was already quite dry, and covered with embers and withered leaves, and whilst I was resting upon my elbow casting my eyes around you may conceive my astonishment to find they were all conversing very composedly in French. A group of finer officers, about twenty, I never saw. They were attired in handsome uniform, and appeared quite unfatigued. At first the extreme exhaustion of my bodily powers led me to suppose my mind was disordered, and that this was a mere fantasy. I looked around for my friends of the 28th but none were to be seen. My companions were all French. Whilst for a few minutes in this state of amazement, our bugle sounded, and it gave me strength to jump up. I rushed to the tree from whence I had proceeded, and got on the rugged road, and was again in darkness, but met my Sergeant, of whom I immediately learnt that these men were the Chasseurs Britanniques, a French Regiment in our 7th Division, and adherents of the Bourbons.[1] They had been ordered up to our assistance, had come too late, and had halted on one side of our path, while the 28th were on the other.

Continuing next morning our retreat through these mountain fastnesses, we arrived at an open but narrow valley with a streamlet to ford, and rising ground on the opposite bank affording an advantageous position to oppose the French. The 28th ascended this eminence, and here we came to a temporary halt of about an hour. Sir Rowland Hill dismounted among us, and at a point jutting forward seated himself to reconnoitre with his telescope, in which he continued long and anxiously employed. The French were now collecting below within pistol shot of

---

[1] The Chasseurs Britanniques was one of the foreign units which served in Wellington's army. Consisting chiefly of Swiss, Italian and Polish deserters, and with an officer corps consisting largely of disaffected French royalists, the unit was not to be relied upon and with its appalling rate of desertion it is not surprising that Wellington gave instructions that they were never to be allowed on piquet duty. Nevertheless, the unit did have its better moments and at Fuentes de Onoro, on May 5th 1811, the regiment acquitted itself well with some well directed musketry which saw off Montbrun's cavalry, an action which Wellington mentioned in his despatch to Lord Liverpool. (*Despatches*, Wellington to Lord Liverpool, 8th May 1811, VII, 530.)

us — but a mutual understanding suspended hostilities and the most perfect silence prevailed at this picturesque spot.

Our attention was fixed in the direction of Sir Rowland's spyglass where we beheld the French army defiling very leisurely in their loose greatcoats, cross belts and fur caps, and winding down amidst the rocks and trees to follow our footsteps. Conjectures during this silent survey were being formed, of their numbers, now increasing into a dense column, quite close beneath us. At length Sir Rowland arose, and gave the order to move on again, being probably of opinion that their force was too great to be resisted.[1] For two days more we continued this harassing retreat but on the morning of the third day we were roused from a deep sleep we were enjoying, worn out with our fatigues, by an order to stand to our arms. At this moment the Brigade Major rode up to our Adjutant requiring an officer immediately from our Regiment to conduct the wounded to the rear. Lieut. Bridgland took out his pocket book, and found I was next on the roster for this duty, and I accompanied him to the place where they were collected on bullock cars, wrapped up in their blankets, with their caps and accoutrements on the upright poles of these clumsy vehicles, the wheels of which are of solid wood and make a dismal creaking — the more so with such a burden placed upon them. By slow degrees we proceeded into the open plains on the high roads to Vittoria. My servant attended me, and had obtained a fowl, which he boiled, and with a Spanish loaf and some good wine I was refreshed upon this slow journey. In the meanwhile great events were occurring.

Lord Wellington had received early intimation of our retrograde movements, and had made his dispositions accordingly, so that when Soult arrived in sight of Pamplona, he perceived to his dismay that his Lordship had drawn up four Divisions of his Army to oppose his progress.[2] This was the momentous battle of the Pyrenees that took place on the 28th July, whilst I was moving slowly onward

---

[1] In fact, D'Erlon did very little to follow up his success at Maya. He remained at the Col de Maya whilst Darmagnac marched south into the valley of the Baztan as far as Elizondo, Hill's former headquarters.

[2] Whilst the fighting at Maya had been in progress on July 25th, a second French attack took place to the south-east, at Roncesvalles. Here, Lowry Cole, commanding 13,000 men of his 4th Division, was attacked by two strong enemy columns under Clausel and Reille numbering 20,000. As at Maya the fighting was fierce and the British forced to give ground but only after a prolonged struggle. During the late afternoon a thick mist came down, bringing the fight to an end. Unfortunately, Cole lost his nerve and, fearing the French might take advantage of the cover to get round his right flank, he drew his men off and retreated south in the direction of Pamplona. He duly wrote to Wellington, informing him of this course whereupon the latter sent an urgent letter to Cole, with orders that he was to halt at Zubiri where there was a good defensive position. Indeed, Picton was already there but the order arrived too late and the two nervous generals continued south as far as Sorauren, giving up much ground to the enemy, much to Wellington's dismay. Little wonder, therefore, that he was moved to write, 'All the beatings we have given the French have not given our generals confidence in themselves and in the exertions of their troops. They are really heroes when I am on the spot to direct them, but when I am obliged to quit them they are children.' (Wellington, quoted in Fortescue, *History of the British Army*, IX, pp.255-256.)

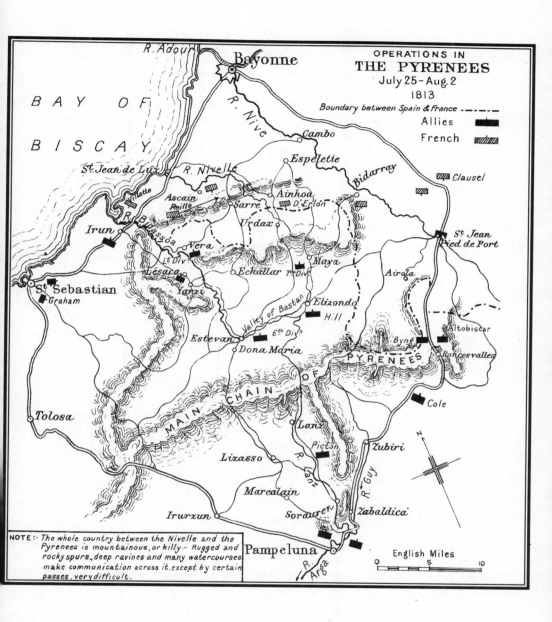

OPERATIONS IN
THE PYRENEES
July 25 – Aug. 2
1813

Boundary between Spain & France ──·──·──
Allies
French

R. Adour
Bayonne
BAY OF
BISCAY
R. Nive
Cambo
Espelette
St Jean de Luz
R. Nivelle
Bidarray
Clausel
Villatte
Ainhoa
Ascain
Reille
D'Erlon
Sarre
Urdax
St Jean
Pied de Port
Irun
R. Bidassoa
Vera
Lt Div.
Echallar
Maya
Airola
Lesaca
7th Div.
St Sebastian
Yanzi
Elizondo
Graham
Hill
Valley of Bastan
Estevan
6th Div.
Byng
Dona Maria
PYRENEES
Roncesvalles
Cole
Tolosa
MAIN
CHAIN
OF
Lanz
N
Picton
Zubiri
Lizasso
R. Lanz
R. Guy
Marcalain
Zabaldica
Irurzun
Sorauren
Pampeluna
R. Arga
English Miles
0   5   10

NOTE:- The whole country between the Nivelle and the
Pyrenees is mountainous, or hilly.- Rugged and
rocky spurs, deep ravines and many watercourses
make communication across it, except by certain
passes, very difficult.

with the wounded in the previous conflict and approaching so near the battlefield that some fear was entertained for our safety.[1]

A very fine unclouded day, with the sun burning hot on this dusty road, brought us to a village called Bario Plana in the British rear. At this place I had a sad and toilsome task to attend, with those already in charge, to the fresh claimants for assistance. The houses in this village were thrown open for the reception of the wounded coming from the field, and where our surgeons were collected. The first I had to assist in alighting wounded from his horse was our Brigade Major, with many other poor fellows, who were obliged to undergo immediate amputation, the further particulars of which I will not describe to you.

Eight officers of ours were killed or wounded at that fatal pass of Maya, and Major Bradby as well as Col. Paterson, wounded at Vittoria, I am sorry to think are not expected to recover.[2] Within a few days more I arrived here, and obtained a very good billet in this Depot for the wounded. Some here luckily are not desperate cases, with a Captain of ours among this number. I have just returned from a morning's ride to survey the ground where we were so hotly engaged, and it is something singular that we were opposed to the 28th Regiment in the French service on that occasion.[3]

The tranquil aspect of this sanguinary spot round the village we were the only tenants of — during that day — was quite in accordance with our melancholy feelings for the slain buried there. Some remnants were left distinguishable as belonging to our Regiment, but I am glad to say they had little to do in the last

---

[1] The battle of Sorauren is often called the battle of the Pyrenees, whereas in fact it was just one of three actions, Maya and Roncesvalles being the other two, that made up the battle of the Pyrenees. The fight at Sorauren took place over three days, July 28th-30th, although there was very little real fighting on the 29th. The two armies, commanded by Soult and Wellington respectively, were drawn up on two very steep ridges, with the French making a succession of attacks on the Allied ridge. These met with some success at first but were eventually beaten back by a combination of British and Portuguese musketry and bayonet charges. The morning of July 30th revealed the French to be moving off to the north whereupon Wellington turned his guns on them before launching his infantry to hand out another thrashing to the French. Soult's attempt to relieve Pamplona was thus thwarted and another battle honour added to the already long list of Allied triumphs in the Peninsula.

[2] Actual 28th casualties at Maya were one officer and 8 men killed, and 6 officers and 112 men wounded, while one officer and 31 men were reported missing, many of whom, like Keep, probably rejoined their unit during the night. Many, however, were taken prisoner. (For casualty figures at Maya see Beatson, *With Wellington in the Pyrenees*, p.299.)

[3] The French 28th of the Line formed part of Darmagnac's division. There were quite a few occasions in the Peninsula where British regiments met their numerical French counterparts, notably at Badajoz, where the British 88th (Connaught Rangers) fought the French 88th Regiment, and, more famously, at Arroyo dos Molinos where the 34th (Cumberland) Regiment took a number of prisoners, including the regimental band with drums and drum major, of the French 34th Regiment. Edward Fraser, in his *War Drama of the Eagles*, claims that the 28th Regiment captured the 'eagle' of the French 28th Regiment at Maya, a claim wholly unsubstantiated. There is certainly no record of such a feat and, indeed, Fraser himself gives no source for his claim. (See Fraser, *War Drama of the Eagles*, p.260).

battle to add to our long list of killed and wounded; this victory is considered one of the most masterly of his Lordship's achievements — by echelon movement of the other Divisions Soult's design to relieve the starving Pamplonians was completely defeated, and they have been driven back over that very pass from which we were forced to retreat before them, and our Regiment has now resumed its station, and with the next detachment in a few days I shall proceed to join them again.

God bless you my dear Father. I hope you will be pleased with the agreeable news this long letter contains, and believe me to be, Your affectate Son, W. T. Keep.

In a few moments I find we shall be again on the move, Heaven bless you, till I have next an opportunity of writing. Affectionate regards to all at home.

Pass of Maya
17th September 1813

My dear Samuel,

Promises are only fine things when performed — and I know you will not have forgotten mine to write to you, and will be anxious to hear often from me, now I am in the midst of such stirring scenes of events. My last letters were written at Vittoria, where I had arrived at a very apropos time to afford me rest, after our rapid marches and toils upon these mountains, at the foot of which we are now again stationed. Soult's defeat by Lord Wellington at Pamplona was a lucky event, for if he had succeeded in relieving it we must have laid siege to that formidable place, and perhaps altogether changed our alignment. I passed a few days very quietly at Vittoria in the company of the invalids after the battles fought, where many were getting on their legs again to resume their duties in the field, and I set out to join the Army with a detachment under Captain Baker of the 34th with a Lieut. Kerr Ross of the 92nd Highlanders and a Lieut. Myers of the 66th. By easy marches through Biscay, well supplied with good provisions to help us on our way, we reached a point affording the first glimpse again of the wide ocean. Since I had beheld it last, I had traversed the whole length of Spain to Portugal, not having once put foot in the stirrup, except at Vittoria to revisit the field of our engagement, and during the battle, when I was sent upon the Adjutant's horse, in a great haste to order up the ammunition. My legs therefore have done me good service, and I find myself very well cut out for a soldier in bearing privations. I threw many anxious glances upon that wide sea that separates us, and thought of days past, and wished you was with me at that pretty part of the coast where we had arrived. At a hamlet with a few houses we rested, after a pleasant day's march, and my active servant Robert got me a good dinner in a billet I went to by myself (as the Gents I was travelling with were strangers to me) and here I had paid some attention to my toilet and equipment, and sat down to it in a secluded farm house surrounded with orchards and orange trees. After this repast two very pretty girls, about 16 and 18, favoured me with their company — why or wherefore it was impossible to tell — their pretty tongues in the Basque language being quite unintelligible to me — as mine was to them. I was left entirely to guess who or what they were, but my eyes convinced me they were extremely attractive — modest behaved and well dressed. I must let you think me egregiously vain in saying more upon this unexpected favour than I would do with anybody else. These girls in this sequestered part of the coast it is to be supposed had never before seen Scotch soldiers in kilts, or red coats at all; their fancies were pleased perhaps at the sight of our first approach, and one under their roof was an object of such curiosity to them that they couldn't resist its gratification — still I was surprised to be left so entirely alone with them during the whole of this fine afternoon and evening. As we could not speak a single word to each other to be understood, you will wonder how we amused ourselves. There was nothing in the least giggling or silly about them — but it was all serious work in dumb show as far as conversation went. This will remind you of "Drink to me only with thine eyes and I will pledge with mine etc", but they did more, for they danced and sang to entertain me, having a tambourine for the music. (You must know, a chere amie is not unfrequent among us.) Dashing damsels accompanying some officers (one very much like a wife to a Captain of the 28th) came to request a peep at the bull fight at my billet in Vittoria. How this love making is brought about appeared difficult to imagine, until I came here, and found that signs only were required to be interpreted.

After the dance a large trunk was opened, and its manifold treasures of lady's apparel etc displayed to my wondering gaze with marks of trepidation, tender looks etc, which unluckily I could only meet with responsive nods of satisfaction, for it was totally impossible without the aid of speech to make any arrangement for elopements. Some tragic occurrences with proud relatives armed with stilettos I had heard of, these dangers however I might have disregarded. But marching with a detachment prevented the hope of escape from pursuers, so that on the next morning I was obliged to take an eternal farewell of my fair Biscayans. Had I stayed longer with them I think it very likely I should have been deeply enamoured. The chances to realise the blissful pictures imagination paints are so few that I was very sorry to be forced to leave them behind, and they so engrossed my thoughts that I scarcely noticed anything on our line of march till we reached the Pyrenees, and there I shook off my moody fits of despondency to join again my gay companions. Our losses here, and at Vittoria, had brought from our 2nd Battalion more of those who had fought in previous battles to encounter fresh perils, and by my promotion as Lieut I now belong to that Battalion again, with Alexander, Hill and others, but our Colonel seems to be disinclined to part with us yet and we are glad to remain with them for the present. These fine young soldiers, Lieuts Shelton, Gilbert and Clarke, have come to take the place of our Light Infantry officers killed — for poor Col. Paterson is dead, and Bradbey (this brave officer's relations lived at Southampton and were acquainted with Lord Cavan's family).

My messmate at Berry Head, poor Byrne, was killed at Vittoria, and many others have fallen victims to this long and desperate war. Bradbey's predictions in his letter I gave you an extract from when there, have been too truly and unfortunately verified in his own person. He commanded the Light Companies on the 25th July, in front of us, but I could only describe what I saw myself on that occasion in the position we were placed in. Since my return I often wander through the high fern upon the mountain tops here, and meet with skeletons bleaching in the wind, or mouldering there. I have heard that Delmar's remains could only be distinguished by a fragment of his shirt with his initials. Birds of prey and the elements soon reduce them to dust or to a state like dried mummies, with the body entire and bones loose in them. The beauties of nature are thus blended with objects terrible to contemplate.

We pass our time very agreeably, being encamped half way up the mountain in huts and tents, the officers strange to say being unsupplied with the latter, are forced to get them how they can. Sir William Stewart (who is extremely popular with the soldiers of all classes) one day riding past a road where Hill, Tatlow and I were in a hut built by our servants, and furnished with poor protection against the weather, he stopped his horse and enquired if that was the only accommodation we had. Upon our informing him it was, he told us to send to his quarters, where we should find a tent at our service. Returning thanks for his kindness, this we did, and obtained a very good one. But as the devil would have it, when we were attacked, our servants in the hour of retreat thought it best to hide it from the French in a field of Indian corn, from whence we found it had been taken on our return. A more surprising occurrence than this took place one day on the march, for whilst our Army was advancing in front an enterprising French cavalry officer in a defile upon the road came upon our baggage in the rear.

Col. Nixon, a very gallant officer of ours, was in charge of it, whose nerves were not liable to be unstrung at any time, when taken off his guard. An anecdote is told of him, giving good proof of this, at the recollection of which our officers often laugh. A hermit's cell, or Demon's abode (so called) in a deep cavern in a mountain pass, was spoken of as containing a giant few had the courage to remain in the presence of. Some well acquainted with the trick took Nixon to see him, and in a dark recess this formidable combatant they found seated with a large club in hand; by mechanic contrivance he was made to rise suddenly and wield this weapon. Most men started back at the least on this unexpected movement, but Nixon fell into a bold attitude of immediate defiance, not shrinking at all from the meditated blow. Yet on this occasion he was compelled to yield part of our baggage and that of the 14th Light Dragoons to the French. It was an unavoidable affair — most dextrously achieved. Our one eyed donkey escaped them with Nelson's and my traps.

Upon the heights of these towering mountains, after a fatiguing journey to ascend them, we spend hours in the enjoyment of the glorious prospects around us. The French dreading us no more than they need to, have left entirely their farms and homesteads, and nothing can surpass the lonely aspect of these dwellings, where the sheep and horses are untended in the valleys, grazing in the meadows, or feeding at the haystacks, and the poultry relapsing into a wild state, quite at freedom. These are strong temptations, not only to our men but to the bold Bascoes, and at first it was an act of daring to descend to them few could resist. Alexander and I went one day down, and opened gates that had ceased to admit the owners, and entered orchards for fruit which no footsteps had long visited. The fearful silence of these places is now often broken by the sharp report of musketry that reaches our ears when reclining on the turf above; for the French peasants have been getting more incensed daily at these trespasses. The consequence has been that several times a day, parties armed have been put in requisition to descend and bring marauders off in safety, and this has occurred so frequently that our men are now strictly forbidden to make such inroads on the enemy. Yet you may suppose all this has greatly tended to our diversion, and added interest to the strip we are engaged in. These mountains are very abundant in cherry trees, which seem to be in their proper element here. They shoot up like poplars, with long and straight branches, one of which makes a good dessert for a party after dinner. They are very fine, and much superior to any I ever saw in England.

Being desirous a few days ago to reach one on a pinnacle by the side of a precipice, I had a narrow escape of my life; for it was surrounded entirely with small stones, about the size of a walnut, and on approaching it, the whole body of them thus disturbed gave way, and rattled down like an avalanche, threatening to carry me with them. I never was in a more dangerous situation, and had great difficulty to extricate myself from it. Thick slabs of slate and stone lay on these mountain tops in some places, very handy to be rolled below, and it is curious to watch their descent into the deep chasms when sent edgeways from the brink of the precipices, cutting the trees to pieces in their fall with hollow reverberations.

The course of events in this war with Bonaparte appears yet on the defensive, and Engineers have been busy on the slopes of the mountain paths constructing little fortifications called Block Houses. It was my turn of duty lately to be posted in one of them with Captain D'Arcy of the 39th (the same Gent who played Lampedo in the Honey Moon) and here we were much more seriously employed, though the chance of the French advancing again was not very great — but the wooden tower we were shut up in (formed of the trunks of trees driven into the earth in a circle with platforms and loop holes to fire through, with a garrison of 30 men) was provided with sufficient annoyances in case they did so. The whole floor of the interior was a magazine of combustibles, consisting of shells we were ordered to roll down should the French attempt to advance by that path, and merely covered with bullocks' hides, one imprudent spark falling here must have blown us to atoms. D'Arcy and I were left to get through as well as we could our 48 hours' sojourn at this post, and so gentlemanlike and pleasant a companion made them pass quick enough. Indeed our routine of duties is not devoid of interest, and time seldom flags. At the picquet station in front of us, you may imagine me at morning's dawn going with the relief, leaving the camp far behind, and from the tops of these mounts winding down the long descent on the French side of them, but halfway only, to the still and forsaken valleys beneath, where our sentinels are placed, and where indeed we feel to be left alone. The fear of surprise at night keeps our eyes open (for lately a Portuguese picquet was bayoneted to a man being careless in their watch) not only therefore at the risk of life but with the importance of the command upon which the safety of the Army rests, are we forced to keep a sharp look out. To visit hourly sentries removed from sight, know the countersigns to give, clamber over rocks and precipitous paths with no light but the stars over head to guide one's steps, are anxious duties to perform. Well repaid however by a return to camp, where like families full of domestic cares you would laugh at our contrivances, to furnish a breakfast or dinner, get sugar, tea or butter. Stout women with baskets on their heads containing butter wrapped in fern come to sell it to us, and excellent it is, and some of our wags have good fun with them, making a dodge round the tents to perplex them, and answering their cry of 'Mantica' — the Spanish name for that desirable article. This is sport you would chime in with, on a fine sunny morning, and think it a very delightful picnic party to associate with. I have now been, I hope you will say, sufficiently descriptive of our pursuits.

The dear pretty cottage at home gives me pleasure to look at it, and fancy portrays all you have described to me in your last letter, and our little sisters running about in the garden there. Give kindest love to my dear Mother and all when assembled together, And believe me to be, Dear Sam, Your affectionate Brother, W.T. Keep.

Chapter Seven
The Nivelle and the Nive

William Thornton Keep next wrote to his mother when Wellington's army was firmly established upon French soil, having crossed the Bidassoa river, which marks the border between Spain and France, on October 7th 1813. The invasion of France had been a great success for Wellington, whose men crossed the Bidassoa near its mouth at the Bay of Biscay. Soult had a front of some sixteen miles to defend with just 47,000 men, barely enough to fight a major battle let alone defend such an extensive position. His main fear was that Wellington would move round his left flank and in so doing would pin the French against the sea. Believing this to be the case he neglected to defend the coastal section of his line in any great strength, believing it to be impassable. He was to be proved sadly mistaken and at dawn on October 7th the 1st and 5th Divisions of the Allied army, supported by units of Portuguese and Spanish troops, waded across the shallow river estuary and flushed the surprised defenders from their positions on the French side of the river. Further inland, the men of the Light Division attacked the enemy positions atop the Bayonet Ridge above Vera and by the end of the day, at a cost of around 800 casualties, Wellington's men found themselves standing on French soil at last.

Keeps division, the 2nd, played little direct part in the operation, save for a diversionary role, along with the 6th Division, which was intended to keep the French guessing as to where the invasion would really take place. The 2nd Division made demonstrations around Maya the 6th Division similarly at Roncesvalles, all the while teasing Soult's left flank.

Wellington consolidated his position on the right bank of the Bidassoa but could not turn his attention to a full-scale invasion of France until the French-held fortress of Pamplona surrendered. In the meantime, Soult retreated to the line of the river Nivelle, where forts and redoubts were constructed atop the hills that run along both banks of the river with the great mass of the dominating Rhune mountain as the key to the position. These forts were fairly formidable in places, such as the Signal redoubt above Sare, each representing a stiff climb for the Allied soldiers before they could actually get at the forts themselves. On October 25th the governor of Pamplona finally surrendered which gave Wellington the freedom to concentrate on the job in hand, namely the crossing of the Nivelle.

Ten days before this event William Thornton Keep was writing to his mother, keeping her abreast of events in the Peninsula. It was to be the prelude to an eventful six weeks which would see him fight his way across the border into France during the battle of the Nivelle and play a part in the next action of the war, the battle of the Nive. Keep's regiment, the 28th, played a significant part on the final day of this latter battle, officially called St Pierre. As we shall see, however, it was to be the last battle he fought in.

Puerto de los Aldudes (or the Doubts)
31st October 1813

My dearest Mother,

Since my last letter to Samuel, we have been so much shifted about, that I have not had time to write with any satisfaction to you. Our Brigade (now called the 2nd, and commanded by General Pringle) moved again to Roncesvalles and marched from thence on the 6th October to this Pass, which is 3 leagues from our old station, and one of the loftiest on this chain of mountains. Our attention has been confined to the possession of it, in a state of great uncertainty as to future operations, but the long meditated invasion of France is now about to take place. The English papers as you must have perceived, have been teeming with opinions upon it, conceiving Lord Wellington would never undertake it, and should he do so, presuming to predict it must terminate in the retreat if not destruction of his army etc. Every hillock and bush these prophets have told us, we shall find defended by the French peasantry, and our difficulties immense and insurmountable.[1] All this however will not prove sufficient to deter us from attempting it, and very soon too, but for the present we have been put into cantonments, in consequence of the inclemency of the weather. For upon the heights from which we have just descended you will be surprised to hear we were completely enveloped in snow. Such an event in our bivouacs demanded immediate exertion, and for some days we had good success in clearing it away. But a few nights after we had such a heavy fall of it that a new disaster occurred we were unprepared for, the weight of it having forced the poles through the canvass of the tents and down they came while we were sleeping. And the additional ones that had been served out with fresh supplies of blankets and grog were ineffectual to protect us from being frozen to death. Consequently we were removed in to the houses in this valley where the temperature is so different, that we are now very warm and comfortable and the more so in being billeted on this very hospitable people in this quiet vale. This is another most agreeable transition in the vicissitudes we have encountered, and we have made ourselves so at home here that we shall be reluctant to leave it again.

---

[1] On the contrary, Wellington's men found the French people to be fairly hospitable, once they were certain that they were not to be plundered or their villages burned as they might have expected. Wellington took great pains to ensure that the locals were not harmed in any way, issuing a number of General Orders to the effect. It is a mark of Wellington's determination that his operations were not to fall foul of any guerrilla movement, the like of which had dogged the French for the previous few years in Spain and Portugal, that he sent back over the Pyrenees some 20,000 Spaniards following a series of incidents where French properties had been burned and looted by them. The Spanish reaction, after years of similar treatment at the hands of the French invaders, is understandable but such revenge was beyond Wellington's tolerance.

Alexander and I are surrounded by young families of most amusing children, with whom it is our frequent pleasure to frolic. Think of my surprising these little Bascoes with "Fly away Jack", a marvel they never before beheld, and of course thought me a most expert conjurer, and Alexander teaching them our language, words of which these British descendants certainly pronounce as distinctly as we can. All this happens to the great satisfaction of the parents, as Alexander generally contrives to get something besides to regale them with being very fond of them and is even thinking of clothing them for he is as liberal as a prince with his money.

These domestic endearments incline us to forget the serious task yet in hand, for the state of European affairs it seems won't admit of the Campaign being closed with the approach of winter, as heretofore. Very audible whispers of hostile intentions soon to be put in play reach our ears, and bid us prepare for fresh conquests on the French soil, to which as yet we are such strangers. Our position now is somewhat like what it was at Coria, with this addition, that Spain is become almost as free from the French as Portugal was, except towards the East, where Lord William Bentinck is employed.[1]

The subject that I intended to put in the foreground of this letter I find is left to the last. You may easily conceive that it relates to the contents of your last letter, in which there is so much to regret and rejoice at. To condole with you on the loss of Lady Cavan is a painful task, because I know how greatly your happiness must be affected by it, next to the death of your dear Mother, the greatest you have met with in this world; yet you keep up your spirits my dear Mother, and believe there are other friends yet left, to appreciate your good qualities and afford consolation.

With respect to your sketch of my future fortunes, which I have read with such surprise and delight, what can I say adequate to my sensations? Can I encourage the hope of being thus rewarded for my toils in this Campaign? I should indeed be a fortunate fellow in that case. The pecuniary advantages would be no small defect to one so poor as I am. The crisis is now at hand, either to embrace this prospect opened to me, or see it for ever close and my name put upon the half pay list. But I still flatter myself if the war continues and his Lordship is employed, my chance is pretty good — Lord Kilcoursie, Duncombe, and Captain Harvey having left the service, and the death of poor Lambert are strange coincidences in my favour. Col. Belson has written to the Adjutant General about our return to the 2nd Battalion. What do you think of my getting leave of absence that I may be on the spot in case of Lord Cavan's appointment. At all events should his Lordship write to you about me, pray tell him that I am in expectation of being sent home,

---

[1] Sir William Bentinck had arrived at Tarragona on June 17th 1813 to assume command from the hapless Sir John Murray whose indecision there was to lead to his court martial in 1815, although he was acquitted of most of the charges. The operations along the east coast of Spain were never really more than a diversion despite some notable actions, such as Ordal and Castalla. Bentinck himself was apparently one of four names put forward by Lord Liverpool to act as Wellington's second-in-command in the Peninsula although he declined the offer as he was too pessimistic as to the eventual outcome of the war.

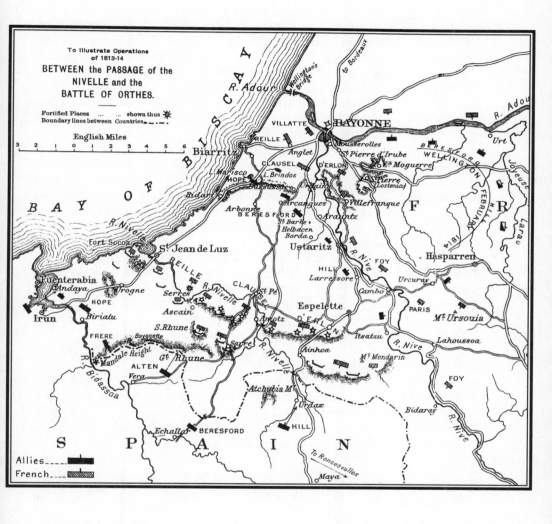

To Illustrate Operations
of 1813-14

BETWEEN the PASSAGE of the
NIVELLE and the
BATTLE OF ORTHES.

Fortified Places ... ... shown thus ✳
Boundary lines between Countries. _ . _ . _

English Miles
3 2 1 0 1 2 3 4 5 6

as I now properly belong to the Battalion in England. If I am appointed to his Lordship's Staff there will be no difficulty in recalling me from this country to join him, which you must understand could not be done if I belonged to the first Battalion while they are on service. I quite agree with you in thinking that Eaglehurst must have lost its attractions in the present state of his Lordship's mind, and that he will be anxious to seek relief by being actively employed somewhere. The command in India is just given to Lord Moira, but I see the Sussex District is vacant by the removal of Lord Chas Somerset to the Cape of Good Hope.

I suppose I shall eat my Christmas Dinner on this side of the water, and shall certainly now not have the opportunity before leaving Spain of gratifying my curiosity with the sight of Madrid, but I must inform you that the Spanish aspect of the country is quite altered, either by the elevation of the ground, or change in northern latitude, so that these Mountains are covered with turf, green as Dover cliffs, and other variations in climate make it very closely resemble our native land. I only just detain the enclosed, to pop in a few words more to embellish as it were the dear little Draft, and render the receipt of it more gratifying to you. I have this morning received it from our Paymaster, Mr Dewes, who I vanquished after a long encounter, in which he has proved himself a generous antagonist, having besides the said Draft, given me 5 guineas in gold.

I beg my dear Mother that you will make no reservation of it, to repay my debts, for I have still enough in arrears to pay those few myself, in the event of my getting leave to go home, when I shall receive an order payable on my arrival in England. Our army is now concentrated round this point of the coast, and communications opened with the ports here, so that we have a much speedier intercourse with England,[1] and receive most bountiful supplies of all that is essential to our operations, fresh troops constantly arriving, and the Spanish and Portuguese armies being united with us, no trifling obstacles will impede our entrance into France, particularly as Bonaparte has his hands too full with the allies in the north to send reinforcements.[2] The ardour of our soldiers are animated which tends likewise to promise good success; though I am sorry to say we have had some desertions to the French. I picked up a printed Bill lately, addressed in English to our men, offering great encouragement to it, and of money to be realised by skilful workmen in different trades at Paris, "a weak invention of the

---

[1] Once the French had been driven back over the Pyrenees Wellington was able to begin using the ports along the northern coast of Spain to land supplies. Bilbao, Santander and Passages were the principal ports. The speed at which supplies reached the army was further improved owing to the close proximity of the army to the coast, a far cry from the previous years when supplies, once landed at Lisbon, still had to be transported deep into the heart of the Peninsula. One of the best studies of the supply system can be found in Ward's *Wellington's Headquarters*, pp.66-101.

[2] Napoleon did indeed have his hands full when Keep wrote this letter. The French had been defeated at Grossbeeren (August 23rd), Katsbach (26th), Hagelburg (27th), Kulm (30th) and Dennewitz (September 6th). Napoleon's victory at Dresden on August 26th-27th did little to offset these defeats and worse was to come, on October 16th-18th, with his crushing defeat at Leipzig, the so-called 'Battle of the Nations'. Although the battle had been fought almost two weeks before Keep wrote his letter it would be a month before news reached the Allies.

enemy", that it is to be hoped will fall short of the mark it was destined to hit. A few prisoners is all the triumph the French have yet got from us, and those were taken at Maya, where we had such disadvantages to contend with.[1] They laid hold of Captain Irving of the 28th, and Sherer of the 34th[2] (our Rolando in the Honey Moon) and I should have been taken, if I had not had the Colours to save at all risqué. I have received a note lately from my old school fellow, Farmer, who is now a Lieutenant in the 95th, in another part of our lines, and hope to see him again on a nearer approach of our Divisions, when we enter France.

I am in the best health and spirits, and remain, My dear Mother, (with love to Sam and all at home) Your affectate Son, W. T. Keep.

N.B. The singular name of this place arises from its being a questionable point, whether in France or Spain.

Cantonments on the banks of the Nive, France
4th December 1813

My dear Mother,

Our late operations have occupied so much of my time and attention that although you have always engrossed a portion of my thoughts, I assure you this is the first moment I could well have availed myself of to commit them to paper.

I don't mean to say that I might not have written since the 31st October, the date of my last, or that you should suppose we have been marching and manoeuvring ever since that period, but we have been so unsettled that really I felt disinclined to give you an account of our movements. The comfortable house at which I was quartered in Aldudes did not prevent my being somewhat unwell there. Our doctors have observed that the soldiers are never in better health than when in a state of activity, and I must now tell you that in July when in the Valley

---

[1] Altogether, the British suffered losses at Maya of 1,484 which included 349 missing. The majority of these, if not all, were made prisoners by the French. The 1/28th itself had 32 men listed as missing, most of whom were undoubtedly taken prisoner. The largest number of missing was sustained by the 2/34th, which regiment listed 88 officers and men, most of whom were taken when the piquet on the Aratesque hill was overrun early in the fight. (

[2] Moyle Sherer was taken prisoner by the French at Maya when his piquet, on the Aratesque hill, was cut off by the encircling French. 'The contest now,' wrote Sherer, 'if contest it could be called, was very unequal; and, of course, short and bloody. I saw two-thirds of my piquet, and numbers, both of the light companies and my own regiment, destroyed. Among other brave victims, our captain of grenadiers nobly fell, covered with wounds; our colonel desperately wounded, and many others; and surviving this carnage, was myself made prisoner. I owe the preservation of a life, about which I felt, in that irritating moment, regardless, to the interference of a French officer, who beat up the muskets of his leading section, already levelled for my destruction.' (Sherer, *Recollections of the Peninsula*, pp.258-259.)

of Maya, much sickness had befallen us, and on the morning of our engagement I was under Dr Dakers' hands with dysentery, who very considerately came to recommend me not to accompany the Regiment on that day, which advice I did not then follow, being anxious to see what was going on. The great exertion however I then underwent entirely removed the complaint, and I was quite well by the time I got with the wounded to Vittoria. But I had fresh symptoms of it on my return to the mountains, and the time had now come to try again the same mode of cure, which I am happy to say has been equally efficacious.

As I think my Father will be more interested than yourself in what I have to relate, I will not curtail it, nor yet make it I hope too tedious for you to peruse. Although our 1st Division had planted their standards on the left bank of the Bidassoa, the centre and right wing of our Army had not advanced a mile in the country before we assembled on the 9th to put beyond a doubt our being in the French territory.[1] We marched on the 5th November from Aldudes, that night encamped in the valley of Bastan and on the 6th pitched our tents on the same ground we occupied on the memorable 25th July. The 1st and 3rd Brigades joined us by the 8th with some Portuguese Battalions and on the 9th artillery was taken up the heights.

Everything was now in preparation to advance, and the soldiers were congratulated in General Orders upon the auspicious moment that had at length arrived of invading France. Soult it was well known had for the last three months been throwing up works and entrenchments.[2] Lord Wellington had already reconnoitred these positions and depending upon British Valour for success the troops were now leading to the attack. At about 4 o'clock on the afternoon of this day, the order came to stand to our arms.

Our Division once more ascended the heights, and we rested there to await the approach of night and rising of the moon, which was to light us on our way to the enemy's camp. We were now within an hour's march of the French advanced guard. In the meanwhile the soldiers were desired to cook their provisions for the

---

[1] Units of the 1st and 5th Divisions of Wellington's army crossed the Bidassoa on October 7th 1813 and finally set foot on French soil after years of hard fighting. Soult considered the western end of his line, adjoining the Bay of Biscay, to be impassable to Wellington and so concentrated his forces to meet what he thought would be an attack upon his left and centre. As it turned out, Allied movements here were simply diversions and, whilst Soult fretted and waited, Wellington's 1st and 5th Divisions crossed the river at dawn, meeting very little resistance. In the centre, the Light Division stormed the heights above Vera and by the end of the day the Allies were firmly established on French soil. At this point, however, Wellington halted and waited for news from Germany before deciding upon his next move. Also, the fortress of Pamplona remained in French hands and any advance would have to wait until it surrendered, which it did on October 31st.

[2] Soult's positions along the line of the river Nivelle stretched from the shores of the Atlantic, on the French right flank, to the pass of Roncesvalles, on their left. This twenty-mile front was marked by a series of forts and redoubts, some of which contained artillery. The weakness of Soult's position lay in the fact that the twenty miles were defended by just 63,000 overstretched troops, whereas Wellington, who could pick his point of attack, could call upon 80,000 troops, although 20,000 of these were Spaniards, many of whom had yet to see any action.

next day. Precautions were taken to conceal as much as possible these movements, and the men kept entirely on the Spanish side of the mountain to light their fires, and the whole face of this ground was now covered with our assembled forces. As the hour was still distant in which we were to approach the foe, the men who chose were permitted to take their last nap in Spain, and here you may suppose time flew on heavy wings with the sleepless whose minds were filled with restless thoughts on this night before the battle. The Germans attached to our Division, as is their custom on these occasions, chanted their war songs — a rather doleful mode of passing the time, that aided those inclined to doze.[1] A little after midnight, a silent intimation was given, just as the moon appeared to fall in, and this was an appropriate signal, but as yet it only shone full orbed, on a dim tree on the horizon, but increasing every minute in lustre, sufficient to guide our steps. The wheels of our artillery had been bound in straw to prevent the sound of their approach over the rugged road — and no noise was heard but of falling waters to the deep cavities around us as we proceeded forward. The enemy's picquets had been sometime withdrawn from the foot of the Pyrenees, being too far removed from their entrenchments in front of us, but horse patrols were to be expected on the bridle paths which we accordingly avoided by advancing slowly over the most difficult ground and enclosed fields. Our light companies under skilful officers being in advance of us, stole forward with good heed to foes that might be lurking in ambush. Frequent pauses happened in our progress, with nothing but the tramp of our feet as yet to disturb the stillness.

Some time before day break we found it prudent to halt, and the men were ordered to pile their arms, and take another hour's repose, in a place sufficiently secure, surrounded with groves of trees. Not long after, by some strange accident, one of the men's pouches exploded, and a momentary panic ensued, all starting from sleep imagining the French cavalry were amongst us. Our Adjutant, a fine old soldier, much beloved by the men, soon reassured them, and they afterwards took a good long rest. I was awoke just as dawn appeared, which was remarkable from the sky being so deeply tinged with red, and ushered in by as loud a peal of artillery as I ever heard, from a distance however, and evidently not in our front.

With the utmost haste we now advanced, and small arms began immediately to sharply rattle, and the French picquets to retire. Our Brigade was attached to the 6th Division to aid them in a desperate attack upon the strongest point of the Enemy's entrenched camp — their lines extended along a ridge of mountains covering the whole of our front, and formed their last barrier to our approach into the plains of Gascony (where we now are).

This position was a most formidable one, but we heard that it was less so towards the sea, and this gave us hope of Lord Wellington's turning their flank there with our left, as we did at Vittoria. But that was not his Lordship's design in the present instance, as we afterwards heard, it being intended that we should force

---

[1] These doleful airs sung by the German troops in Wellington's army evidently made an impression upon their British comrades and are mentioned by Cooke, in his *Memoirs of the Late War*, I, p.245 and in Malcolm's *Reminiscences*, p.263, amongst others.

the enemy's centre.[1] Our right was sufficiently protected by a strong body of Spaniards. After repulsing the picquets, we continued to move forward, under as much cover as possible from the artillery in front of us, which seemed to be particularly directed at our column, and the only danger we were in this day was from cannon shots, and you may conceive the trouble they occasioned amongst compact bodies of troops. When within ten minutes march of the foot of this mountain, from which the enemy were so cordially saluting us, we had the pleasure of witnessing one of the finest military achievements of the campaign. A thick wood covered its base, through which we had expected instantly to penetrate, instead of which we were halted, and in double quick time the whole of the 6th Division ascended it, having to our great surprise been concealed from us by this wood, at which point they had arrived by a different route.

Four Columns were to be seen at the same instant climbing the Mountain at various and nearly perpendicular parts of it, bearing with them ladders to scale the works. They didn't fire till they had completed their ascent, during which they were exposed to a terrible discharge of musketry and artillery. When they reached the summit, they formed, and rushed on with the bayonet, and soon afterwards the whole line of French works were in flames. Our Brigade cheered them all the time ascending, and no doubt added to the consternation the sudden onset and bravery of these fine fellows must have spread among the foe. We directly followed them to the scene of action, which surpasses description, presenting to view all the burning havoc of war, not only from the explosions that had taken place, but the fire kindled on every thing that was combustible. It has never fallen to my lot to witness such murderous strife as must here have ensued. Each bank of entrenchment (of course having no walls of brick or mortar) being taken by a Coup de Main.[2]

---

[1] Wellington's plan for the attack on Soult's positions of the Nivelle was, in a way, a reversal of that which he had used when crossing the Bidassoa the previous month. On that occasion the diversion came in the west, allowing the 1st and 5th Divisions to cross close to the estuary of the river. Now, against the French line along the Nivelle, the demonstrations were to be made against the seaborne sector by Hope's 1st and 5th Divisions, whilst the main thrust came from the Allied centre, by Beresford with the 3rd, 4th, 7th and Light Divisions, and from the right, by Hill with the 2nd and 6th Divisions. The attack, on November 10th, was a complete success and once the Light Division had stormed the French positions on the commanding Rhune mountain, the key to Soult's line, the outcome of the day was never in doubt. By early afternoon the French were in total retreat having suffered 4,351 casualties to Wellington's 2,450. The best account of the battle can be found in Beatson's *Wellington: The Bidassoa and Nivelle*.

[2] Keep's division, the 2nd, acted in support of the 6th Division during the battle of the Nivelle. The 6th Division were ordered to attack the French redoubts in front of Ainhoa. These commanding hills were stormed with great success, the majority of the French troops abandoning their positions after setting fire to their hutted camps. On the extreme left flank of the French position the fighting was much harder, with the 2nd Division attacking the redoubts at the Col de Finodetta. These hills are steep and bare and the French troops, under Abbe, fought with great gallantry. However, once the 6th Division had broken through on their right, retreat became inevitable and Abbe withdrew his men towards Espelette. Charles Cadell, serving in Keep's regiment, left an account of the battle in his *Narrative*, pp.184-189.

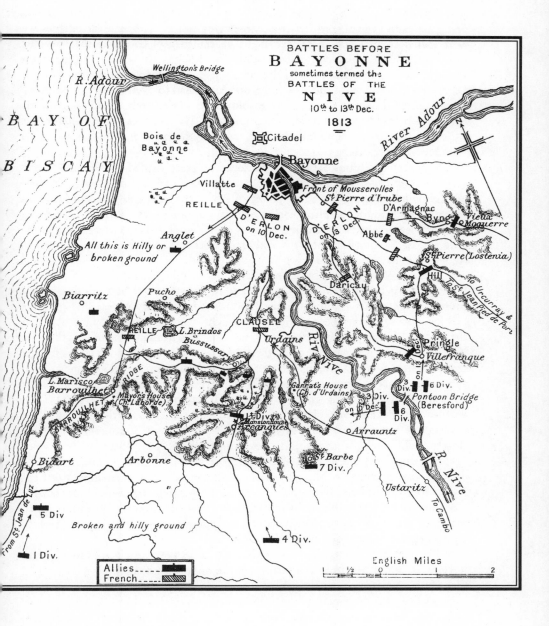

BATTLES BEFORE
BAYONNE
sometimes termed the
BATTLES OF THE
NIVE
10ᵗʰ to 13ᵗʰ Dec.
1813

R. Adour

Wellington's Bridge

BAY OF

BISCAY

Bois de
Bayonne

Citadel

Bayonne

Villatte

River Adour

N

Front of Mousserolles
St Pierre d'Irube

REILLE

D'ERLON
on 10 Dec.

D'ERLON
13 Dec.

D'Armagnac

Byng

Vieux
Moguerre

Anglet

All this is Hilly or
broken ground

Abbé

St Pierre (Lostenia)

Hill

To Urcurray &
St Jean Pied de Port

Biarritz

Pucho

Daricau

REILLE

L. Brindos
Bussussar

CLAUSEL

Urdains

Riv. Nive

Pringle

Villefranque

L. Marisco
Barrouilhet

RIDGE

Mayor's House
(Ch. Laborde)

BARROUILHET

Garrat's House
(Ch. d'Urdains)

1ˢᵗ Div.
Mansion House
ARCANGUES

Arrauntz

3
Div.

6 Div.

6
Div.

3 Div.
on 13 Dec.

Pontoon Bridge
(Beresford)

R. Nive

Bidart

Arbonne

St Barbe
7 Div.

Ustaritz

To Cambo

From St. Jean de Luz

5 Div.

Broken and hilly ground

1 Div.

4 Div.

Allies ......
French ......

English Miles

½   0   1   2

The day was won and the victory ours, for the retreat of the French was precipitate and general, and the troops requiring rest after their great fatigues we were halted at once, and slept that night on the field of battle, in the huts our ingenious enemies had constructed with the boughs of trees for their own accommodation. In other parts of this strongly fortified field, you will read in His Lordship's Despatches of the difficulties our Army had to overcome, and the many encounters of this busy day entirely employed it; so that only when the sun was going down could we find respite from our toils. We had then indeed a quiet but afflicting scene to witness, in collecting together the wounded. Alexander and I were busy in performing this service.

We entered a hut of the French darkened by green shaded boughs, and to our surprise found a black man, probably of some band in their service, badly wounded and expiring, but a fine young officer of the 51st, going on horseback to the rear, was truly to be pitied, being deprived of both eyes. With this exception there was less to shock the feelings — most of the wounded as is usual being in the arms and legs, and not so apparent, and many of them it is to be hoped destined to recover and may be as well as ever.

Several rivers, neither broad nor deep, but winding abruptly in this part of France, obstruct greatly military operations; so that as yet we have advanced but a short distance, and are still in the neighbourhood of the Pyrenees. The river we had just passed, where these battles were fought, was the Nivelle, but proceeding the next and following days after the French we came in sight of another called the Nive, and were checked in our progress by a tete de pont, or entrenched bridge, that presented a very ugly appearance, bristling with cannon, and defended with abbatis, chevaux de frise, etc, from which however we diverged along its banks until we came to a rising ground, where in front some chance offered of being enabled to ford this river. Here we assembled, and Col. Ashworth of the artillery was ordered up with some guns to cover the movement, if attempted. But Sir Rowland Hill having a suspicion of the place ordered an immediate reconnaissance (it being supposed the enemy were laying in wait, in great numbers, on the opposite banks, concealed there by bushes and willow trees). A small party of the 34th were ordered from the ranks for this purpose, while we awaited the issue. It was a fine afternoon with a beautiful landscape view, and scarcely a breath of air to move the leaves. Col. Ashworth had a nine pounder ready to awaken presently with its report this tranquil vale.

The 34th men approached a gate leading to a field on the edge of the river and were crossing it when from the bushes on the opposite side that fringed its banks the white smoke of a few muskets from different parts of them showed the enemy's line of concealment at once, and killed two or three of these poor soldiers — at the same moment a shot was fired from our nine pounder, and then immediately all was still as before. The bugle sounded to recall the 34th party, and the peaceful serenity of this pretty valley was no further disturbed, and we have contented ourselves since in remaining on this bank, where we are now stationed.[1] At first we bivouacked within ten minutes' walk of the house I am at present in, but in consequence of the heavy rains that have fallen here lately we have been ordered into (we should be glad to hear) permanent cantonments for the Winter. The risks we have run have been less deplorable in the result, than might have been expected, the system of tactics obliging one General or the other to yield the field to an opponent who has succeeded in turning or breaking the line, without the necessity of personal contests, for which we are none of us provided, so that we have no actual fighting, and when it does take place it is of very short duration, but is generally avoided, as at Maya, where the 92nd and ourselves were not required to fight the battle out, our defeat being decided by other operations. Perhaps this is the least objectionable and most humane method upon which war can be conducted.

I am now living under the roof of an honest old Gascon, who is a Miller by trade, within sound at this moment of the incessant clack of his water wheels. I hope my dear Father and you will not find this long detail equally tiresome to listen to, if read aloud, it being all about Military Manoeuvres, but I intend to enclose a letter to Samuel upon other particulars.

I am in very fair health, and tolerable spirits, and remain, Dearest Mother, etc.

P.S. By the surrender of Pamplona[2] the French have relieved themselves from starvation, and we shall now have the agreeable task to feed them on their way to England as prisoners, so that fortress is off our hands, and that more fatal one besides, St Sebastian.[3] A private of ours was found among them at Pamplona, at

---

[1] The river Nive was crossed by Hill's 2nd Division at daybreak on December 9th by two fords close to the broken bridge at Cambo. George Bell, of the 34th Regiment, in the same brigade as the 28th, wrote a good account of the operation. 'The troops were now assembled in perfect quiet. No drum or bugle was sounded — not a word was spoken — all as still as death, waiting the signal gun to make the rush. The outposts on the riverside had their orders not to take any advantage of the enemy when, just at dawn, bang went the first cannon. The French were under arms in a moment. Our pickets on the river bank gave them the signal to clear off. They took the hint, got out of the way a little, halted, and formed up on the defensive. Bang went another gun, and now the field-day began. Our men had slung their pouches behind their necks, resting on the pack, to keep their powder dry, as the river was swollen. The grand rush was now being made under cover of our guns. We took the stream; some killed and wounded went away with the current, for the French kept up a fire on us now, which was quite awful. We made good our footing on the right side, fought on all the day, and calling the roll at night, we found there were many widows.' (Bell, *Soldier's Glory*, pp.107-108.)

[2] Faced with starvation, and cut off from the main French army, the governor of Pamplona, Cassan, surrendered on October 31st. Cassan had earlier threatened to blow up the ramparts in an attempt to secure an honourable capitulation, to which Wellington responded by threatening to shoot every officer and NCO as well as one tenth of the garrison if he did so. Cassan finally surrendered at the very moment when Wellington ordered an assault to be made. The garrison marched out and were transported to England as prisoners of war.

[3] Although the 28th took no part in the storming of San Sebastian on August 31st, the regiment was, in fact, represented by a sergeant and six grenadiers. Apparently, Sergeant Ball and six other men of the 28th were sent to Passages by Colonel Belson to

first supposed to be a Deserter, but since proved an excellent soldier taken prisoner by them. He gives a shocking account of the famine — by which they were reduced to the necessity of feeding upon horseflesh, dogs and cats, etc.

Banks of the Nive
5th December 1813

My dear Samuel,

You will be rejoiced to hear that we have arrived in France with so little injury to the 28th, having not half a dozen wounded, and thus fortunately have escaped the hazards of crossing the Pyrenees, and hard day's work on the banks of the Nivelle.

We are now all quartered on the margin of the Nive, and in some suspense about what is to be done next, but the weather proving so opposed to any change in our position, that we are becoming reconciled to it. I am in a small room in a Mill, with a window overlooking the river, and a French sentry so close to me on the opposite bank that in an instant he could shoot me through the head, should I pop it out to take a look at him.[1] But a sort of truce is now prevailing to prevent any fear of that sort, and the two armies merely separated by a narrow but deep current, are on the most friendly terms with each other, notwithstanding which we expect an order to advance, and are only waiting I believe for the waters to subside to cross this river.[2] The country is so peculiar in the intersection of these streams that we are all drawn together, both French and English, to this point of the coast, and we seem now to have met for the first time in order to become

---

buy tobacco, tea and sugar. They were given 2,000 dollars which had been collected for the purpose. They reached Passages on August 30th but upon learning that San Sebastian was to be stormed the next day, Sergeant Ball spoke to his men, telling them that there had hardly been an action in the Peninsula at which the 28th had not been present and that they should volunteer for the storming parties. The men agreed, the money was placed with a commissary for safekeeping and on August 31st Ball and the six grenadiers duly took their places in the storming parties. All survived safely, the money was reclaimed and the goods duly purchased, and the party returned to rejoin their comrades with a glowing testimonial from Colonel Belson. The story is related in Cadell's *Narrative of the Campaigns*, pp.176-178, and in Brodigan's *History of the 28th Regiment*, p.68-69.

[1] Cadell also mentions a position from which a French sentry on the opposite bank of the Nive, 'was within half musket shot, absolutely looking into our windows.' (Cadell, *Narrative of the Campaigns*, p.189). Was this the same billet as Keep's?

[2] Fraternisation was fairly widespread in the Peninsula but when Wellington's army crossed over the border into France it became very common indeed. There are numerous accounts, many of them quite humorous, of these unofficial 'meetings', most of which took place at the respective picquet's of the two sides. A fair selection of these can be found in Brett-James' *Life in Wellington's Army*, pp.292-309. It must be borne in mind that this feeling of mutual friendship existed only between the British and French and that there was understandably little love lost between the French and Spanish troops.

mutually better acquainted. One hour before daylight we turn out (the time at which most attacks are made) when we are under arms on the pleasant banks of this little river, where in darkness we stand prepared, and watch the morning's earliest beam. When we see the sun has fairly swept away the mists of night, joy returns to our hearts with the promise of another day's peace, and the bands of the different Regiments on both banks appear to rival each other's strains. The French I think in this respect excel us; to me at least there is a tune played by them that falls so sweetly soft upon the ear I can never forget it. It seems to echo and repeat again, — All-is-well — all-is-well — the cadence of this tune under the circumstances is greatly affecting.

We have the pleasure to meet here Regiments we never saw before, but often heard of; and the country, and houses, are crowded with our men. The French people returning are amazed at the bad opinion they entertained of us before our arrival, as they have found their little property safe, and now offer us all the comfort their homes can afford.[1]

At first we had such fine weather that we remained out of doors, and the battle of the 10th has left some pleasant impressions of our last encampments. We spent the evening of that eventful day on the field, and Hill and I took a seat at sunset on the green turf there to contemplate the wide spread of France before us, and distant sea; other parts of our Army were still in pursuit, and when darkness was shutting up the prospect the flashes of their muskets were visible enough, though we were far beyond the sound of their report. The French appeared to have led a pleasant life on that ground, and greatly surpass us in their camp contrivances.

Having fewer tents, they had been at the trouble of forming in basket work most convenient habitations, which we took possession of, as they very kindly left them uninjured (being as I think rather partial to us). Col. Belson and many officers preferred them to their own tents, yet we had some comic alarms of fire, without any water to extinguish it, from our imprudence in making too careless and jovial use of them.

We have now bid a final adieu to the mountains where we so often spread our boat cloaks upon the sweet scented heath, or places covered with wild strawberries or wild potatoes, that never grow bigger than filberts. Our servants formed our bedsteads with sticks run into the ground, shaped like hammocks, and wattled

---

[1] The French people quickly realised that their fears for the safety of themselves and their property once Wellington's troops entered France were unfounded. Indeed, they found the British troops to be generally well-behaved and their system of paying for local produce welcome. There were, of course, incidents of misbehaviour but on the whole the relationship between the British soldiers and French population was good. A few days after the battle Charles Cadell, of the 28th, wrote, 'The people did not know what to make of us at first; but from the judicious proclamations of the Commander-in-Chief, recommending them to remain in their houses, and assuring them that everything would be paid for, they soon gained confidence. The poultry of France, of which we had heard so much, but of which we had yet seen nothing, began to make its appearance, and to our astonishment, we found it was kept in the garrets of the houses.' (Cadell, *Narrative of the Campaigns*, p.190.)

round, about a foot deep, which was filled with leaves to supply the place of a feather bed.

Hill's handkerchief that saved his life had nineteen holes in it as exactly cut as if with scissors, and the contusion completely blackened his body; but he is now quite recovered. Escapes like this we are always hearing of. One happened to Captain Carthew of the 39th equally remarkable. He suddenly lost the use of his limbs while in the battle, and at first the surgeons couldn't discover any cause for it, but it soon began to show itself in his legs, which both became black as charcoal. It was therefore supposed a cannon ball must have passed between them.

Nor were such dangers the only ones we had to congratulate ourselves on escaping. On our march to Vittoria in June we met with an awful visitation from a thunderstorm, one peal of which was so sharp and terrific that immediate destruction followed, and a whole section of the 34th Regiment very near me were thrown down, and Lieut Mastermind and a horse he was riding struck dead, and his clothes instantly burnt to a cinder.[1] With a heavy rain pelting, and another thunder clap expected, as we were crossing a plain, we could only turn out the pioneers to bury this fine young officer where he fell.

Our losses, though they have not abated our spirits, have diminished our strength, but more officers and men are constantly joining us from England. Our old friend Colonel Ross has arrived to supply poor Paterson's place — who supplied his so fatally — and Captain Carrol to command the company to which I belong in lieu of Meacham, who was severely wounded in the arm — and Captain Briggs, an old companion and gallant officer at Berry Head, and four Ensigns just appointed.

I am sorry to tell you Nelson and I have had the misfortune to lose both our animal and baggage, through neglect of our servants and men in charge of them. I am therefore left quite destitute, with scarcely a change of linen, and this has been a sad loss to me of my nice pannier, and its few contents. My host, the Miller, is a merry Old Gascon with a wife and young family, the latter only coming occasionally to see them, with a Maiden Aunt, who is staying here at present and is a most lively good looking young woman about 30, with all the manners of an amiable old maid. Luckily she can speak very intelligible French, which is unusual in these parts, and with her I feel very much at home, and am becoming extremely interested in events here. Her sorrows and apprehensions she confides to me, for

---

[1] The officer's name was actually Masterman, who had been wounded at the storming of Badajoz in April 1812. His death is mentioned in the memoirs of Captain John Patterson, of the 50th Regiment. 'While we were advancing towards the Pyrenees, a most tremendous storm burst upon the column, as it was marching over the crest of a lofty ridge. The thunder rolled in fearful peals, and the forked lightning, attracted by the polished fire-arms and bayonet points, flashed about our heads in an awful manner, threatening destruction to our troops. Lieut. Masterman of the 34th was struck by the electric fluid, with such fatal violence that his death was instantaneous; his features scorched and blackened, and his body burnt almost to a cinder, presented a frightful spectacle as he lay extended on the road.' (Patterson, *Adventures*, pp.319-320.) The incident is also mentioned by Sherer in his *Recollections,* the author serving in the same regiment (Sherer, *Recollections of the Peninsula*, p.245,) by Bell, (*Soldier's Glory,* p.77) and by Cadell of the 28th. (*Narrative of the Campaigns,* pp.158-159.)

the Miller is in our pay. A messenger from Sir Rowland bought him ten guineas for information about the depths of the river, and I suspect he has engaged himself for a further gratuity to lead us across. The solicitude therefore of his family, I can fully participate in from his undertaking this dangerous service.

I must now conclude, so God bless you my dear Sam. In the hope of our success, and of being enabled to give you good tidings of it, I remain, etc , W.T.K.

General Depot for the wounded
Espelette
20th December 1813

My dear Father,

I fear ere this reaches you, you and my dear Mother will have heard of my having been wounded in action with the enemy on the 13th of this month in front of Bayonne.[1] However this letter will soon I hope relieve you from all unpleasant suspense about me, for although I have been unfortunate enough to receive a severe wound in my face, I am happy to say the Surgeons pronounce me in perfect safety. A merciful Providence has again protected my life amidst the greatest of dangers, for it was next to impossible I could have escaped on the 13th as I commanded a Company (the Captain being absent on the baggage guard) of which most of the men were either killed or wounded. I can only give you a brief account of our proceedings since my last, dated at the old Miller's, which I suppose you must have received about this time. I described to you that the Nive separated the two armies, and that we had reason to conclude Lord Wellington's intention was to cross that river. Sentries lined both banks of it, and the French had planted cannon opposite the points at which it was fordable. Mutual civilities and harmony subsisted however between both parties, and we had every day some friendly chat with the French officers, who like ourselves expressed an anxiety for a general cessation of hostilities. During this peaceful posture of affairs, Sir Rowland received his Lordship's orders to make a general attack upon the enemy in our front, and to carry these fords. This order arrived on the evening of the 8th, and on the following morning, long before daylight, we were under arms in waiting for the signal to rush down to the river's bank, and dash in upon the startled foe (for of course if we could it was intended to take them by surprise). By a well concerted plan, many Regiments of different Divisions plunged at the same instant into the stream, our line extending a great distance down its banks. (According to the usual routine of tactics, any portion of these, overcoming

---

[1] This was the battle of St Pierre. Officially, it forms part of the battle of the Nive, which was fought between December 10th to 13th. Owing to the fact that the battle on the 13th was fought on the right bank of the river around the village of St Pierre it attracted that name. However, it is shown as the Nive on battle honours and medal clasps.

resistance, and advancing rapidly would cut off the retreat of the remainder of the French to their main body, on their right wing.) The 28th happened to be the leading Regiment of the Brigade and we had the brunt of it, but from the above cause it was of a very short duration, for the 6th and other Divisions on our left so gallantly and quickly succeeding, the enemy had no time to lose, and had we been later it might have been better, and thus detained the French longer in our front. But as it was, they contented themselves with one discharge of artillery, and not much more of small arms, before they entirely decamped to avoid being taken prisoners.

Yet some were caught, and it was comic when we got over to find those few left behind so chop fallen at our success, and more so on taking possession of the new ground on that side of the river; for there we immediately went to breakfast, in the French houses of a small town very near us, as nothing further was remaining at that moment for us to do. The French people here, particularly the women, seemed highly rejoiced at the sight of us, and we all tried to make friends among them, in catering for a breakfast, which you may suppose after wading the river, and escaping cannon shots and bullets, was very pleasant employment.

Our loss has not been much there, Captain Taylor unfortunately severely wounded, a light infantry Sergeant killed and some few men; much less than we expected, for it did not promise such easy work. I was with the 2nd Company in front (the best place as it turned out for the shots flew over our heads when up to the hips and breast in water.) Col. Benson was very near me, and I felt rather uneasy about his horse, lest it should be wounded, and kick and plunge and retard my advance. We however were untouched, but not so with those behind us. Yet altogether it could not have been more judiciously managed. The French behaved extremely well in retreating so quickly, and we were very glad not to have to run after them. I had so often forded rivers between Lisbon and the Pyrenees that a wetting of this kind was unthought of, and indeed it soon drips off. We had just time to breakfast, and then pursued our march, changing our front considerably to the left and towards Bayonne, and about an hour or two before dark we came up with the French the aspect of things now looking very black and hostile, and preparing us for more difficult work, the 28th still keeping the lead of the Brigade.

It was only at nightfall and after considerable difficulty that we could dispossess them of the ground they occupied, and here we sustained a greater loss than we had done in the early part of the day, having many men killed at close quarters firing through a hedge. Luckily I was out of this death dealing strife (the worst a soldier can have to perform) being with the other part of the Battalion on the slope of a Hill to protect us from artillery, but with fixed bayonets expecting to be ordered forward. The French, however, retired and a heavy rain set in with darkness, and we were all drenched to the skin long before morning as our baggage and tents did not come up, nor cross the river that day, it being uncertain how things would terminate.

On the 10th, 11th and 12th we continued approaching Bayonne, on the 12th the French having retired under its walls, and the wet weather still continuing we were again put into houses. During these operations Lord Wellington had been attacked on his left by Soult, when our Army was divided by intervening streams, for whilst Sir Rowland was crossing and advancing from one point, the French Marshal crossed at another, and attacked Sir John Hope's army, in which however he was repulsed. His next effort was to drive back our right from the ground we had gained, while he had been thus fruitlessly employed on our other flank.[1]

But this we frustrated by a hard battle with forces much more numerous than ourselves. We heard of this intention early on the morning of the 13th and sent our baggage to the rear, and prepared to receive him. The attacking party I always think has the advantage, for their movements are previously decided upon, whilst that acting on the defensive is often divided, from ignorance of the points on which they may be attacked. This was our case, for our Division had no immediate support to expect from the rest of the army.

Lord Wellington was so concerned at the odds against us that every effort was made to send troops in time to our assistance, but before they arrived we had fought and conquered and the combined forces of the French were completely defeated. When the foe was fast retreating I am told the meeting between Lord Wellington and Sir Rowland was most gratifying to both, particularly the latter, to whom his Lordship expressed his approbation in the warmest terms, declaring the Victory was all his own.[2]

And now my dear Father I shall defer giving you an account of this battle, to speak of the wounds I have received in it. The bullet having entered at the corner of my mouth, passed under the tongue, and lodged in my neck, and fracturing the jawbone in its progress. The consequence has been an immense swelling, black as my hat, and frightfully disfiguring, for my neck has been swelled to a level with my breast, and that has been tinged of a deep gamboge; all this is now gradually

---

[1] With Beresford and Hill having crossed the river Nive Wellington's army was thus divided into two, something which Soult was not slow in taking advantage of. On the morning of December 10th, he attacked Hope's 1st and 5th Divisions on the Allied left as well as the Light Division on the right. The Allied troops were driven back in a series of small, confused actions although the line was stabilised by the end of the day and the French attacks beaten back. Soult persisted with his offensive over the next two days in actions on the left bank of the Nive, although all were ultimately beaten off. The fight on December 13th, known as the battle of St Pierre is dealt with shortly. Oman's account of the fighting between December 10th-12th can be found in his *History of the Peninsular War*, VII, pp.233-261.

[2] On the night December 12th, the pontoon bridge over the Nive, linking Hill and his 14,000 troops with the rest of the Allied army, was broken by the swollen river owing to heavy rains. This in effect isolated Hill and afforded Soult an opportunity to bring some 35,000 of his men against him. The attack was duly carried out on December 13th in what is known as the battle of St Pierre. Soult was able to use the bridges in Bayonne to transfer his men easily from the left to the right bank of the Nive but he knew he had about four hours to win the battle, four hours being the amount of time it would take for Wellington to come to Hill's assistance. The fighting amongst the lanes and hedges of the three spurs over which the battle was fought was fierce and for a while it looked as though the French attacks would prevail. Indeed, only when Hill had used up nearly all of his reserves did the battle finally turn in his favour and when Allied reinforcements from the 3rd, 4th and 6th Divisions began to arrive the battle was as good as won. Hill finished the fight with his own troops and when a relieved Wellington arrived he extended his hand to his trusty subordinate, saying, 'Hill, the day is your own.' (Sidney, *The Life of Lord Hill*, p.267).

disappearing, and the injury I have sustained is not dangerous from the direction the ball took. But it might have separated the arteries in my neck and been fatal from haemorrhage, or done other mischief as the Doctors inform me. The Surgeon was with me this morning, and says I am doing very well, and that my neck will soon be healed, so that there is no fear of inflammation or anything of that sort ensuing from it, and I therefore beg you will believe there is no reason for my dear Mother or you to make yourselves at all uneasy about me. Under such circumstances it would be a sin to complain, others being much less fortunate. One poor fellow, a Captain Bulstrode of the 66th, had his lower jaw bone carried away entirely by a canister shot, and his tongue the Doctor says hangs down in a most frightful way upon his breast. This case, without mentioning others, will be enough I am sure to reconcile you to what has befallen me, and to induce you to unite with me in thanks to God it was no worse.

I shall certainly write to my Mother in the course of another week to let her know how I am going on, And remain my dear Father, Yours etc. W.T.K.

Espellete (Espelette)
28th December 1813

My dearest Mother,

I am happy to inform you that I am progressing most favourably, and my wounds healing with astonishing rapidity. And as I promised to write, I cannot fail to do so, although I have only to repeat that everything is going quite well with me, and I am in a most comfortable billet with Captain Wolfe of the 28th, likewise wounded, though not dangerously, but in the leg. And with him, I am very lucky to find an associate most agreeable to me. I assure you we are very snug in our present quarters, and getting quite domestic. We had no plumb pudding on Christmas Day, but mustered a suet one, and fancied the sweet things, but I am unable yet to take any but spoon victuals, and it will be some time before I can venture upon anything else.

Now that I am so much at leisure, I will describe to you more particularly past events that led to my disaster. The severity of warfare is most felt when it is mixed up with the peaceful occupation of life, and is quite out of all character when it involves those so commendably employed. Our poor Miller and his wife and sister never supposed he was to be made an Instrument to our designs. That pretty and genteel old maid, who seemed to be so completely out of her element at the Mill, afforded me much that was exceedingly touching to witness and listen to. Such as, the tears and entreaties of the old man, not to be too rash in his undertakings, etc. All of which I was myself an interested spectator in, as the dangers of it were certainly to fall to my own lot. We could therefore very well sympathise together in the meditated project. On the night before it took place I drank tea with them all, and as the hours waned (so anxiously awaited by thousands) it was a trying scene to them.

I slept for a few hours, but got up long before daylight again, when a trusty Corporal came to take the Miller away, and then the most painful moment had arrived of separation. His post was a most dangerous one, having to lead the foremost men forward at the peril of his life, and especially should he wilfully misconduct them. But this I saw there was no fear of; he was to receive 40 Guineas for this service, and another ten I believe when we got safe over. I then had to take leave of them myself to join the Regiment, which I found collected round the walls of a convent or large building in deep silence, where we awaited a discharge of artillery that was to be the signal.

The good old Miller escaped and we arrived on the 12th at a part of the country where our soldiers were put into every house that could be found to avoid the rain. This separated us completely from one another on a very dark night, and the officers were ordered to remain in the same houses with the men, a very unusual thing, but not without sufficient cause, for we were now amongst people whose business it was to gather in the vintage, and whose cellars were filled with casks of wine. In consequence of this, I passed a night amidst the greatest miseries, and had no sleep until within an hour or two of daybreak.

The poor woman who was in this house alone came to tell me of the excessive bad behaviour of the men, who had broken open her cellars, and taken the shoes from her feet. I therefore went below to look after them, and sent Robert to the Adjutant to acquaint him of this and to send me aid to take away the delinquents, but when a file of the Guard arrived under a very steady Corporal he informed me the Adjutant could send no further assistance, as the same and worse conduct was going on with the other companies of the Regiment. (War is in itself so irrational a pursuit, that human reason, distracted by it, has, when opportunities occur, always these results.) The Corporal, though a powerful man, was levelled to the ground immediately with his men, by these intoxicated soldiers, and I found there was nothing to be done, except by remaining myself among them, being a check upon their committing further mischief, as they professed to be willing to obey my orders in that respect. When I saw them all falling asleep, I continued to contribute to that object by remonstrating with them, and then left them. Just before dawn of day, Robert came to tell me the French were advancing.

This information had a most surprising effect upon the men, who turned out with the greatest steadiness, and fell into their ranks, so that when I marched them up to the Regiment they were in perfect order. The artillery was reverberating around us, and we were moved forward directly, under the direction of an Aide de Camp, for as the light increased, and day advanced, it became evident the French had commenced an attack upon us.

Captain Carol being ordered away, I was the only officer going into action with the Company, and when the Regiment had halted for a few minutes our Adjutant passing down the ranks told Col. Belson in a loud voice there was no officer but myself with it, to which the Colonel replied in the same loud tone "Then let Mr Keep command the Company". This was complimentary, and I felt the importance of it, but unluckily discovered I had left my sword at my billet, and sent Robert directly to request Alexander would send me one, which he did; and then we advanced again forward; and here Col. Ross and General Pringle, both on horseback, were quite close to me, the Colonel having a sore throat with flannel bandages round it, and the General in loud conversation with him about the picquets. We came then upon an open space with a bank formed by the side of this wood, where we halted a long time; and I never was more surprised to find whilst we were seated here, and the men eating what they had about them for a breakfast, that random shots were flying among us, one of which a soldier by the side of me took from amidst the brushes in his pack. Looking over this bank into the wood, I perceived men skirmishing from behind the trees, but the Regiment were acting so completely under orders that no one thought of interfering in what was going on, and as if it was no business of ours to notice it.

Presently however Sir Rowland's Aide de Camp, Captain Egerton, pricking his steed gently forward over rough ground, intimated that we were to advance. In a moment the whole Regiment entered the wood under Col. Belson's command, and here beneath trees scattered at distances about, with fallen leaves up to our ankles, we moved forward in a very good line, the skirmishers of the enemy retreating very slowly, and turning their backs most unconcerned to us.

We came at last to the extremity of this wood, where the Regiment stopped, as there was a somewhat steep descent in front, and open fields, with a wood on higher ground opposite to us, occupied by the French with artillery. The other companies of the Regiment were partially concealed and sheltered by some of these trees growing on the edge of this bank, but only one or two were near the left of my Company, and of course we were immediately exposed to view, and a cannon shot struck the breast of my left hand man, and the breath of life was wrested from him with a dismal shriek. The rank closed up, and our firing directly opened upon the numerous skirmishers crossing this field. In the centre of it was a small house, having only one window over the door, and here the most dreadful hand to hand fighting was going on between the French and some Portuguese; and such as was terrible to behold. In the meanwhile we did not interfere, but encompassed this small field on three sides of it, a French close column being in our front, and Captain Hartman with a company of the 28th on the right hand side of this square with the distant open country opposite to him in front. Nor did the French skirmishers run there to give any assistance, but were the bravest men I ever saw, for they retreated most leisurely, though now receiving the fire of our whole line, returning it as they retired, to the column opposite, across this little field. Many of my men were killed or wounded in a short time, and Ensign Waring was for a few minutes by the side of me before he was struck, and Nelson on my left, firing like Robinson Crusoe from a tree, with men loading the muskets for him, as he is an excellent shot, but he was soon wounded, and then came my turn from the enemy as I suppose on the opposite height, and more distant, though the French column there I did not see deploy (or form into line) but it could not have come from the skirmishers, for they being below me, the shot would not have descended to my neck. The bullet struck me down, and covered me with the crimson fluid, spurting like a fountain from my mouth, whilst I was laying on my back. The blow was severe, it was like a cart wheel passing over my head, but this was instantaneous only, for all pain ceased, and I was left in full possession of my senses, with the warm drops falling upon my face. After a minute or two I got again upon my legs and went only a few paces to the rear before I saw our Assistant Surgeon under a tree, attending some soldiers there. He directly examined the wounds I had received, and cut the ball from my neck, and told me I was safe,[1] but he had scarcely uttered the words when a cannon shot struck the top of the tree, reminding us both that we were still in the way of them, so that at once we moved further into the wood, where his attention was called to others, and I left him to proceed, but had not gone far before I came to a farm house[2] in the large kitchen of which the wounded had come before me, and one or two young women ran directly to assist me, which they had a very good opportunity of doing, for there was a large boiler on the fire, with jugs of warm water and several dishes, into the latter I was surprised at the quantity of blood that flowed from my mouth, and it was some time before I could remove it effectually from my face and hair and eyes,

---

[1] Gunshot wounds to the neck of this nature were not viewed with any seriousness by surgeons of the day. In his *Principles of Military Surgery*, p.357, John Hennen wrote, 'Simple incised wounds on the back of the neck, although sometimes penetrating to a great depth, and even uncovering the vertebral arteries, are not beyond the reach of simple bandage....In the simple superficial gunshot injuries, no peculiarity of treatment is required'. The elasticity of the skin on the face and neck enabled a simple field dressing to be applied, thus the surgeon was allowed to simply cut out the ball from Keep's neck. The more serious wound was to the jaw, the fracture of which would have taken much longer to heal. Hennen was Deputy Inspector of Military Hospitals in 1818 and had served in the Peninsula. His book contains over seventy case histories of all sorts of wounds sustained in the Peninsula and at Waterloo. It demonstrates that the surgeons in Wellington's army were a far cry from the popular image of being merely 'lopping off limb' merchants and could, in fact, perform successful operations such as the removal of a bullet from the brain.

[2] This farm house was almost certainly the Chateau Larralde, which lay in the rear of Pringle's position. Pringle's brigade, including Keep and the 28th, were positioned on the left flank of Hill's force in front of the Chateau. They were attacked by Darricau during the day but the French appear to have attacked without any real conviction, and, certainly, the thickly wooded ground prevented them from attacking in any real formation. The casualty figures for Pringle's brigade bear testimony to the lightweight nature of Darricau's attack, 145 killed and wounded out of a total of 1,784 casualties altogether during the battle. The 28th suffered some 101 of the casualties in Pringle's brigade, by far the heaviest, with the 2/34th suffering just 5 casualties and the 1/39th 18. (Oman, *History of the Peninsular War*, VII, 548.) There are very few good accounts of the fighting on Hill's left flank and even fewer detailed maps. A large round hill dominates this part of the battlefield but nobody appears to have occupied it, the battle being confined to the ground immediately in front of the trees in front of the chateau. Cadell, in his *Narrative*, pp.197-203, wrote of the fighting as did Bell, of the 34th. Curiously enough, Bell, in his *Soldier's Glory*, pp.110, claims that the chateau actually fell to the French during the fighting. 'The Chateau of Villefranche, which was in our rear when we commenced operations in the morning, was well in our front before twelve o'clock, i.e. we had to abandon it to a superior force, and this caused our fellows to get furious. It had been taken and retaken several times today, but we held it at last.' I find this hard to believe as it would have left the French well in the rear of Hill's centre. Also, I have found no other accounts to support Bell, who goes on to say that the British troops abandoned the chateau to the French and moved to their right. This would have severely exposed Hill's left flank and rear. As Bell wrote his memoirs some fifty years afterwards, I am inclined to view his account of the fighting at the chateau with great suspicion.

for my cap had fallen off and rolled away, and at the moment I got up I couldn't find it, and the shots were flying too quickly to look for it.

The wounded in this kitchen were seated against the walls, and none apparently requiring such aid as myself. When I had cleansed my face I left the farm house, and proceeded to a small collection of cottages very near me. Descending a small declivity in front of this village, I perceived women assembled at the doors, and here I met my hostess of the previous day, that poor distressed creature, who I had been up all night with to protect from our soldiers, who had got drunk and staved her wine casks. She lifted up her hands in malediction upon the author of all these calamities at the sight of me, covered as I was with blood still flowing over my clothes and hands, and without a hat, and in a fit of distraction punning upon his name and calling him no Bonaparte mais malaparte, with many Jesu Maries! in commiseration of my misfortune. This procured me immediate reception into a comfortable but small dwelling with some kind young women, where I was followed by Dr Dakers who came very anxiously to see me, and carefully looked to my wounds, advising me to get to bed. In such a scene of confusion, I was glad enough to do so, you may be sure, as night was now approaching. The place was so crowded that the front room of this cottage was immediately filled with very boisterous artillerymen, and the females were glad to shut themselves up with me in the adjoining back room, where however there was only one comfortable bed and bedstead. These three young women therefore spread some clothes upon the ground at the foot of it for themselves and insisted upon my occupying it. They were in some uneasiness at being discovered, bolted the door and placed chairs against it. This I found they had good reason for, as the artillerymen carousing began to talk very loud, and as I lay I heard such things related by them as fully assured me it was no more than a necessary precaution. At night these good females came in turns to my bedside to attend upon me, as the blood at intervals bubbled forth so fast it threatened to choke me. I was quite speechless with the swelling, not knowing what was the extent of the injury, and my mouth in that state that I didn't dare to move my tongue, even to ascertain it, except by degrees.

In the morning Robert came to me, with his arm in a bandage, having been wounded, but not dangerously (Officers' servants are always with their masters when in action[1]) and he procured me a forage cap, and by the authorities I was furnished with a horse and left my good angels behind me, to meet again with kind people here, where Wolfe and I are now residing. Thus my dear Mother you may fancy all the rest that has occurred to me, in the endeavour to swallow food to strengthen me, and give good hopes of my speedy restoration. As I cannot talk,

---

[1] Soldiers who were employed as Officers' servants were, nonetheless, expected to be well versed in drill, and indeed, soldiers who were not perfect were not able to become servants. Although acting as servants these soldiers were expected to have with them their arms and accoutrements at all times and were to maintain their equipment to a high standard. They were also expected to perform their share of guard duty and fell in with their respective companies for parades, reviews and inspections. As Keep says, they fought alongside their masters and, presumably died alongside them. Being an officer's servant was not, therefore, an excuse for dodging regular duty.

Wolfe does his utmost to amuse me, and has a book of anecdotes to refer to, but some of his own are equally entertaining, and we have newspapers from England occasionally, where I read of nothing but rejoicings for victories. When the public mind is thus occupied they little think of the mangled heaps that are stretched upon the field of battle. I am told that in which we contributed to the late glorious achievement was so covered with the French and Portuguese slain that it was a grievous task to bury them, and exceeding anything before witnessed.

How strange it appears that all these horrors should arise from the ambition of an individual, when he himself might his "quietus make with a bare bodkin", an acre of ground suffice to maintain him, and a few feet of it to hide his remains from the world. The French officers on the banks of the Nive were kept in great ignorance of passing events. To enlighten them a little we threw over the papers containing patches of Bonaparte's defeats. The French here certainly show no signs of attachment to him, and without that how unenviable must the condition of such potentates be.

I can add nothing more at present my dear Mother, but to request you will make your mind perfectly easy about me, and to express a hope of getting home soon, as I am now, with the loss of baggage and in my present state, quite hors de Combat and only fit to return to the 2nd Battalion and Old England again. The Spanish Officers here invited us last night to a Ball, but of course we couldn't accept it, and besides had nothing gay to sport in, as we could wish as British officers.

We have no news from the Army. Everything quite in status quo. Marshal Soult is not recovered yet from his late defeat. We hope to see a good account of our gallant Division, but shan't I suppose receive the Dispatch for some time.

God bless you my dear Mother, Believe me, etc., W.T.K.

Chapter Eight
Return to Plymouth

The fighting in front of the Chateau Larralde during the battle of St Pierre was the last action in which William Keep was ever to take part. The wound to his neck and jaw ensured his return to England and he would miss the remaining fighting in the Peninsula. On February 23rd 1814 Wellington's men crossed the Adour and the blockade of Bayonne began, but not before Soult had managed to slip away with his army to the east, leaving behind a garrison under Governor Thouvenot, to be watched by the men of the 1st and 5th Divisions under Sir John Hope.

The main Allied field army under Wellington continued east and on February 27th fought its last major battle in the open field at Orthes. Here, amidst the green, wooded spurs that reminded many a soldier of his homeland, Wellington attacked Soult and after heavy fighting forced him to retreat in the direction of Toulouse. There were a number of small but sharp fights during the pursuit, notably at Tarbes and Aire before the final battle of the war, which came on April 10th when Wellington's men made a series of assaults on the French positions around the town of Toulouse. The fighting here was bloody, confused and, to some extent, unnecessary, Napoleon having abdicated in Paris some four days earlier. Nevertheless, news travelled slowly and the killing and wounding of 4,558 Allied and 3,236 French soldiers was the price to pay for the lack of urgency in communicating the news south. And yet there was still one final, and most definitely unnecessary, drama which was played out on April 14th when Governor Thouvenot, acting purely out of malice, launched a sortie from the citadel of Bayonne against the troops blockading the town to the north. 843 Allied casualties were the price of this folly, including Sir John Hope himself who was taken prisoner during the fight.

The Peninsular War officially ended on April 17th 1814 when Soult signed an armistice. British troops remained in France until June and July 1814 when they began sailing home from Bordeaux. The Portuguese and Spanish troops, with whom the British had shared their dangers, glories and miseries during the last six years, returned home also, and there were sad scenes as the comrades in arms bad farewell to each other. Wellington himself issued his final General Order from Bordeaux on June 14th 1814, thanking his men for their efforts during the past six years and asking them to accept his thanks.[1] His briefly-worded order ran to just 174 words, scant recognition for his men compared with the lavish praise which was to be heaped upon Wellington by the government upon his return to England. The order was read out before slowly, one by one, the regiments of one of the finest armies this country has ever possessed, were scattered across the seas to

---

[1] General Order, Bordeaux, 14th June 1814.

England, Ireland and America. As the great historian of the war, Sir William Napier, later wrote, "thus terminated the war, and with it all remembrances of the veterans services."[1] What a pity this great army could not have been assembled one year later when, after his escape from Elba, Napoleon was finally defeated on the undulating plains of Waterloo. Surely the outcome of the battle on June 18th 1815 would not have been the close run thing that it was had the army of Badajoz, Salamanca and Vittoria been present. on that great, fateful day. Keep's comrades of the 28th were present, however, and they gave a magnificent account of themselves in the tradition of Wellington's Peninsular veterans.

William Keep himself was still recovering from the wound he received at St Pierre and he was never to see active service again. These final letters see him having to go through the process of appearing before a Medical Board before finally being allowed to return to England as unfit for service.

Fontarabia
18th January 1814

My dear Brother,

As I think, notwithstanding the very favourable report I made to my Mother last month, my further advancement towards recovery may yet leave much anxiety on your minds about me, I avail myself with pleasure of an opportunity to write, to assure you that I am still improving and only wearing now a black handkerchief across my head, which permits some signs of the appearance of my face presented before I was wounded.

An order came to remove us further to the rear, and I proceeded on horseback from Espellete with my wounded companions to this very retired place. On the journey I met an old school fellow of ours at Norfolk House, that capital Arithmetician and good looking little fellow, Walters, now a Commissary's clerk, in charge of stores going up to the army, and mounted on a mule, with a stylish cap decorated with gold band and tassel. As we were moving at a canter, in opposite directions, you may suppose our surprise at this rencontre, but as I couldn't pull up to talk we could only exchange most significant glances.

This nook of the coast is so crowded with troops of all arms that when we arrived at St Jean de Luz it was difficult to find a place of shelter for the night. A storm had just visited this sea port, and added to the apparent confusion and bustle the place was in, and a heavy rain falling. I was left at the door of an inn, whilst an old soldier named Dunstan, now in my service, was seeking a billet for me. I had waited a full fifteen minutes in the dark entry of this house, just far enough within to escape a bespattering from the rain. The wind still blowing in heavy gusts had stirred up such a commotion in the bay, that what with the darkness and noise of the waves beating over the rocks and shingles on the beach I thought it about as dismal a night as I had ever beheld. Having the ocean directly in front of me I was

---

[1] Napier, *A History of the War in the Peninsula*, VI. p.656.

forcibly reminded of dangers past in an hour so dark and tempestuous. But my attention was suddenly called away to a loud noise at the top of a narrow flight of stairs behind me, and in a great hurry and alarm a female descended them with a light in her hand, exclaiming in French at the sight of me "Sir, Sir, have you seen my wicked little boy, my poor little son?"

This was a delicate and pretty young woman about twenty four, who told me she feared he had thrown himself from the cliffs into the sea, for having reproved him he had threatened to destroy himself, and after a long search he was no where to be found.

I endeavoured to offer all the consolation in my power, told her I had not seen him, but hoped there could be no occasion for such fears. To this she only replied by giving me a very deplorable picture of his desperate disposition etc (and at the same time her fondness was evident, for the tears she was shedding about him) and then entering into general conversation, with all that freedom and fluency of utterance for which the French women are so remarkable, in less than five minutes made me acquainted with every particular of her domestic affairs, by which I learnt that she was a widow whose husband had died six months after her wedding. But the volubility of her tongue was checked as by a sudden recollection in the midst of this, and gently placing her hand upon my arm, she asked how long I had been there, and apologising for her remissness begged me to walk up stairs until the rain was over.

I told her that having come some distance, I was impatient to procure quarters for the night, and understood her house was already too much crowded to afford me a bed. That is true, said she — the town is full of the military at present, but ... and something I thought she would have added if more than the wish to accommodate me, had been in her power. Here our conversation came to a stop, for my fair companion's thoughts again reverted to the object of her solicitude, from whom they could scarcely be said to have wandered, our discourse having been momentarily interrupted by some expression of maternal uneasiness. This was like a signal of distress to me, to the sound of which I felt ashamed to be thought for a moment indifferent, and without considering what I was doing, my hand came in collision with hers that held the candlestick, which occasioned her to relinquish it, and I advanced to the door without any direct intention, but as the eye rests ever unsatisfied upon vacancy, having raised the light above my head the more effectually to dissipate the surrounding obscurity, I espied on a sudden the youthful delinquent, popping back from the window of a chaise that stood within three paces of me a little to one side of the door. Now it happened that in turning too quickly round to communicate the pleasing intelligence a current of air extinguished the candle, and by a simultaneous movement of my pretty hostess we came in direct contact with each other. These circumstances combining, I made no hesitation in throwing my arm round her neck, and whispering what I had to say in her ear. In a few words it was agreed between us that whilst she went for a light, I should stand sentry over the chaise, to intercept our prisoner if he attempted to escape, a duty I entered upon with as much promptitude as though immortal laurels were to be obtained by the performance of it. As soon as she returned, we opened the Chaise door, and I had the satisfaction of beholding the penitent runaway imploring forgiveness from his delighted Mother. This adventure procured me good quarters for the night, and the next day we arrived here.

Fontarabia is a town very inconveniently situated at the extreme corner of Spain, bordering on the river Bidassoa, and Bay of Biscay. Extensive sands receive the waters of this river which runs so shallow that it admits of no shipping whatever.[1] On the opposite bank is the French town called Andaye (Hendaye). Both places are very pretty, but secluded. Fontarabia shows some remains of ancient fortifications, for such they seem, and to have been long since in ruins. The town consists of one street facing the river, and a suburb called the Marina, built on the sands of this turbulent and mighty bay. The wounded officers are quartered in Fontarabia, and a large Convent on the French side at Andaye is occupied by the men. But we have so many medical officers and others here (among the rest a very dashing sporting Chaplain) that the place is very crowded, and we are forced to submit to great inconvenience, more so than being doubled up, as we used to call it, at Berry Head, for Waring and I, being junior Officers (Captain Wolfe has a billet to himself) we are obliged to sleep in one bed. But that is nothing, for a married couple and 3 Spanish damsels occupy this room as well as ourselves. A double recess contains a bedstead each, and the girls (fine young women) repose upon the floor.

The Patron's wife is a middle-aged woman, very interesting, but much to be pitied, being in very delicate health, which our presence here does not tend to improve. Waring is wounded in the leg, and goes upon crutches. He is a very handsome dashing youth, with a good deal of roguish fun in him. The girls you must know come to bed when they think we are asleep, and pin themselves into the bed clothes, we being quite strangers to them.

A few nights ago, Waring laid a train of gunpowder round the bed, and fired it, and you may suppose the fun of their jumping up, enclosed as they were. But it did no mischief except to alarm them a little, and these girls are rather better pleased than offended with our jokes, but Waring is very gentlemanlike and does not carry his frolics beyond due limits. Yet we are now growing very serious from the increased illness of the poor married woman, and have dropped all such tricks. During the day we adjourn to a sooty cavern (as it appears to us) where a fire is kept, and cooking performed. Here we smoke Brazilian tobacco, Waring having a fine Turkish pipe, and teaching me to do the same, which I had learnt a little of at Berry Head, and now find is beneficial more than otherwise to my wounded face.

---

[1] At the time of the Peninsular War the estuary of the Bidassoa was wide but fairly shallow, owing to the extensive sands that extended into it. Indeed, Wellington's men were able to wade across in relative ease on October 7th when the invasion took place. George Bowles, of the 1st Foot Guards, considered the crossing a bit of a joke (Malmesbury, *A Series of Letters*, II. p.385) whilst Rees Gronow, of the same regiment, also considered it very easy, adding that it was merely an affair of outposts. (Gronow, *Reminiscences*, p.13). Today, the estuary has been dredged to such an extent that it is only possible to cross the river by boat. An interesting comparison can be made between the photograph of the estuary in Beatson's *Wellington; The Bidassoa and Nivelle*, opposite the title page, and the colour plate number 32, by Andy Cook, of the same place, in my own *Fields of Fire*, to see how the estuary has changed over the years.

When at Espellete I received a long and amusing letter from Taylor, dated from Manchester, in which he paints his interview with you in droll colours. He says when he first called you was not at the office, and so he strolled into the Abbey, where he stayed some time "holding high converse with the mighty dead". He says you talk very like me, and describes his introduction very funnily. He mentions the cottage, which he calls a nice cottage, and says my Mother received him very kindly, and showed him the assenting Gentlemen I bought from Walcheren, also his astonishment at the London Theatricals. He begged me to write to him whenever I can steal a moment from the funking situations that must surround me, to tell him "how we fought and conquered" and with it "all my travel's history". I complied with his request a little while ago, in which I told him that a letter from his facetious hand coming to us in these times was like the radiant orb of day, breaking through regions of dark clouds after a tremendous storm. I might have told him more than I did, that his feelings were too acute, and his mind too reflective for such scenes as we have been engaged in.

The wounded here are doing very well. A young Surgeon who attends us relates many wonderful cases. A stout Highlander complained of one of his legs being so heavy that he couldn't raise it from the ground, and upon lifting his kilt a spent cannon ball was found lodged in the fat of his thigh. Waring's servant's life was preserved by his breast plate, and his own great coat was riddled with holes. The smallest movement has its consequences, and the men therefore are as little interfered with as possible in action. The worst and most disagreeable idea that presents itself is of being thrown into the ground on the field, for all are immediately striped naked, and I have seen twenty together thus prostrate, without a rag to cover them. The French imprudently offered a large booty to our men — the waist bands of their trousers containing often a store of dollars most ingeniously concealed. This you must think is no very creditable incentive to their exertions, and war is positively become no less than deliberate murder and assassination, for the instruments of destruction absolutely from habit have long ceased to intimidate both parties. Yet these scenes of warfare are pursued amidst the tranquil charms of nature in most novel and often delightful places, but the wounded are generally soon withdrawn from sight.

At the Pyrenees I nearly stumbled over the body of a Corporal named Mutton, in going to take the Colours (No Sunday Morning's work was that for you or Taylor to have been present at, much as you would have enjoyed the beauty of the scene in a quiet survey of it). This excellent soldier had his accoutrements for the day brightly polished, but a bullet in the temple had deprived him of life, and when I inquired of Tatlow what had occurred, incredulous of Delmar's fate, I found he was equally unfortunate, and dead as mutton indeed. On that very morning the Regimental barber had cut his hair, and I had observed how very youthful and well he looked, and never saw him more, poor fellow. He was of a quiet, pensive but most amiable disposition. He died instantaneously, surrounded by his friends, on the Sabbath morn, in that elevated and beautiful spot, in a glorious cause.[1]

---

[1] Keep refers here to the fight at Maya on July 25th 1813.

Lord Wellington has been here, to inspect the position of some Congreve Rockets,[1] but I had not the pleasure to see him. Nelson says he looks very well, and is very stout and broad across the shoulders. He approached me one day very close on the march and almost brushed my elbow, as he was mounting a bank, and then appeared the neatest dressed man I had seen for some time, with small cocked hat, blue coat, and white muslin cravat, and his horse furniture in the finest order; and I thought he had somewhat the look of a Statesman or General of Engineers.[2]

Give me credit for this long letter, equal I think to the most lengthy of your circulars, and collect me all the news in reply to it, both of the office and all that is going on at home, and believe me to be, my dear Sam, Yours etc, W.T.K.

P.S. The jolly old Miller and family came out on the road to salute me with kind greetings when proceeding to the rear.

Fontarabia
27th February 1814

My dearest Mother,

I am not so well inclined as I have been, to take up the pen to address you — feeling unwilling to impart to you anything to disturb the pleasing expectations my previous letters may have inspired. Do not however suppose it is about myself only, that I am possessed with this feeling for it refers equally to melancholy scenes which I have lately been witnessing, and the illness and death of the poor woman, not only in the same house but *room* where Waring and I have been billeted here.

I have besides been made aware of another cause to prolong the suspension of my recovery, to what the Doctors call an indefinite period, for although the tendency to heal has been so soon effected, yet from fragments of jawbone being still liable to come away in splinters I am subject to fresh

---

[1] The Congreve Rocket had been invented by Sir William Congeve and had first been used in 1805. Wellington himself distrusted them and, indeed, the rockets, once fired, often had a unfortunate tendency to turn upon their firers. However, they were used to great affect during the crossing of the Adour, in February 1814, when a couple of them burst amongst French troops who were threatening the bridgehead made by a small party of Wellington's troops who had crossed the river on rafts. At Waterloo, Wellington ordered Captain Whinyates to leave behind his rockets and use ordinary guns. The commander of the Royal Artillery, Lieutenant Colonel George Wood said, "It will break poor Whinyates' heart to lose his rockets", to which Wellington replied, "Damn his heart, sir, let my order be obeyed".

[2] The blue coat, mentioned by Keep, appears to have been Wellington's habitual dress in the Peninsula although there exists, in the Wellington Museum in Waterloo, a buff coloured coat, said to have been worn by him in Spain. Whilst Wellington cared little for the appearance of his men, provided they came armed with sixty rounds of ball ammunition, he himself took great pains to ensure that he was well turned out at the best of times and, indeed, was frequently to be found discussing the latest fashions or the cut of his coat.

swellings of the face, that make it very uncertain when I shall be quite restored; such is my present state, and while this has been going on a fatal illness seized the Mistress of the house and a Spanish doctor has been in constant attendance upon her, until her death, which as she was a Catholic gave rise to many ceremonies that we have been forced to witness, and even join in, our feelings being so awakened to the mournful scene around us, and this has been the most singular one you can perhaps imagine. Brought here by the strange accidents of war, we are more the objects of surprise to the natives than they to us, as we have been sometime among their country-men, and the group around us were all true Spanish, though Biscayans in that house; but as we could talk a little only of their language to be understood, all we could do was to look on, and leave them to observe us in speechless wonder at our ways, so contrary in many things to their own; and whilst the poor Invalid was in a dying state, we had no place to retire to, but the little recess where our bedstead stood. At night it is usual for certain priestly persons to parade the street, crying out for customers, as is common elsewhere with Sunday commodities in the day. A bell man accompanies the cry of 'Sacramento' and here it being needed, up the staircase they ascended in full congregation, the chief leader closely resembling our Parish Beadles. During this ceremony, with all these people present, Waring and I had our noses just peeping above the bed clothes.

More important things it seemed remained to be done after the poor woman was dead, for a large table, as if for a feast, was prepared, and a cloth laid, with glasses, half filled with water, into which little pellets of bread were cast. On the next day the body itself was placed upon this table, sewed up in black silk, round which all the friends assembled to be devout and merry by turns. Waring hobbles about with a wound that deprives him of the use of a leg, but not otherwise of serious consequence, and he joined in these ceremonies, to add to the grotesqueness of them with crutches in hand, and funny forage cap on his head. He is the son of the beautiful Mrs Esthen (that was) the Actress, and his father is an M.P., and he inherits splendid eyes and fine complexion, and is a very stylish man about 18, very well versed in all that is going on in London, and fashionable circles, and though not at all enthusiastic displayed great nonchalance in action.

The Biscayans here are chiefly mariners and fishermen, very fair and good looking young fellows; and I was much amused among a crowd of them on the beach this morning, in possession of what seemed to them great curiosities, for we are such a nation of traders that our Merchants are not idle, and do not lose the opportunity of introducing their goods here. They were laughing over some cotton hand kerchiefs from Manchester, in which a most capital mode of recommending them to notice had been adopted, for caricatures had been printed on them of Bonaparte's reverses of fortune, and defeats in Russia etc, with other comic subjects. At Coria a sutler came from England to sell different articles to us, and he had shifted his ground to St Jean de Luz, and being as you may suppose much in want of every thing since the loss of my baggage, Wolfe had the kindness to lend me his horse, and I rode over to him lately to get what was most essential, but as he had only shoes and boots, stockings and shirts and eatables, to dispose of, of course I could not get a refit, nor should I attempt it as a new military cap, coat etc must come from England, but at present I see no need to be in a hurry about that, besides which, whatever my ulterior prospects may be, I now belong to the 2nd Battalions till quartered in Devonshire. Col. Nixon and Mullins have gone over to take command of them.

I am sorry to hear Col. Belson is somewhere in sick quarters in the rear. He has been very kind to me, particularly in the last instance, for Waring tells me, by a new order from the Prince Regent, having commanded the Company on the 13th, will put an extra £150 in my pocket; with this agreeable news I shall conclude for the present. With kindest love to all at home, remaining my dear Mother, Your affectionate son, W.T.K.

Fontarabia
20th March 1814

My dear Mother,

Another month has passed away without much occurring to retard its progress, or cure of my wounds, yet somehow both have been slowly moving forward, with a sort of weariness at the delay that detains me from you, as I am now longing to see you all again, and to be better informed of many things than your last letter could give me sufficient details of.

Last week a Medical Board assembled here, before whom Waring and I appeared, and a Report has been sent up to Headquarters, without our being at all aware of the result, nor do we expect yet for some time to be informed of it, but suppose it will be the means of sending us home.

I hope therefore we shall have the pleasure to embark together before long. This young Gent is very kind in the loan of many things to me I couldn't do without, yet he has been as unfortunate as myself in the loss lately of his baggage and animal, a continued system of robbery of this kind going on, and the carelessness and negligence of our officers has given too much encouragement to this practice. Most of the horses and mules are worth £20 and it is no difficult task to move off with such property in safety on the borders of two kingdoms at war with each other. If Marshal Soult hadn't decamped there might have been a Melee of both armies confined in such a narrow space, for never I think were so many men in hostile array seen within so small a compass and our having possession of the coast has facilitated the arrival of a constant addition to our forces. Another battle you must have heard has taken place at Orthes,[1] where the 28th have experienced a further loss of its finest Soldiers;

---

[1] The battle of Orthes was fought on February 27th 1814 and was the last major action to be fought in the open field by Wellington in the Peninsula. During the battle the Allied army drove Soult's troops from their positions along the main Dax-Orthes road, inflicting casualties on them of around 4,000, of which some 1,300 were taken prisoner. Wellington's losses were put at 2,164, including the Commander-in-Chief

Captain Gale and Captain Carrol, and Lieutenant Gordon, killed, and Captain Baker likewise, and Lieutenant Myers who came up with me from Vittoria, besides numbers wounded. Such dreadful warfare cannot it is to be hoped long continue. To tell you how many of our officers have died in torment would make you shudder. Now that I am no longer exposed to such dangers I need not conceal from you that war is a heart sickening and most revolting scene of bloodshed, from which I am very happy to escape. After a term of service that has gone beyond what I might have expected from September last, I am inclined now to enjoy at least a respite, and the tranquillity of this place would have been most agreeable, but from the death of that poor woman.

I have now a billet to myself, on the marina or sea beach, and can find no other fault but that it is too lonely and deserted for my spirits, sometimes when I return to it at night, for during the day, having the full use of my legs, I ramble a good deal about this delightful neighbourhood, the inviting scenery of which has possessed an interest to lead me on, some striking object generally presenting itself to excite my curiosity. I came the other day to a tower and courtyard with an inscription over the gateway to Philip the 2nd of Spain, overgrown with weeds and wallflowers, and where no marks of recent visitants were to be seen. And upon a small vessel wrecked in a late storm, with Don Amigos (the two friends) her name, inscribed upon the stern. Thus have I wandered about without meeting a soul, until the stillness of every thing around has startled me with the rustling of a bird even in a bush to a consciousness of being so completely alone. Our officers have been very remarkable in their fear of assassination in this land of strife, which I have hitherto been surprisingly exempt from in my thoughtlessness and pleasure amidst scenes so new to me, but since that melancholy event at our billet, nervousness now possesses me, that makes me limit my walks, and moreover a mysterious circumstance has in no trifling degree added to this feeling.

The room I occupy has a bedstead in a recess, or alcove (such as might ornament your garden) with folding doors in lieu of glass windows, and unpainted wooden balcony in front, and everything indicated it to have been some time without a tenant, as if it was a sort of haunted house, for the owners had apparently forsaken it, and only a queer looking man to be seen at night to fasten the heavy portal of a stable underneath.

At first I slept pretty well here, though awakened by strange noises now and then, but a few nights ago, being rather surprised at this, I sat up in bed to find out what it was that so disturbed me, and you may imagine my surprise to hear outside this house a distinct sound I had been long familiarised to, of ramming down cartridge in a musket. It was so continued and often repeated that I got up, put on my trousers, and opened the window shutters, and found it was a beautiful night, with the moon bright and clear, shining upon the tranquil waters of the Bay, the waves of which were gently rippling upon the shore. And as I felt extremely uneasy and desirous to know the cause of my alarm, I stooped

---

himself, slightly wounded by a spent ball towards the end of the fight. During the battle, the 28th fought as part as O'Callaghan's brigade of the 2nd Division.

over the balcony as far as I could reach, to observe who and where this person was, but could see no one, nor yet sufficiently under the spot where I stood, and as I was not acquainted with the fastenings below, and unable to seek them in the dark, this has remained an inexplicable riddle to me, but being repeated on more than one night at the same hour and place, I was considerably annoyed at it, and desired my good old soldier and servant Dunstan to bring his things and sleep in the same room with me. I know not how I can have given offence to any one here, and am therefore the more astonished at it, as I have thought it indicative of some evil design. The brother of the woman who died certainly looked angrily at Waring and me, when our servants have made too free with an old chair to light the fire, but otherwise I am not aware of any other cause for his displeasure.

I am on the very best terms with my good neighbours, in proof of which it is only necessary to say that when Dunstan passes them on the marina they have always a friendly salutation for him, as 'Come esta usted, Portico, Come esta Signor Hermoso?' which means 'How do you do, Portico How does Signor Hermoso?' (Hermoso implies, I must tell you, good looking and handsome which these fair damsels very flatteringly apply to me.) Dunstan is a jovial old soldier, who on approaching frequently enlivens them with a merry stave, and chatters to them in Spanish. We have no very recent news from the Army. I write occasionally to Alexander; Col. Ross now commands the Battalion, to whom he is the right hand and factotum. He met with a serious accident, but is now quite recovered, and writes in the best of spirits.

In the cheerful hope of soon meeting, I must now bid you farewell, remaining, my dearest Mother, Yours etc, W.T.K.

Commercial Inn, Plymouth
17th April 1814

My dearest Mother,

Last night at seven o'clock I had the inexpressible pleasure of landing once more in this happy Island, after a voyage of eight days from Passages in the Cyrus Transport. We encountered a stiff gale on the 14th otherwise we made a very favourable passage.

Everything looks new and delightful on this my native shore. The bustle of coaches, shops etc are most agreeable novelties, for such to me they now appear. The contrast is so great that I dreamt of nothing else last night, and this morning awoke with the ringing of Bells and sounds I had long been disused to. I have just partaken of an excellent breakfast, consisting of luxuries I had nearly forgotten the taste of. Good Heavens — what eventful times! The inhabitants here are all in commotion with the tidings of peace, and Bonaparte's Abdication etc. This is all news to us.[1]

When we left Spain Bayonne had not fallen, but was expected to be attacked hourly, and Lord Wellington had fought another battle with Soult, now only to be deplored from the casualties that occurred in it. I have been improving hourly, and my wound is healing again, more broken particles of the bone having exfoliated, so that I may truly call myself a lucky fellow.

If you didn't receive my last from Fontarabia, this will not a little surprise and please you. Waring came home in the same ship with me in a similar state of destitution to make any tolerable appearance out of doors impossible without being stared at. I want at present both money and clothes to enable me to leave this, having been forced to borrow some things of the Captain of the Cyrus and his mate even to come here. The paymaster is at hand however, and I have plenty of money to receive for these purposes, but this being Sunday I cannot seek what I want nor get cash until I write to our 2nd Battalion or go to them.

They are at Kingsbridge Barracks within 25 miles of this; under these circumstances I shall not be able to get to London before Friday night, but I calculate I shall certainly arrive by that time. I am all impatience you may be sure to commence the long journey and to see you again. If Sam will wait for me at the White Horse Cellar on Friday night, we can take a Hackney Coach and proceed together. I am informed the Coach will be in about 6 o'clock. I am in high spirits in anticipation of having more good news to impart to you when we meet, till when, adieu dear Mother, Says yours etc., W.T.K.

Plymouth
Tuesday Morning

My dear Sam,

I have been most unpleasantly detained here by the want of both money and clothes, as I stated in my last, and it was only last night the tailors brought the things I had ordered, all of which I have returned, as none of them fit me. I am therefore about to proceed in my present trim, in the blood stained coat in which I was wounded, with a cloak to conceal it. I wrote to Kingsbridge, but could not obtain any money from thence, for being on leave absence I was informed my supplies should be drawn from Macdonald in London, and I accordingly received an order for £30 which I couldn't get cashed till this

---

[1] Napoleon abdicated on April 6th 1814 although Wellington did not hear of it until April 12th, by which time he had lost 4,500 casualties in an assault on the French defences at Toulouse. Upon being informed of the abdication Wellington cried, 'You don't say so, upon my honour! Hurrah!' before snapping his fingers and spinning round on his heel. (Longford, *The Years of the Sword*, p.344.)

morning. I can conceive your disappointment at not finding me at the cellar last Friday, but it could not exceed mine, at being kept here from the causes I have explained to you. Tomorrow morning at five I shall positively start, so that if you will go once more to Piccadilly we shall certainly have the felicity of meeting there. I have had great difficulties to contend with from the time I left Fontarabia, but happily they are all over, for the 200 miles remaining is nothing now I have got the money in my pocket. I shan't come by the Mail Coach, but by different stages so as positively to arrive on Friday night by 6 or 7.

Waring and I expected to have fought another Battle on the Seas before we reached old England, a strange sail having hove in sight which our Commodore took to be an American. He ordered the Cyrus to stand by him, and prepare for action, and the rest of the transports to spread their canvass and proceed homeward without us. Our guns were there fore loaded, though we had but a few of them, decks cleared, and rigging in readiness. Some time elapsed as she approached, and proving to be a large ship 'of most warlike appointment' we fully expected to witness a naval engagement. We couldn't but admire the gallant style in which our little commodore in a small Brig of War bore down upon her, with his ports open and guns ready to give her a broadside, she seemed unwilling to lay to in obedience to the first shot fired. After keeping us some time in this unpleasant expectation, she displayed her Ensign, and proved to be a Swede from the East Indies.

My last night in Spain was likewise full of disasters, the order being sent from Headquarters for us to proceed to England just as the fleet was on the eve of sailing as we heard from Passages was detained after Waring had started till sunset at Fontarabia and obliged to make a night march of it, along a road infested by robbers (one of our men, a servant of Captain Wolfe's, having been murdered by them only a few days before, while in charge of some horses conveying forage) and this road we had to pass over. Old Dunstan accompanied me with a loaded musket, and being on foot we proceeded unmolested, but having mistook the road at a cross turning continued on the tramp till 10 at night and arrived at last at the station of a Spanish Regt 2 or 3 leagues from our proper destination. I made myself known to their officers assembled at supper, and they found me a bed for the night. The next morning we crossed the country, and arrived at the heights overlooking the harbour and shipping of Passages just as the sails were unfurled and they were working their way out to sea for England. I had no time to lose therefore and hastened to get an order to embark, but was obliged to take a boat, and hail the Cyrus to get on board. Had I been five minutes later I should have lost my passage.

Passages is a town within, and at the waters edge of this beautiful harbour,[1] the entrance to which is so narrow it will only admit one ship at a

---

[1] The entrance to the harbour of Passages is indeed beautiful. It is also one which provides sailors with a test of their seamanship, particularly in bad weather, with its narrow entrance and high cliffs on either side. It is situated just a short distance to the west of San Sebastian and today provides the Spanish fishing fleet with a perfect harbour, much as it did the merchant ships and the Royal Navy in Wellington's day.

time, but the water as smooth as a lake, enclosed by the high lands around it, in the centre of which stands St Sebastian. I little expected to find this terrible fortress in so lovely a situation.

Sailing from this fine port, it is difficult to say which is the most beautiful, my last view of Spain or first of England, with its deep green turf and little red tiled houses — the picturesque and bold scenery of Mount Edgecombe, with its country seats embowered and verdant recesses made the comparison a fair one between the two, but the chief thing that enhanced the latter in my estimation was its being my native soil and containing those most dear to me, and whom in the joyful expectation of soon meeting, I remain my dear Samuel, Yours etc, W.T.K.

P.S. The tailor was very rude, and would not leave the suit without immediate payment, and to apologise for it told me an officer of the Berry Head Garrison but not of the 28th, had been shipwrecked, and left without a thing to cover him, and was the only person saved, by his extraordinary skill in swimming, which indeed we had proofs of there; and he had been obliged to apply to the Right Hon. Relatives of this ungrateful officer for payment, hitherto without success.

Chapter Nine
Aftermath

Wil`liam Keep landed at Plymouth on the very day that Marshal Soult
signed the armistice document which officially brought the Peninsular
War to an end. The wound suffered by him at the battle of St Pierre
meant that he would see no further active service and he went on half-pay, being
granted a pension of £70 per annum in addition, dated from December 13th 1813.[1]
Some fifteen years later, on December 1st 1828, Keep submitted a form to the War
Office with details of his service adding that he was 'desirous of serving. As it may
be necessary to be more explicit, I beg to observe that I shall always be ready to
serve if required, but am not desirous of returning to the full pay unless with the
prospect of promotion thereupon to a company.' Apparently, Keep's wound
incapacitated him from following any occupation. However, he never did return
to the Colours and it is just as well that at the fairly young age of 23, with no
occupation and, given his previous financial difficulties, he had been granted the
£70 per annum pension. In fact, it is possible that this amount was actually as
high as £200 per annum including a grant of £100 for his wound.

In 1819, Keep married Anne Colley at Marylebone. This apparently caused
great upset because he had been engaged to someone else but at the last minute
changed his mind and eloped with Anne, his fiancee's maid. Both families were
described as 'relentless' in their reaction to the presumed scandal. Four children,
all daughters, were born to Keep, one of whom was born on the Isle of Wight.
They lived happily in north London at 13, Rochester Road, Camden Town,[2] at
least from 1841 where they are recorded for the census. It was in the garden that
Keep and his old friend, Henry Alexander, used to refight their old Peninsular
battles. By then, Alexander had transferred to the 12th Light Dragoons with
whom he was killed in action in 1847.[3] Just round the corner from Keep's
house, in Camden Road, lived a Robert Maundrell, one of whose daughters was
married to a Mr Macleod, who in 1881 was a paymaster in the Royal Navy, and
this family knew the Keeps well. Either the Royal Navy Paymaster or his son
was the Robert Macleod who was still in touch with William's surviving
daughter, Julia, age 88, in 1914. Either way, Robert Macleod must have known
various details about William Keep, not only from Julia, but also from Vittoria
Alexander,[4] Henry Alexander's daughter, who married Robert Maundrell's

---

[1] This chapter is based upon very thorough research work carried out by Professor
Roy Newton and Mrs Joy Newton, to whom the editor is eternally grateful. Roy and Joy
negotiated a veritable labyrinth when unravelling not only the source of the Keep letters
but his family background also.

[2] The house still stands today, a fine Victorian building.

[3] Henry Alexander's service record with the 28th Regiment can be found on page,
footnote of this book.

[4] Henry Alexander had been wounded at Vittoria on June 21st 1813.

brother-in-law, Frederick Gilder and was therefore, as he said in one of his letters, his aunt. A great coincidence. Vittoria died in Australia in 1914 aged 77.

We know from Robert Macleod that there was a miniature on ivory made when William Keep was in the 77th Regiment and that he received a General Service Medal with clasps for Vittoria, the Pyrenees and the Nivelle. It is certainly very strange that he was not awarded a clasp for the Nive, the action in which he sustained his wound, and indeed, Robert Macleod said that William Keep always thought there should have been another clasp. Julia Keep said that after his death she and her sister Honora were obliged to sell them. The Regimental Museum obtained the medal but this, together with all other property and possessions could not be got out of Burma in 1942 when the battalion of the 28th, which had been one of the two peacetime garrison battalions there, had to leave hurriedly in the wake of the Japanese onslaught.[5] There was a framed silhouette of William Keep which still survives and is on show in the Soldiers of Gloucestershire Museum in Gloucester.[6]

William Thornton Keep died on January 31st 1884, two and a half months after his 92nd birthday, a rather astonishing fact given the severe nature of the wound which he sustained in December 1813. He had purchased grave number 1275 in Highgate Cemetery for the sum of £3 3s on December 7th 1884 and it was there, on February 6th 1884, that he was laid to rest.[7] It is sad to relate that he had already seen his eldest daughter, Sophia Margaretta, buried there in 1844. Another daughter, Matilda, was buried in the same plot in 1852, and his wife Anne, in 1856, before he himself was buried there. In 1908 his daughter Honora Elizabeth was buried there and, finally, in 1923, Julia. Today, the grave is overgrown and the headstone missing.

Keep's mother would not let him have the original letters and so he made copies of them in 1830 and it is these letters which are now in the possession of the Soldiers of Gloucestershire Museum having been given them by Julia Keep along with the silhouette.[8] The original letters went to William Keep's sister, Julia Matilda, but his daughter, Julia, did not know what became of them. Perhaps they were destroyed, or maybe they are still out there somewhere, sitting in somebody's attic. Robert Macleod did, in fact, try and get the letters published in 1914 but without success and a letter exists from Julia Keep to Macleod thanking him for the interest he was showing in her father. It may be of some comfort to them that after all these years, the letters have finally been published and that many people will now be able to enjoy the story of a young officer in the British army of the early 19th century and his years spent in the service of the king.

---

[5] Apparently, there existed an album with photographs of Peninsular veterans of the 28th which was also lost along with other possessions in Burma.

[6] Family tradition has it that for years, the silhouette was believed to be that of the Duke of Wellington on account of the rather distinctive bridge of the nose.

[7] The Grave Register states that the grave is 14 feet deep, with six burials.

[8] Julia Keep was then living at 6, Glynfield Road, Harlesden, and she donated them to the museum as there was nobody else to leave them to.

Bibliography

Beatson, F.C. *With Wellington in the Pyrenees, Being an account of the Operations between the Allied Army and the French from July 25 to August 2 1813*. London, 1914.

Beatson, F.C. *Wellington: The Bidassoa and Nivelle*. London, 1931.

Bell, Sir George. *Soldier's Glory, being Rough Notes of an Old Soldier*. London, 1956.

Blanco, Richard. *Wellington's Surgeon General: Sir James McGrigor*. Durham NC, 1974.

Brett-James, Anthony. *Life in Wellington's Army*. London, 1972.

Cassels, S.A.C. (Ed). *Peninsular Portrait, 1811-1814. The Letters of Captain William Bragge, Third (King's Own) Dragoons*. London, 1963.

Brodigan, Lt.Col. F. *History of the 28th (North Gloucestershire) Regiment*. London, 1884.

Cadell, Charles. *Narrative of the Campaigns of the Twenty-Eighth Regiment, since their return from Egypt in 1802*. London, 1835.

Carr-Gomm, F.C. (Ed). *Letters and Journals of Field Marshal Sir William Gomm, GCB, from 1799 to Waterloo, 1815*. London, 1881.

Cooke, John. *Memoirs of the Late War: Comprising the Personal Narrative of Captain Cooke of the 43rd Regiment of Light Infantry*. London, 1831.

Cooper, John Spencer. *Rough Notes of Seven Campaigns in Portugal, Spain, France, and America, during the years 1809-1815*. Carlisle, 1869.

Eadie, Robert. *Recollections of Robert Eadie, Private of His Majesty's 79th Regiment of Infantry*. Maggs, London, 1987.

Embleton, G & Windrow M. *Military Dress of the Peninsular War*. New York, 1974.

Esdaile, Charles. 'Heroes or Villains?' *History Today*, Vol. XXXVIII, April 1988.

Fletcher, Ian. *The Waters of Oblivion: The British Invasion of the Rio de la Plata, 1806-07*. Tunbridge Wells, 1991.

Fletcher, Ian, (Ed). *A Guards Officer in the Peninsula; The Peninsular War letters of John Rous, Coldstream Guards, 1812-1814*. Tunbridge Wells, 1992.

Fletcher, Ian, (Ed). *For King and Country; The Letters and Diaries of John Mills, Coldstream Guards, 1811-1814*. Staplehurst, 1995.

Fletcher, Ian. *Fields of Fire: Battlefields of the Peninsular War*. Staplehurst, 1994.

Fletcher, Ian. *Wellington's Regiments: The Men and Their Battles, From Rolica to Waterloo, 1808-1815*. Staplehurst, 1995.

Fletcher, Ian and Poulter, Ron. *Gentlemen's Sons: The Foot Guards in the Peninsula and at Waterloo*. Tunbridge Wells, 1992.

Fortescue, Sir John. *History of the British Army*. 13 Vols. London, 1910-1930.

Fraser, Edward. *War Drama of the Eagles*. London, 1912.

Gates, David. *The British Light Infantry Army*. London, 1987.

Gleig, George. *The Subaltern*. London, 1825.

Grattan, William. *Adventures with the Connaught Rangers, 1809-1814*. Cambs, 1989.

Gurwood, (Ed). *The Despatches of Field Marshal the Duke of Wellington, During his Various Campaigns in India, Denmark, Portugal, Spain, the Low Countries and France, from 1799 to 1818*. 12 Vols. London, 1834-1838.

Gurwood, John. (Ed). *Selections from the Despatches and General Orders of Field Marshal the Duke of Wellington*. London, 1842.

Hamilton, Lt. Gen. Sir F.W. The *Origin and History of the First or Grenadier Guards*. 2 Vols. London, 1874.

Havard, Robert. *Wellington's Welsh General; A Life of Sir Thomas Picton*. London, 1996.

Haythornthwaite, Philip. *Uniforms of the Peninsular War*. Poole, 1978.

Haythornthwaite, Philip. *Wellington's Military Machine*. Tunbridge Wells, 1989.

Hennen, John. *The Principles of Military Surgery*. Edinburgh, 1820.

Leach, John. *Rough Sketches of the Life of an Old Soldier*. London, 1831.

Longford, Elizabeth. *Wellington: The Years of the Sword*. London, 1969.

Mackinnon, Colonel Daniel. *Origins and Services of the Coldstream Guards*. 2 Vols. London, 1833.

Mackesy, Piers. *British Victory in Egypt, 1801: The End of Napoleon's Conquest*. London, 1995.

Malcolm, John. *Reminiscences of a Campaign in the Pyrenees and South of France*. Cambridge, 1996.

Malmesbury, Earl of. *A Series of Letters of the First Earl of Malmesbury, His Family and Friends, from 1745 to 1820*. 2 Vols. London, 1870.

Nosworthy, Brent. *Battle Tactics of Napoleon and his Enemies*. London, 1995.

Napier, Sir William. *History of the War in the Peninsula and the South of France, from the Year 1807 to the Year 1814*. 6 Vols. London, 1828-1845.

Oman, Sir Charles. *History of the Peninsular War*. 7 Vols. Oxford, 1902-1930.

Oman, Sir Charles, *Wellington's Army, 1809-14*. London, 1913.

Patterson, John. *The Adventures of Captain John Patterson, with Notices of the Officers, &c of the 50th, or Queen's Own Regiment, from 1807 to 1821*. London, 1837.

Raymond, John. (Ed). *The Reminiscences and Recollections of Captain Gronow, Being anecdotes of Camp, Court and Society, 1810-1860*. London, 1964.

Robertson, Sergeant D. *Journal of Segeant D. Robertson, late 92nd Highlanders, during the Campaigns between 1797 and 1818*. Maggs, London, 1982.

Robinson, H. *Memoirs of Sir Thomas Picton*, London, 1836.

Robson, Brian. *Swords of the British Army: The Regulation Patterns, 1788-1914*. London, 1996.

Sherer, Moyle, *Recollections of the Peninsula*. London, 1824.

Stanhope, Philip Henry. *Notes of Conversations with the Duke of Wellington, 1831-1851*. London, 1888.

Sydney, Rev. E. *The Life of Lord Hill*. London, 1845.

Ward, S.G.P. *Wellington's Headquarters. A Study of the Administrative Problems in the Peninsula, 1809-1814*. Oxford, 1957.

Woolwright, H.H. *History of the Fifty-Seventh (West Middlesex) Regiment of Foot, 1755-1881*. London, 1893.

Index

Index